Agile Application
Lifecycle Management

Agile Application Lifecycle Management

Using DevOps to Drive Process Improvement

Bob Aiello and Leslie Sachs

◆◆ Addison-Wesley

Boston • Columbus • Indianapolis • New York • San Francisco • Amsterdam • Cape Town
Dubai • London • Madrid • Milan • Munich • Paris • Montreal • Toronto • Delhi • Mexico City
São Paulo • Sydney • Hong Kong • Seoul • Singapore • Taipei • Tokyo

For information about buying this title in bulk quantities, or for special sales opportunities (which may include electronic versions; custom cover designs; and content particular to your business, training goals, marketing focus, or branding interests), please contact our corporate sales department at corpsales@pearsoned.com or (800) 382-3419.

For government sales inquiries, please contact governmentsales@pearsoned.com.

For questions about sales outside the U.S., please contact intlcs@pearson.com.

Visit us on the Web: informit.com/aw

Library of Congress Control Number: 2016936588

ISBN-13: 978-0-321-77410-1
ISBN-10: 0-321-77410-8

Text printed in the United States on recycled paper at RR Donnelley in Crawfordsville, Indiana.
1   16

In loving memory of:

Bob's mother and grandmother, two exceptional women who encouraged him to embrace all of life's challenges and develop an inner compass for the surest path forward,

and

IT expert and dear friend, Ben Weatherall, a pillar in the CM community who was always eager to share his best practices and tirelessly promoted the value of a modified agile–scrum development methodology. As an editor, I appreciated and chuckled along with our readers at the many zany characters he would weave into his articles for CM Crossroads. He was proud of his involvement with both professional associations, such as the IEEE and ASEE (Association of Software Engineering Excellence—The SEI's Dallas-based SPIN Affiliate), and social and charitable organizations. An enthusiastic resident of his Fort Worth, Texas, community, Ben was an active participant in his local Shriners' "Car-vettes" group and could be counted on to lend a hand whenever their presence was requested at an event. Ben was a man of deep faith and, over the years, we had many engaging discussions about matters much more significant than configuration management.

Each of these three individuals was dedicated to balancing a strong work ethic with an equal commitment to their personal relationships; we cherish their legacy.

Contents

Preface

This is an amazing, and perhaps chaotic, time to be involved with the technology industry. The demand for talent, skills, and commitment to excellence has never been higher. Developing software and systems has become a remarkably complex task, with many factors affecting the success of the development effort. Learning new development frameworks and adapting legacy systems to meet the need for continued growth and flexibility require the modern IT professional to be able to press forward, while understanding the limitations imposed by earlier conditions. Teams may be located in one specific "war" room or distributed across the globe and frequently working at different hours of the day, with varying languages, cultures, and expectations for how they will operate on a daily basis. The project itself might involve writing complex application software or customizing a vendor package as part of a systems (versus software) development effort. The competition for specialized technical resources motivates many organizations to allow flexible work arrangements, including telecommuting along with choosing office locations convenient to attract local candidates. Technology professionals must often choose between the demands of high-paying (and often stressful) opportunities and trying to maintain a comfortable work-life balance. The Internet has clearly become the backbone of commerce, and companies are expected to continuously align themselves with growing Web capabilities in order to achieve and maintain success.

Pragmatic Focus

This book focuses on the real world of creating and implementing processes and procedures to guide your software and systems delivery effort. The views expressed in these pages may make you feel uncomfortable, especially if you view yourself as an agile purist. We are going to challenge assumptions regarding the way things are being done today, and we are going to encourage you to participate in a discussion on how we can do a better job of developing software and systems. We are going to stipulate up front that our views may not always be applicable in every possible situation, but all that we write is based upon our real-world experiences or that which we have heard about from reliable sources. This is not a "feel-good" book about agile. This is a book about creating processes and procedures to guide you in overcoming the day-to-day challenges of developing complex software and systems. We look forward to hearing from you as you read through these chapters!

Successful organizations need to support complex technologies, most often with a significant Web presence. Even companies going out of business are expected to have a functioning Web presence capable of handling the peak transaction requirements of customers and other users. In practice, these complex development efforts necessitate effective processes and methodologies to meet both the demands of today and those that will surface in the future. This book will describe best practices for designing the appropriate application lifecycle management (ALM) processes necessary to successfully develop and implement complex software systems, whether your team is writing the code or customizing a system that you have purchased from a vendor. We will discuss both agile and non-agile methodologies to empower the reader to choose the best approach for your organization and the project that you are trying to complete. Our goal is to increase and enhance the reader's understanding and ability to apply these principles and practices in your own environment. We often work in the imperfect world of having to support lifecycle methodologies that are not always optimal. In fact, we are usually called in when things get really bad and an organization needs to figure out how to incrementally improve processes to improve quality and productivity. In our opinion, the most effective methodology to emerge in the last decade has been agile.

Agile configuration management and, by extension, agile application lifecycle management have become two of the most popular software development methodologies in use today. Agile has resulted in indisputable successes boasting improved productivity and quality. My 25-year (and counting) career has always involved software process improvement with a particular focus on configuration management. As a practitioner, I am completely tools and process agnostic. I have seen projects that successfully employed agile methods and other efforts that thrived using an iterative waterfall approach. Still, *all* organizations need a reliable and repeatable way to manage work, allowing full traceability and clear, complete communication. Years ago, the IT community looked to the software development lifecycle (SDLC) to guide us in understanding what needed to be done by each member of the team on a daily basis, although the SDLC process documentation often sat on the shelf along with the outdated requirements specification from the latest software or systems development effort. When purchasing commercial off-the-shelf (COTS) products became popular, we began to use the term systems development lifecycle to refer to the work, at times spanning months or even years, to customize and configure COTS systems. We will discuss the differences between software and systems lifecycles further in Chapter 1. Whether applied to software development or systems customization and configuration, the SDLC, in practice, generally only referred to the required activities to create and maintain the system. Some vendors marketed efforts to customize and configure their solution as production lifecycle management (PLM) solutions. Many companies struggled with improving programmer productivity, and some tried to use the Software Engineering Institute's (SEI) Capability Maturity Model (CMM). These efforts often had limited success, and even those that succeeded had limited return on their investment due to the excessive cost and effort involved. The SEI chartered a series of Software Process Improvement Networks (SPINs) throughout the United States, which provided speakers and opportunities to meet with other professionals involved with software process improvement. I had the pleasure of serving for many years on the steering committee of one of the SPINs located in a major city. Today, most of the SPIN presentations focus on agile practices, and most of the attendees are interested in establishing scrums, iterative development, and agile testing. Agile has certainly had a major impact on software process improvement, although not without its own inherent challenges and limitations. Application lifecycle management has emerged as an essential methodology to help clarify exactly how software development is conducted, particularly in large-scale distributed environments. ALM typically has a broader focus than was considered in scope for an SDLC and helped to resolve many of the most common challenges, such as providing a comprehensive software development methodology helping each member of the team understand what needed to be done on a daily basis. At its core, the ALM enhances collaboration and communication. DevOps is a closely related approach that is particularly effective at driving the entire ALM.

DevOps and the ALM

DevOps is a set of principles and practices that improve communication between the development and operations teams. Many DevOps thought leaders acknowledge that DevOps is also effective at helping development interact with other groups, including quality assurance (QA) and information security

(InfoSec). In this book, we will broaden that definition to show that DevOps is essential to enhancing communication between every other group that participates in the ALM. We will be discussing DevOps throughout this book and in detail in Chapter 12. DevOps principles and practices are applicable to the interactions between any two or more groups within the organization and are essential in driving the ALM.

The initial goal of any ALM is to provide the transparency required to enable decision makers to understand what needs to be done and, most importantly, approve the project, including its budget and initial set of goals and objectives. Providing this transparency is precisely where IT governance plays an essential role in helping to get the project approved and started.

IT Governance

Effective software methodology today must have a strong focus on IT governance, which is essentially the control of the organizational structures through effective leadership and the hands-on management of organizational policies, processes, and structures that affect information, information-related assets, and technology. Fundamentally, IT governance provides the guidance necessary to ensure that the information technology organization is performing successfully and that policies, processes, and other organizational structures are in place so that essential organizational strategies and objectives are achieved. Organizations with excellent IT governance enjoy improved coordination, communication, and alignment of goals throughout the entire enterprise. IT governance is closely related to, and must align with, corporate governance in order to ensure that information technology can help drive the business to success and profitability. The initial goals of IT governance are to define policies, clarify the objectives of corporate governance, and ensure that the information technology organization aligns with the business to provide essential services that enable the business to achieve its goals. From an IT service management perspective, IT governance helps drive the development and deployment of services that help achieve value; these include fitness for purpose (utility) and fitness for use (warranty). IT governance is also concerned with establishing the most efficient organizational structure that will allow technology to be delivered successfully as a valued corporate asset. In this context, management is also responsible for providing adequate resources while maintaining necessary budget and financial controls.

IT governance cannot exist in a vacuum. Management requires accurate and up-to-date information in order to make the best possible decisions. Department managers and teams must provide valid and relevant information so that management understands the risks, challenges, and resources required for success. IT governance enables the business by ensuring that informed decisions are made, that essential resources are available, and that barriers to success are removed or identified as risks. Risk management is essential to effective IT governance. Risk is not always bad, and many organizations thrive on well-defined risk. IT governance provides the essential information that is needed to enable senior management to identify and mitigate risk so that the organization can successfully operate within the global business environment.

IT governance has the unique view of seeing the organization as part of an ecosystem, with the focus on competitors and outside forces, including regulatory requirements that affect the business and business objectives. Information security and business continuity are special areas of focus for IT governance, as it is essential to ensure that the business can operate and thrive regardless of challenges, such as competitive forces and other external pressures. Other considerations of IT governance include data privacy, business process engineering, and project governance.

Closely related to IT governance, and often mentioned in the same sentence, is compliance with regulatory requirements, industry standards, and internal audit requirements. IT governance helps all relevant stakeholders within the entire organization understand what they need to do in order to meet and comply with all regulatory requirements. Effective IT governance enables businesses to implement organizations with organizational structures that operate successfully, while providing the necessary information to help senior management make the decisions, which then propel the organization to achieve improved quality, productivity, and profitability. With this guidance from senior management, the next step is to ensure that all of the stakeholders understand their roles and what needs to be done on a day-to-day basis. This is exactly where application lifecycle management comes into the picture.

Application Lifecycle Management

Application lifecycle management (ALM) evolved from the early days of process improvement to provide a comprehensive software development methodology that provides guidance from requirements gathering, to design development, all the way through to application deployment. In practice, ALM takes a wide focus, with many organizations establishing an ALM to manage their entire software and systems delivery effort. Even nondevelopment functions such as operations and the help desk can benefit from a well-defined ALM. Some organizations implement ALM in a way that would not be considered agile, using a waterfall model that has a heavy focus on completing the tasks in each phase before moving on to the next. Configuration management, consisting of source code management, build engineering, environment configuration, change control, release management, and deployment, has been a key focus of ALM for some time now. Another central theme has been applying agile principles to support and improve configuration management functions.

Agile CM in an ALM World

Agile configuration management (CM) provides support for effective iterative development, including fast builds, continuous integration, and test-driven development (TDD), that is essential for successful agile development. In a comprehensive lifecycle methodology, agile CM can make the difference between success and failure.

The Definition of Agile ALM

Agile ALM is a comprehensive software development lifecycle that embodies the essential agile principles and provides guidance on all activities needed to successfully implement the software and systems development lifecycle. Agile ALM embodies agile CM and much more. Agile ALM starts with tracking requirements with "just-enough process" to get the job done without any extra steps, or what agile enthusiasts often call "ceremony." This is often accomplished by creating user stories, which need to be under version control just like any other artifact. Testing throughout the lifecycle also plays a significant role in agile ALM and may even be used to supplement requirements documents that are often intentionally kept brief in an agile world. Agile ALM focuses on iterative development that requires a minimum amount of process, with an emphasis on proven practices that include iterative development, strong communication, and customer collaboration. Understanding agility is much easier when we examine the process methodologies that have come before.

Understanding Where We Have Come From

Understanding where we have come from should always start with reviewing the essential principles of process improvement. For example, most practitioners will confirm that process improvement needs to be iterative, pragmatic, and continuous. One excellent source of valid principles for process improvement may be found in the work of W. Edwards Deming. Many of Deming's teachings[1] provide principles that are practical and form the basis of quality management.

Principles of Process Improvement

Process engineering focuses on defining the roles, responsibilities, and essential tasks that need to be accomplished in order for the process to be completed successfully. Processes themselves need to be understood, clearly defined, and communicated to all stakeholders. Complex processes are most often created in a collaborative way and usually take several iterations before they are comprehensive or complete. Processes may need to change over time and may be loosely defined early in the lifecycle, but usually require greater clarity and discipline as the target delivery date approaches. Too much process is just as bad as not enough. Therefore, the best processes are Lean with few, if any, extra unnecessary steps. Quality must be built into the process from the very beginning, and it is essential to maintain an honest and open culture to achieve effective processes and process improvement.

Mired in Process

Bob worked in an international financial services firm that was deeply mired in process. The CEO of the company once commented in a town hall meeting that they realized they had too much process, and their solution was, unfortunately, to add more process. The organization had a deeply held belief in process, which also had a high degree of ceremony. The dark unspoken secret, however, was that many people simply chose to work around the burdensome processes, which required far too many documents. Most people in the organization become quite clever at gaming the system to deal with the burdensome requirements of the organizational processes. But because the culture was so focused on process, it was considered disloyal to complain or attempt to push back on this. The organization wanted to grow, but just about every effort took far too long to complete.

---

1. Deming, W. Edwards. (1982). *Out of the Crisis*. Cambridge, MA: Massachusetts Institute of Technology, Center for Advanced Engineering Study.

Right-sizing processes is essential for organizational success, as is effective communication. Application lifecycle management has its own terminology, which needs to be understood for effective communication among all stakeholders.

Terminology

Every effort has been made to use terms that are consistent with industry standards and frameworks. Please contact us via social media with any questions or via the website for this book as noted on the next page.

Use of "I" versus "We"

Although we do everything as a team, there were quite a few places where it was much easier to write in the first-person singular. Bob is also much more technical and "hands-on" than Leslie, so when you see first-person singular "I" or "my" you can safely assume that this is a first-person account from Bob.

Why I Write About Agile CM, DevOps, and Agile ALM

Agile configuration management and agile application lifecycle management provide the basis for essential best practices that help a software or system development team improve their productivity and quality in many significant ways. DevOps and the agile ALM help ensure that teams can produce systems that are reliable and secure while maintaining high levels of productivity and quality. As is often the case, early life experiences have greatly shaped my view of the world.

Blindness and Process Improvement

Much of how I have approached my life and career has been influenced by the fact that I had a significant visual handicap growing up that could not be safely corrected until I was in my late teens. Consequently, I used Braille, a white cane, and lots of taped recordings ("talking books"). Even when I gained useable vision, at first it was only for short amounts of time because my eyes would fatigue quickly, and then for all practical purposes I would be temporarily blind again (or what we blind guys like to refer to as "blinking" out). My beloved ophthalmologist, Dr. Helen Grady Cole, once noted that my handicap *made* me successful because I learned to achieve against all odds and "move mountains" when necessary. No doubt, you will hear some of that fierce determination in these pages. I am very comfortable when approaching the seemingly impossible and viewing it as quite doable. You will get to hear about some of my experiences in the motorcycle gang of para- and quadriplegics with whom I proudly associated during my most formative years.

Classroom Materials

University professors who would like to use our book for a class in software engineering or software methodology are encouraged to contact us directly. We are glad to review classroom materials and would guest lecture (via Skype where travel is impractical) if appropriate and feasible. Obviously, we are glad to answer any and all questions related to the material in the book.

Website for this Book

Please register on our website at http://agilealmdevops.com and connect with us on social media to engage in discussions on Agile ALM and DevOps!

Who Should Read This Book

This book will be relevant for a wide variety of stakeholders involved in application lifecycle management.

Development managers will find guidance regarding best practices that they need to implement in order to be successful. We also discuss the many people issues involved with managing the software development process.

How This Book Is Organized

This book is organized into 22 chapters divided into four parts. Part I consists of five chapters defining the software development process, agile ALM and agile process maturity, and rapid iterative development. Part II covers automation, including build engineering, automating the ALM, continuous integration, delivery, and deployment. Part III covers establishing essential IT controls, including change management, operations, DevOps, retrospectives, agile in non-agile environments, IT governance, and audit and regulatory compliance. Part IV covers scalability, including integration across the enterprise, agile ALM in the cloud, ALM on the mainframe, QA and testing, personality, and the future of ALM.

Part I: Defining the Process

Chapter 1: Introducing Application Lifecycle Methodology

This chapter introduces application lifecycle management by explaining what you need to know in order to define an ALM that will help you implement a comprehensive and effective software or systems lifecycle. We discuss how to implement the ALM using agile principles in a real-world, pragmatic way that will help guide the activities of each member of your team, whether you are creating new software or customizing a commercial package. Systems lifecycles are a little different than a software development lifecycle and are usually associated with obtaining (and customizing) a project from a solution vendor. Commercial off-the-shelf (COTS) software is commonly used today to deliver robust technology solutions, but they often require some effort to customize and implement. In this chapter, we introduce the core concepts and then build upon them throughout the rest of the book

Chapter 2: Defining the Software Development Process

This chapter helps you understand the basic skills of how to define the software development process. Defining the software development process always sounds straightforward until you actually start trying to do the work. Many tasks are involved with any software or systems lifecycle, and a well-defined process must provide guidance on exactly what needs to get done and who is responsible for completing each task.

Chapter 3: Agile Application Lifecycle Management

In this chapter we discuss the core strategies that will help you create a flexible and robust software and systems development lifecycle while ensuring that the values and principles of agility are understood and maintained.

Chapter 4: Agile Process Maturity

In this chapter, we will examine the factors that affect agile process maturity from a number of different perspectives. Many technology professionals find that they must implement agile processes in a large organizational context, including managing teams that are composed of many scrums, totaling scores or even hundreds of developers working from a variety of locations. Scalability is certainly an essential aspect of agile process maturity. Mature agile processes must be repeatable for each project in the organization and have sufficient support for project planning. We also need to understand how process maturity affects non-agile development methodologies, including waterfall and other process models.

Chapter 5: Rapid Iterative Development

In this chapter, we discuss rapid iterative development and its impact on software methodology that came long before agile development reached its level of popularity common today. We consider what we learned from rapid iterative development and how it may be applied in practical situations today.

Part II: Automating the Process

Chapter 6: Build Engineering in the ALM

This chapter helps you understand the build within the context of application lifecycle management. We discuss essential aspects of automating the application build, with particular attention on techniques for creating the trusted application base. We also discuss baselining, compile dependencies, and embedding version IDs as required for version identification. We discuss the independent build and creating a fully automated build process. Building quality into the build through automated unit tests, code scans, and instrumenting the code is an important part of this effort. Finally, we will discuss the ever-challenging task of selecting and implementing the right build tools.

Chapter 7: Automating the Agile ALM

In this chapter we discuss how application lifecycle management touches every aspect of the software and systems lifecycle. This includes requirements gathering, design, development, testing, application deployment, and operations support. Automation plays a major role in the agile ALM, which sets it apart in many ways from other software development methodologies. We also explain why it is essential to appreciate the big picture at all times so that the functions that you implement are in alignment with the overall goals and structure of your ALM.

Chapter 8: Continuous Integration

In this chapter we explain that continuous integration (CI) is an essential practice that involves putting together code that has been created by different developers and ascertaining if the code components can compile and run together successfully. CI requires a robust automated testing framework, which we will discuss further in Chapter 20 and provides the basis for ensuring code quality through both static and instrumented code scanning. Continuous integration often involves merging together code that has been written by different developers and is essential for code quality. The fundamental value of this practice is that integrating a small amount of code as early as possible can avoid much bigger issues later. It would be difficult to imagine an effective ALM that does not embrace integrating code frequently, although I will also discuss a couple of situations where it is difficult or even impossible to achieve. When code cannot be integrated early and often, there is increased risk, which must be identified and addressed. It is also important to understand that continuous integration relies upon many other practices, including continuous testing, effective build engineering, static and instrumented code analysis, and continuous deployment, discussed in Chapter 9.

Chapter 9: Continuous Delivery and Deployment

In this chapter we explain how continuous deployment (CD) is a methodology for updating production systems as often as necessary and generally in very small increments on a continuous basis. It would be difficult to understand continuous deployment without discussing continuous integration and delivery. The terminology for CD has been confusing at best, with many thought leaders using the terms *continuous delivery* and *continuous deployment* interchangeably. We discussed continuous integration in Chapter 8. Continuous delivery focuses on ensuring that the code baseline is always in a state of readiness to be deployed at any time. With continuous delivery, we may choose to perform a *technical deployment* of code without actually exposing it to the end user, using a technique that has become known as *feature toggle*. Continuous deployment is different from continuous delivery in that the focus is on immediate promotion to a production environment, which may be disruptive and a poor choice from a business perspective. We will help you find the right balance so that you can support your business by promoting changes to production as often as desired.

Part III: Establishing Controls

Chapter 10: Change Management

In this chapter we examine how change management is a broad function that helps us plan, review, and communicate many different types of planned and emergency (unplanned) system modifications. Changes may be bugfixes or new features and can range from a trivial configuration modification to a huge infrastructure migration. The goal of change control is to manage all changes to the production (and usually QA) environments. Part of this effort is just coordination, and that is very important. But part of this effort is also managing changes to the environment that could potentially affect all of the systems in the environment. It is also essential to control which releases are promoted to QA and production. Change control can act as the stimulus to all other configuration management–related functions as well. Throughout this chapter we will discuss how to apply change management in the ALM.

Chapter 11: IT Operations

In this chapter, we will discuss how to create an effective IT operation group that is aligned with your agile ALM. The IT operations organization is responsible for maintaining a secure and reliable production environment. In large organizations, operations often resembles a small army with too many divisions to navigate that is also often held responsible when things go wrong. Developers, working on the bleeding edge of technology, often regard their colleagues in operations as lacking technical skills and ability, which is true in so far as operations resources tend to focus more on the day-to-day running of the systems. Understanding these different perspectives is a key aspect of our DevOps approach to the agile ALM.

Chapter 12: DevOps

In this chapter, we discuss DevOps as a set of principles and practices intended to help development and operations collaborate and communicate more effectively. DevOps is truly taking the industry by storm and, in some circles, reaching almost mythical proportions. I hear folks suggesting that DevOps can help solve almost any issue, which given the versatility of its cross-functional approach, is a view that has some merit, but some groups are losing sight of what this methodology is all about and how it can really help us implement the ALM.

Chapter 13: Retrospectives in the ALM

This chapter discusses the practical application of retrospectives to support application lifecycle management. The first section of this chapter will examine the main function of retrospectives, namely, to evaluate what went well and what needs to be improved. But that's just the beginning. Getting accurate information from all stakeholders in a retrospective can be very challenging. If you are successful, the retrospective can help drive the entire ALM process. Retrospectives require leadership, and this chapter will provide guidance on how to succeed if you are responsible for implementing this function. We will discuss how to employ retrospectives to support ITIL incidents and problem management, along with other industry standards and frameworks. Crisis and risk management are also key considerations along with IT governance and compliance. Retrospectives take on a different tone when used as vendor management tool. We will complete this chapter by considering how much process is necessary, how to deal with politics (or, more accurately, *relationships*), and the use of effective metrics to drive the process improvement journey.

Part IV: Scaling the Process

Chapter 14: Agile in a Non-Agile World

In this chapter we discuss that being agile in a non-agile world can be very difficult, and at times even seem impossible to accomplish. We have often found ourselves in organizations that insisted on a waterfall approach. What is most difficult is trying to predict things that are just not possible to ascertain up-front. Many are unaware that waterfall was originally envisioned as an iterative process because today it seems that some organizations expect their employees to be able to predict the future to a degree that is simply not reasonable. The real problem is that these are the same organizations that expect you to make the project actually conform to the plan once it has been developed and approved. Any deviations may be perceived as a lack of planning and proper management. Being agile in a non-agile world can be very challenging and is fraught with its own set of risks and pitfalls.

Chapter 15: IT Governance

In this chapter we discuss how IT governance provides transparency to senior management so that they can make the best decisions based upon the most accurate and up-to-date information. The ALM provides unique capabilities for ensuring that managers have the essential information necessary for evaluating their options. From the CEO to the board of directors, information must often be compartmentalized due to the practical constraints of just how much information can be consumed at any point in time. Achieving this balance empowers your leadership to make informed decisions that help steer your organization to success.

Chapter 16: Audit and Regulatory Compliance

This chapter explains that audit and regulatory compliance require that you establish IT controls to guide the way in which the team works. Your auditors may be internal employees or external consultants engaged by your firm. The internal audit team usually focuses on internal policy, whereas external auditors are often engaged to ensure compliance with federal regulatory guidelines. Although many technology professionals look at audit and regulatory compliance as just something that you have to do, others view it as an obligatory yet unfortunate waste of time and effort. Our focus is on establishing effective IT controls that help avoid both defects and risk. This chapter will help you understand how to use audit and regulatory compliance to ensure that you prevent the sorts of major systems glitches and outages that we read about all too often.

Chapter 17: Agile ALM in the Cloud

This chapter explains how cloud-based computing promises, and often delivers, capabilities such as scalable, virtualized enterprise solutions; elastic infrastructures; robust services; and mature platforms. Cloud-based architecture presents the potential of limitless scalability, but it also presents many challenges and risks. The scope of cloud-based computing ranges from development tools to elastic infrastructures that make it possible for developers to use full-size test environments that are both inexpensive and easy to construct and tear down, as required. The first step to harnessing its potential is to understand how application lifecycle management functions within the cloud.

Chapter 18: Agile ALM on the Mainframe

This chapter explains how to apply the agile ALM in a mainframe environment. Application lifecycle management on the mainframe typically enjoys a specific workflow. Despite a culture that lends itself well to step-by-step defined procedures, ALM on the mainframe often falls short of its potential. Sure, we can specify steps of a process, and everyone accepts that process tollgates are necessary on the mainframe. But that does not mean that our mainframe processes help to improve productivity and quality. It is essential that ALM on the mainframe be agile and help the team reach their goals and the business achieve success.

Chapter 19: Integration across the Enterprise

This chapter explains that understanding the ALM across the entire organization requires an understanding of the organization at a very broad level. It also requires that you understand how each structure within the company interfaces with the others. In DevOps, we call this *systems thinking* when we are examining an application from its inception to implementation, operation, and even its deprecation. DevOps principles and practices are essential in integrating the ALM across the organization.

Chapter 20: QA and Testing in the ALM

In this chapter we discuss how quality assurance (QA) and testing are essential to any software or systems lifecycle. Most technology professionals view the QA and testing process as simply executing test cases to verify and validate that requirements have been met and that the system functions as expected. But there is a lot more to QA and testing, and this chapter will help you understand how to establish effective processes that help ensure your system functions as needed. DevOps helps us build, package, and deploy software much more quickly. Too often, the QA and testing process cannot keep up with the accelerated deployment pipeline. DevOps cannot succeed without excellent QA and testing.

Chapter 21: Personality and Agile ALM

In this chapter we examine key aspects of human personality in the context of the agile ALM. Top technology professionals often have remarkable analytical and technical skills. However, even the most skilled professionals often have great difficulty dealing with some of the interesting behaviors and personalities of their colleagues. Implementing an agile ALM requires that you are able to work with all of the stakeholders and navigate the frequently thorny people issues inherent in dealing with diverse groups of very intelligent, albeit somewhat idiosyncratic, and often equally opinionated, people

Chapter 22: The Future of ALM

In this chapter we discuss what lies ahead for the agile ALM.

Register your copy of *Agile Application Lifecycle Management* at informit.com for convenient access to downloads, updates, and corrections as they become available. To start the registration process, go to informit.com/register and log in or create an account. Enter the product ISBN (9780321774101) and click Submit. Once the process is complete, you will find any available bonus content under "Registered Products."

Acknowledgments

Many people assisted me during the writing and publishing of this book, beginning with a family who tolerates my obsession with writing and broadcasting about configuration management and application lifecycle management best practices. I also need to acknowledge the amazing folks at Addison-Wesley, especially Chris Guizikowski who graciously supported my insatiable requests for books and online materials to read during my writing and gently nudged me to get this work completed. I also have to thank the many thousands of colleagues who collaborate with me on the ground implementing these best practices and all those who shared their thoughts and ideas online. I especially want to thank the thousands of people who have written to me commenting on the books and articles that I have written over what has been more than a decade. Writing, for me, is a team sport, and I am grateful for everyone who connected with me via the various social networks and especially everyone who dropped me a note commenting on what I had written. I have learned from each one of these exchanges, and I am grateful for your collaboration and collegiality.

About the Authors

Bob Aiello has more than twenty-five years of prior experience as a technical manager at leading financial services firms, with company-wide responsibility for CM and DevOps. He often provides hands-on technical support for enterprise source code management tools, SOX/Cobit compliance, build engineering, continuous integration, and automated application deployment. He serves on the IEEE Software and Systems Engineering Standards Committee (S2ESC) management board and served as the technical editor for CM Crossroads for more than 15 years. Bob is also editor of the *Agile ALM DevOps journal* and coauthor of *Configuration Management Best Practices* (Addison-Wesley, 2011).

Leslie Sachs is a New York State certified school psychologist and COO of CM Best Practices Consulting. She has more than twenty years of experience in psychology, intervening in diverse clinical and business settings to improve individual and group functioning. Leslie is assistant editor of the *Agile ALM DevOps journal and coauthor of Configuration Management Best Practices.*

PART I

Defining the Process

Chapter 1

Introducing Application Lifecycle Management Methodology

This chapter introduces application lifecycle management (ALM) process and explains what you need to know in order to define an ALM that will help you implement a comprehensive and effective software or systems lifecycle. We discuss how to implement the ALM using agile principles in a real-world pragmatic way that will help guide the activities of each member of your team, whether you are creating new software or customizing a commercial package. Systems lifecycles are a little different than a software development lifecycle and are usually associated with obtaining (and customizing) a project from a solution vendor. Commercial off-the-shelf (COTS) software is commonly used today to deliver robust technology solutions, but they often require some effort to customize and implement. This is precisely when you might use a system development lifecycle instead of a software development lifecycle, which we discuss further in Chapter 2, "Defining the Software Development Process." Both software and systems development require ALM, to help track and communicate required tasks and deliverables. An effective ALM must be, by its very nature, comprehensive, specific, and traceable. It is not easy to design a software lifecycle upfront, and we will guide you in accomplishing this effort in an agile and iterative way. This is not your typical agile book. We are going to have a difficult discussion about the most pragmatic approach to defining processes that are practical and yet comprehensive. Our approach to this work is very broad, and we touch on functions that are not normally thought of as being part of the ALM, such as internal audit and procurement. *You will be reading about many different processes and functions. Try to ask yourself if this process or function is something that you need now or perhaps should be implemented in six to nine months as you begin to reach your first deadlines. You probably don't need every single function or process that we discuss in this book, and that is fine. Our goal is to help you choose what your ALM will include in a practical and realistic way.* We take this broad and comprehensive approach because the reality is that organizations we have assisted needed to design processes that aligned with the key functions and processes throughout the *entire* organization. We are going to talk about the "elephant in the room," which is our reference to the fact that many companies are implementing processes using agile principles that are customized to their needs and often not completely agile in a textbook way. We are not trying to implement a purist approach to agile development. Instead, we are going to help you take your existing processes and make them better in a realistic and practical way. We have repeatedly seen that our colleagues are very smart and capable people who often make the tough choices required to optimize processes that are the best fit for their organization and the project that they are trying to complete. This book is about designing and implementing real-world processes that are customized to the needs of the organization and can evolve as requirements dictate. We are going to train that elephant and, more importantly, ensure that the team can enjoy open and honest communication. This chapter helps you understand application lifecycle management (ALM) and how to implement all of its features. In this chapter, we introduce the core concepts and then build upon them throughout the rest of the book.

1.1 Goals of Application Lifecycle Management

ALM helps you deliver your solutions faster and with better quality by providing much-needed structure for the entire software and systems development effort, including specific details on the tasks, roles, responsibilities, and essential milestones that help stakeholders track progress. ALM also helps us ascertain and communicate when we will be able to deliver the completed solution. Any parent taking a long trip with small children becomes accustomed to hearing the question, "Are we there yet?" Implementing an effective ALM is indeed a journey, and we need to be able to tell our stakeholders (in this case, my children) when we expect to arrive at the summer camp grounds or waterpark, which is our intended destination. In practice, the ALM essentially defines the rules of the road for the entire lifecycle. This is not a trivial effort, as even a small software or systems development effort involves many tasks, and managing the ALM can be an overwhelming task. It is also not a static endeavor, and any attempt to plan what you do not understand will obviously fail.

Crystal Balls and Application Lifecycle Management

Bob worked with an international firm that had a very strong focus on planning every single step of the development lifecycle. This company felt that planning was essential, and everyone tried to plan out each detail to an extreme degree. Because the culture of the firm focused so much on planning, it was unacceptable to have changes to the plan, and any attempt to deviate from the plan was met with significant consequences in terms of senior management questioning why the plan had been created improperly initially. The end result was that everyone worked to the plan even when it became clear over time that it was not in the best interests of the firm. Managers had to plan out each detail of the effort to a level that was absolutely impossible without a crystal ball, and then everyone focused on making sure that the plan appeared to be correct. There was significant waste as a result, and planning actually became a huge barrier to really getting work done in an efficient manner.

This chapter begins the process of providing a structure to enable you to manage the ALM along with each of the associated tasks that must be completed to implement a software or systems lifecycle. In Chapter 7, "Automating the Agile ALM," we discuss the use of workflow automation to organize the tasks assigned to each stakeholder, and in Chapter 5, "Rapid Iterative Development," we discuss the iterative nature of the ALM. The fundamental goal of application lifecycle management is to provide an appropriate structure to organize and manage the entire software and system development effort. The ALM helps each stakeholder understand what needs to get done on a day-to-day basis. Without a well-designed ALM, your software and systems development effort will be unstructured and most likely will fail. Let's consider why the ALM is so important.

1.2 Why Is ALM Important?

Application lifecycle management is important because it provides the structure to understand and manage the myriad of complexities that are inherent in coordinating the work of many stakeholders. Small projects may only involve 10 or 20 technology professionals, including business analysts, software developers, quality assurance (QA)/testing engineers, project managers, operations, systems

administrators, and, of course, our end users. However, larger projects can involve hundreds or even thousands of stakeholders. Providing clarity to the complex tasks, goals, and objectives of each contributor is essential for any project's
success and the success of the organization itself. The ALM is also important
because it helps provide guidance to everyone involved on exactly what tasks
they should be working on each day. This guidance is particularly important
because large-scale development efforts always have a period that can only be
described as "controlled chaos." This situation isn't necessarily unexpected, so
long as you have the structure in place to help guide the effort. Providing this
structure is precisely where the ALM can help.

> ### Application Lifecycle Management
>
> - Provides structure to the entire software and systems develop-
>   ment effort.
>
> - Clarifies what each stakeholder should be doing on a day-to-
>   day basis.
>
> - Answers the question: Are we there yet?
>
> - Specifies resources needed.
>
> - Identifies impediments to progress.
>
> - Clarifies connections between functions.
>
> - Clarifies the big picture.

Things can get very busy when you are part of a large software or systems
delivery effort. Amidst the noise and "controlled chaos," each member of the
team needs to have a clear picture of their deliverables on a day-to-day basis.
The ALM can provide this clarity through workflow automation, which we
describe more fully in Chapter 7. The ALM answers the essential question of
"are we there yet" by clarifying the tasks that have been completed and the
tasks that remain. More importantly, the agile ALM, supported by workflow
automation, proactively notifies stakeholders of pending tasks and escalates
open items that have missed their planned deliverable date. Project management is certainly an essential function in any development effort, and if you
would like to take a deep dive into agile project management then I recommend *The Software Project Manager's Bridge to Agility* by Michele Sliger and
Stacia Broderick.

The ALM does focus on effective release and iteration planning, thus helping to provide structure around what is often short-term planning that is typically very fluid and, at times, unpredictable. Application lifecycle management helps deal with these shifting priorities by clarifying the resources required for any effort and identifying impediments that could affect the project schedule or any of the deliverables. We discuss technical risk in Section 5.8 from the development view, which can significantly affect project delivery estimates.

ALM is fundamentally different from just a software or systems delivery lifecycle in that it casts a much wider net and can affect almost every function within the organization from the help desk, to the QA testers, to the operations team helping us stay online. Because of this wide scope, the ALM can help clarify connections between functions and helps us understand the big picture. Having a comprehensive approach to application lifecycle management makes the difference between successful organizations and those who risk failure. With this definition of ALM, we understand that the scope is indeed very wide, so the next question is: Where do we start?

1.3 Where Do I Start?

Getting started with an ALM effort involves understanding the business needs and requirements and defining the initial tasks that need to be completed. This effort can be very different based upon the business sector, outside pressures, and internal requirements. We have participated in organizations rushing to get a release to market in order to maintain (or establish) a competitive advantage. Other organizations are obliged to take a much more measured approach. Regardless, getting started usually involves identifying a reasonable pilot and communication with all stakeholders. We usually start by defining a very specific and minimal set of functionality that can truly add value, and we strongly defend against expanding the initial scope as much as possible. Getting something to work right as soon as possible has many benefits. The first is that you have something tangible to show and use to promote further collaboration. The second is that when you are first getting started, you are often dealing with new technology that must be understood, and this is best accomplished via bite-sized efforts. One good way to look at this effort is to consider how to get started with rolling out the tools necessary to support the ALM, and it should not come as a surprise that those of us who support application lifecycle management need to adhere to the same principles and approaches that we are advocating for our colleagues creating business applications. When implementing ALM tools, I like to get something running as quickly as possible. There are several reasons why I have found that what amounts to being an iterative approach works best.

Getting something up and running helps you clarify the vision and technology. This means that getting started often involves getting the iteration completed and shared with all of the relevant stakeholders.

> ### Proof of Technology
>
> In my work, I am often helping teams get started with a new application lifecycle management automation solution. For some organizations, this may involve a simple open-source tool such as Git or Subversion with an integrated defect or task automation tool. In other organizations, my work may involve implementing a full-featured, commercial source code management solution with an integrated workflow automation tool that includes work items such as tasks, defects, or requirements. The very first step is to quickly get a proof of technology or pilot system in place. I then try to get stakeholders to take the new toolset for a spin, and I demo the solution to as many stakeholders as possible. The tool evaluation effort may include development managers, developers, DBAs, project managers, and auditors and data security, along with other stakeholders. I always communicate what I am building, although I do try very hard to push back against customization until the initial system is in use. Then we iteratively improve the product over time.

With any new technology, there is a temptation to try to customize the solution to add features and make the product as productive to use as possible. Although this is obviously a valuable long-term goal, it is also hard to predict how the tool will actually be used—until it is actually in use. We try to get our ALM tools in limited use as soon as possible while continuously teaching and communicating what ALM is really all about.

1.4 What Is Application Lifecycle Management?

Application lifecycle management defines the rules of the road for the entire software and systems lifecycle. Successful ALM provides clarity around the entire delivery effort, from defining requirements to building, packaging, and deploying the code. The ALM can be considered from many viewpoints. Developers need clarity regarding which components they will work with and how they should be structuring their code. Operations needs enough lead time to create the infrastructure, along with estimates for required resources such as memory and disk space. A fundamental consideration is how developers will utilize source code management and workflow automation to achieve structure and clarity around their work. This may include defining how they use streams and components or perhaps a simpler branching methodology, which we discuss further in Chapter 6, "Build Engineering in the ALM." They also need to define how they will handle application builds, continuous integration, and deployment into the initial test environments. The ALM inherently helps us to iteratively define and communicate what we are doing. Of course, the development team consists of many more stakeholders than just developers. For example, the relationship between development and testing should be a fundamental consideration in the ALM.

The QA and testing teams need to be able to understand the requirements and intended use of the system. Requirements management is an essential aspect of application lifecycle methodology, and QA needs to ensure that requirements are traceable and testable. The good news is that the ALM helps us to do this work. Each stakeholder has what can be a very different perspective, and the ALM must be flexible enough to define the work that is being done by each team and help manage change. Good planning does not prevent change. On the contrary, good planning helps to identify, manage change, and most significantly, assess and manage the impact of any changes that are introduced to the plan. Application lifecycle management helps clarify the roles and responsibilities of each of the stakeholders and then proceeds to provide guidance on what each member of the team should be doing on a day-to-day basis.

Scope of Application Lifecycle Management

I have seen team members who struggled to know what to do on a day-to-day basis. The ALM provides this clarity by ensuring that there is a framework for defining tasks, roles, and responsibilities, which is inherent in any process engineering effort. The ALM is different from just a development lifecycle because of its scope and comprehensive view of the entire effort. As a result, it provides a valuable framework for managing software and systems delivery efforts. ALM achieves a very broad scope.

The broad scope of application lifecycle management does incur the risk that it can be too high level and frankly less than useful. Actually, it is our view that effective application lifecycle management should be very specific and detailed, with a practical and applied development methodology. In practice, we usually cannot implement the entire ALM at once. We generally focus on a specific aspect of the process that needs to be improved. This allows us to approach process improvement by creating a series of building blocks. To understand how to implement ALM, it can be helpful to look at the software development lifecycle (SDLC).

1.4.1 Remember the SDLC?

I remember the first time that I got to work on writing a detailed SDLC. It was exciting to brainstorm with colleagues on the tasks that we needed to complete for a successful software development effort. Back then I was a young computer programmer with a few years of experience and a strong interest in industrial psychology. I analyzed the tasks that were completed in each phase of the lifecycle with the same fervor that I imagined Winslow Taylor did in his famous time and motion studies.[1]

Winslow Taylor (1856–1915)

Winslow Taylor was an American engineer who became known for his use of time and motion studies, which he developed into a methodology that he called Scientific Management. Taylor's ideas on efficiency and productivity were both groundbreaking and highly criticized, focusing on a very detailed view of the exact steps taken by workers carrying out a particular task. His work is described in Scientific Management, published in 1911.

At the time that I first learned about Taylor, I was still struggling with severe vision problems and was not certain whether I would be blind or sighted in the coming years. It occurred to me that Taylor's methodologies involving time and motion studies could be used to analyze other types of work to ascertain what jobs could be performed by a blind person such as myself. Later I learned that Winslow Taylor himself had vision difficulties that had affected his own career and educational decisions.

Now software development is certainly quite different from machine shop work in a factory. But, that said, there is considerable value in understanding what is involved with each phase of the software development lifecycle and providing that transparency to each of the stakeholders involved.

Creating an SDLC has typically been described in a waterfall lifecycle, with requirements, design, development, and testing being the high-level phases. The software development lifecycle is intended to help define all of the tasks,

---

1. Taylor, Winslow, *Scientific Management*, 1911.

deliverables, and milestones required to create and implement software systems, but, in practice, it often falls short, and my experience has been that in many organizations the book typically sits on someone's shelf without actually being used. This is quite disappointing because a well-defined SDLC can provide considerable value. We discuss a strategy for defining and automating your SDLC in Chapter 7.

At a practical level, the software development lifecycle helps to clarify all of the tasks required as part of the development effort. It also helps to manage the inevitable expansion in scope.

Managing Scope Creep

Many people get excited when they first review a new system about to be delivered. One of the biggest compliments that you can get is for a stakeholder to start brainstorming about what you can do to improve upon the system that is being delivered. Make sure that you hold the line and deliver the intended functionality as planned, avoiding if at all possible enlarging the scope of the effort—especially when this can affect the project deliverables. Obviously, avoiding scope creep is often impossible, especially when outside market or competitive forces demand more functionality. Regulatory requirements may also place demands upon the development effort. Even in these challenging situations, there is still hope. The ALM helps you assess and communicate the impact of scope creep, including any potential risks that may be incurred when the scope of the effort is expanded.

Software development lifecycles usually start with defining requirements, which gives this methodology an initial focus on understanding the organizational priorities and business focus.

1.4.2 Business Focus

Application lifecycle management must be driven by a pragmatic understanding of the business and business requirements. Technology professionals are notoriously focused on the technical details and often find it difficult to look at the world from a business perspective. I have faced this challenge myself many times while tackling a tough technical problem; my focus is often deep down into the "weeds," and it can be very difficult to pull myself back up and look at things from the point of view of the business end user. In keeping with the wide scope of the ALM, business focus and business requirements must drive the ALM. The

ALM affects requirements in several important ways. The first consideration is to have a well-defined lifecycle, including version control for the requirements themselves.

Obviously, the approach that you take with any lifecycle is directly affected by the business. For example, ALM in a highly regulated environment is very different than what is required for an Internet startup. The requirements themselves benefit from a development lifecycle, and, of course, business and technical requirements should be documented and version-controlled as necessary. Even in an agile environment, your epics and stories need to be under version control, and you may need to manage variants such as the requirements related to a bugfix to address a serious issue such as a regulatory violation. Requirements often need to be under version control and an associated workflow to support a requirements development lifecycle. In some industries, you may be required to maintain traceability between requirements and the test cases designed to verify required functionality. This may sound like an onerous approach with unnecessary extra steps, or what many agile practitioners refer to as "ceremony." I am not advocating any more process than is absolutely necessary to avoid mistakes and their consequences. Less is more, and taking a Lean approach is almost always the optimal approach. However, designing a nuclear power plant actually requires that you not only have adequate documentation, but also verify that the documented requirements are accurate and maintained. The documents in safety systems often become essential artifacts in and of themselves and require a lifecycle to control and document changes. There are many industries where documentation is considered essential.

Documenting Care on an Ambulance

Bob likes to ride as a volunteer emergency medical technician (EMT) on an ambulance. Many times he has helped in major car accidents and other serious incidents. Some patients require oxygen to address breathing. EMTs know that the administration of oxygen must be documented on the patient care report, or else it is as if you did not provide the oxygen at all (and provide an appropriate standard of care). The ALM helps to document the standard of care in developing your software application.

The ALM helps to control the evolution of the requirements themselves. Iterative development results in release milestones that help ensure the requirements are understood at a technical level. It is very common for developers to be given very limited information and be expected to know about details in how the system should work that are neither clarified nor documented. The third aspect to consider is the effort to understand the business requirements by the folks in the business unit itself. Although this need is often not recognized, our business colleagues also benefit from the iterative nature of the ALM as they, too, struggle to understand their own requirements, especially in environments that are changing constantly due to competitive or perhaps regulatory requirements.

Business Requirements and the ALM

Business requirements drive the entire application lifecycle, and thus business requirements also need to drive the ALM. There are three ways in which the ALM affects business requirements:

- Controlling the lifecycle of the requirements

- Releasing iterations to help develop and test requirements

- Helping the business understand the requirements

Addressing the Business Silo

The industry adoption of DevOps principles and practices is bringing into focus the need for better communication between development, QA, and operations. Information security (InfoSec) is also a key stakeholder with a need for better communication and collaboration. Agile does put a much-needed focus on the role of the product owner, including colocation of the product owner with the development team. This is all well and good, but it has been my experience that many organizations often have a silo mentality between each of the technology teams and the business end user. Just as development needs to collaborate early and often with operations, so do the business minds need parameters to guide them in terms of documenting and clarifying business requirements. The business also helps us understand just how much change can be consumed by the end user. In fact, DevOps principles and practices should be used to help improve communication and collaboration between any silos within the organization. One key area to consider is risk and risk management.

Understanding Risk from a Business Focus

Risk is not inherently bad, and some businesses thrive on well-defined and accurately measured risk. I have worked in many trading firms that faced significant risk each and every day. Traders would make excellent decisions that resulted in substantial profits and then the next day, they would make the wrong choice and lose some money. The successful traders had made more good bets than bad bets and made lots of money. There are several important considerations from an ALM perspective. The first is to understand the risk as it relates to business requirements and then align accordingly. If you are in a high-risk business, then taking some well-measured risks might be quite acceptable—even desirable. The second consideration is that the ALM can help the business manage risk by driving technology to provide new services and features that help run the business. The ALM helps manage risk by providing a comprehensive framework to manage the full application lifecycle, especially application build, package, and deployment.

Fragile Financial Systems Infrastructure

In recent years, there have been a remarkable number of very serious financial systems outages, including high-speed trading firms and the trading exchanges themselves. Although many articles discuss what went wrong in each incident, none of them have focused on software methodology. Establishing an effective ALM is the core capability that is necessary to have reliable financial systems that can be upgraded and maintained as needed. Throughout this book, we discuss the fundamental techniques required to implement complex systems, including deploying new functionality and responding quickly to incidents as they occur.

Risk is an essential issue to address and requires an open environment where all stakeholders feel safe expressing their views and opinions. There are many companies where the culture prevents employees from expressing their views, even punishing whistle-blowers who speak up when they see potential issues. Obviously, senior management may have more information and may be right when overruling an employee expressing a view from the trenches. But when the culture rewards silence and obstructs the free exchange of ideas, risk can often be a significant issue with severe incidents and systems outages as a consequence.

Agile practices are very effective, and we speak about them at length in this book. But there are times when you must use non-agile methodologies.

Getting Cut Off by My Manager

Those who know me are aware that I have never been afraid to speak my mind. If you read the foreword of this book, you are aware that I could not see people's faces when I was growing up. Because blind people cannot read expressions on people's faces, we often tend to say what is on our mind without regard for the visual cues that tend to moderate our sighted colleagues. I have had quite a few times when I expressed my concerns only to be cut off by a manager or someone else who had more positional power than I did. Sometimes nothing happened and sometimes systems crashed. The key is to help out without ever uttering an "I told you so," although documenting your position is often a very good idea and has saved my job more than once.

Agile or not, the ALM is an essential part of your software development methodology.

1.4.3 Agile or Not?

Many organizations have project and development management requirements that may affect the ALM. We have often seen that approval for the budget of a project required a waterfall or hybrid agile-waterfall approach where requirements, design, and a project plan were developed to a degree that management felt comfortable approving the budget. Many agile experts insist that the organization completely embrace agile principles and methodology. Although this may be a worthwhile goal, it is often not possible in many organizations. Even if you are in an organization that stubbornly resists becoming fully agile, you can often make your processes a little bit better by embracing agile methods. For some, what I am saying may seem like heresy, but it has been my experience that many companies are successfully employing a hybrid of agile and non-agile methods. There are reasons why this approach may be less than optimal and obviously it carries its own set of risks. But the "elephant in the room" is that many organizations must approach process improvement in an agile iterative fashion, and it is not always possible to just change the entire organization overnight. We discuss this issue further in Chapter 4, "Agile Process Maturity." Whether your organization embraces agile or not, you can improve your development processes by adopting these industry best practices and the ALM is the key to helping you choose the right path and set the best possible priorities. We discuss the agile ALM in Chapter 3, "Agile Application Lifecycle Management."

Being Agile in a Non-Agile World

Being agile in a non-agile world can be very difficult or even impossible to accomplish. I have often found myself in organizations that insisted on a waterfall approach. What is most difficult is trying to predict things that are just not possible to ascertain up-front. Waterfall was originally envisioned as an iterative process, but today it seems that some organizations expect their employees to be able to predict the future to a degree that is simply not reasonable. The real problem is that these are the same organizations that expect you to make the project actually conform to the plan once it has been developed and approved. Any deviations must be perceived as a lack of planning and proper management. Being agile in a non-agile world can be very challenging and fraught with its own set of risks and pitfalls.

The degree of agility does affect how you implement your ALM. Another important consideration is the degree to which your process is mature or in a developing or more fluid state.

1.4.4 Mature Process or Fluid?

Process maturity is an important topic. We discuss agile process maturity in Chapter 4, but your first consideration is really whether or not your organization is ready for a mature ALM process or needs to stay fluid for a while. I try to avoid adding too much process in the beginning of any effort. It has been my experience that process has to evolve iteratively as the need for rules and guidelines organically takes shape. The reason for this is that implementing what can be perceived as too much process will motivate many members of the team to block your advance forward to really having a robust ALM. But catch the team after a systems outage where everyone had to stay up all night and you will find much more support for establishing IT controls to avoid mistakes. Another great motivator for process improvement is the need to pass an audit or meet federal regulatory requirements. Management is often motivated by an audit report or, even worse, a visit from a regulatory authority. This is precisely when you just might get the budget that you need for tools and consulting to help your organization transition to a more effective way of developing systems. It is also essential for process improvement to actually follow agile principles.

Is Your Process Improvement Agile?

Becoming agile is not just for the members of the scrum. I usually go into an organization with an existing set of practices, which may or may not actually be well-defined processes. My phone rings (or I get an email) when they need help. I approach the process improvement effort using the same principles that I am trying to implement. We discuss applying the principles and implementing the ALM in Chapter 4. In most cases, I must approach my work in an iterative fashion. I approach process improvement in an iterative way, and I encourage the teams that I am working with to approach their development effort in an iterative way too. There is a common misunderstanding among some folks that agile and iterative development are synonymous terms. They are not. Agile involves a specific set of principles and practices and is especially focused on the team transforming the way that they work. We discuss this further in Chapter 4, but I also want to point out that there are iterative development methods besides agile, and the ALM does facilitate iterative development whether the team is using agile methods or not.

1.4.5 Rapid Iterative Development

We discuss the iterative nature of the SDLC in Chapter 2 and the iterative waterfall in Chapter 14, "Agile in a Non-Agile World." Whether you are embracing agile or not, the ALM facilitates rapid iterative development, which has long been regarded as an effective software methodology in and of itself. But iterative development is not necessarily agile. Rapid iterative development involves creating runnable versions of the system that can be used to clarify requirements and reduce risk in many important ways. The ALM benefits from an iterative approach and depends upon excellent configuration management best practices.

1.4.6 Core Configuration Management Best Practices

Configuration management best practices [1] are essential for implementing agile application lifecycle and DevOps. Without fully understanding these processes and practices, you just won't get off home plate.

Source Code Management

Source code management is the discipline of safeguarding all of the artifacts that are created to develop your system. Source code management is a key function in configuration management (CM) and directly affects the productivity of your team, as well as the quality of the product being developed. Unfortunately, many organizations overlook the importance of establishing an effective source code management function to implement and support source code management tools and processes. You do not want to make this mistake, and in this chapter, I help you get started in the right direction. I have enjoyed having companywide responsibility for source code management in several large globally distributed organizations. This meant that I had to guarantee that the firm never lost any source code once it was part of a release to production (or even QA). SCM needs to be approached in a flexible and creative way. One size does *not* necessarily fit all, and I have often implemented source code management differently for some development teams than others. But I always focused on meeting the same essential goals as discussed later. I would also say that source code management provides the foundation for the other disciplines of configuration management, especially build engineering, release management, and deployment.

Good source code management starts with making certain all your source code is safely locked down and no important source code (or any other configuration item) is lost. That sounds fairly simple, but many of us recall the massive Y2K efforts that uncovered a remarkable number of critical systems that had been running in production for years without anyone knowing where the source code was located. In some cases, we went searching for the correct version of COBOL copybooks; in other cases, we had to rewrite the entire system from scratch (which was often the right choice anyway). My goal in implementing good Source Code Management is to absolutely guarantee that source code can *never* be lost.

Another important goal of effective code management is to help improve the productivity of your entire team. Effective Source Code Management means that you can manage more than one line of code development at the same time. It also means that you can improve the quality of your code in many ways, including helping to implement automated testing on both a unit and systems level. One of the most important goals of code management is to provide complete traceability so that you know exactly who changed your code and are able to, if necessary, back out the change. We discuss strategies for implementing effective source code management in our book *Configuration Management Best Practices: Practical Methods that Work in the Real World*.

Build Engineering

The goal of build engineering is to be able to reliably compile and link your source code into a binary executable in the shortest possible time. Build engineering includes identifying the exact compile and runtime dependencies, as well as any other specific technical requirements, including compiler (linker and managed environment) switches and dependencies. Build engineering improves both quality and productivity for the entire team. I believe that the build engineering team should consider themselves to be a service function with the development team as their primary *customers*. However, there are times when build engineering must also have the authority to enforce organizational policies. As build engineers, we provide a service to support the development effort, but our primary goal is to help secure the assets of the firm that are built and released through the build engineering function. We discuss build engineering in Chapter 6.

Environment Management

The goal of environment configuration is to always point to the correct runtime resources such as the QA or production database. Environment configuration is all about knowing your interface dependencies and controlling their changes accurately. Done well, environment configuration improves quality and productivity. Done poorly, environment configuration will be the cause of defects, wasted time, and other problems. Ultimately, the goal of environment configuration is establishing and maintaining control as your deliverable code makes its way from development to QA to production. Environment management also has the goal of providing enough test environments so that development can be done efficiently and with the proper utilization of available resources. Best practices in environment configuration will help you develop code faster and with better quality. We discuss environment management in Chapter 7, specifically Section 7.18.

Change Management

Change control is the most central function in configuration management. It is also one of the most underutilized and often misunderstood functions. Large organizations always have a change control board to act as a gatekeeper to control changes to the production environment. This is obviously important, but there is a lot more to change control than just gatekeeping. Some organizations have change control processes to govern requests for change. This is called *a priori* change control. Environment configuration is also commonly controlled by change control. I have seen organizations where there was a robust change control structure arranged in a hierarchy from senior management to the technicians making configuration changes and other organizations where the project managers and development team leads handled change control as an implicit project management task.

The goal of change control is to carefully manage all changes to the production (and usually QA) environments. Part of this effort is just coordination, and that is very important. But part of this is also managing changes to the environment that will affect all of the systems in the environment. It is also essential to control which releases are promoted to QA and production. Change control can act as the stimulus to all other configuration management–related functions as well. We discuss change management in Chapter 10, "Change Management."

Release Management

Release management is a core function in configuration management that focuses on packaging a system for promotion from development to QA to production. If you are supporting a software production company, then "production," for you, may be shipping the product to the customer instead of releasing the code to the production (or QA) environment. Although release management should focus on packaging the code created during the build process, in practice, release management is often viewed as being a very broad function that may encompass both source code management and build engineering. Release management in a corporate IT environment is slightly different from release management for a software product company—although I have worked in software product companies that still maintained separate QA, integration, and production environments as if they were a corporate IT environment, even while shipping the finished product to an end user (or pushing changes via an automated installation process). In this chapter, we focus on defining release management as a function that takes over after the build has been completed and prepares the release for deployment into the desired environment. Once a release has been created, it should conform to all of the standards set by the release management team.

The goal of release management is to create and maintain a repeatable process for packaging a release that includes a clear way to identify every component of the release. Release management must be clearly defined with little or no chance of errors occurring. Generally, release packaging is an automated function that includes creating an immutable ID that is embedded into the release package itself. Release management should also coordinate any dependencies that might be required in order for the release to successfully deploy. Finally, release management should be completely traceable with a clearly defined procedure to verify that the correct components have been deployed into a runtime environment.

Deployment

Deployment is the final step in the code promotion process. Deployment involves taking the packaged release and promoting it into the target environment, which is likely production or perhaps QA. Deployment is also responsible for rolling back a promotion if something goes wrong. If you are able to seamlessly deploy and roll back if necessary, you will be able to significantly reduce a common source of risk (and potential outages). Deployment is usually performed by the operations team, which often has a lot of other responsibilities that need to be fulfilled. I like to see deployment be the simplest step in the release process. This means that all of the prior steps of the process have been successfully completed. Deployment usually also means that control shifts from the release management team to the operations team, which is usually pretty busy with just maintaining the current production systems. The operations team is primarily concerned with keeping the systems running and responding to any events that occur. Therefore, deployment procedures should be kept as straightforward as possible. Your release management team needs to create solid deployment procedures that can be gracefully completed by the operations team. We discuss continuous deployment in Chapter 9, "Continuous Delivery and Deployment."

The main goal of deployment is to promote a release into production without any possible problem occurring. Promoting a release should be like turning on a light switch. If there is a problem with the release, then the operations team follows the deployment procedures to roll back the release so that business can continue while your tech support team figures out how to solve the problem. I believe that the capability to gracefully roll back a release is just as critical a goal as promoting a new release into production. Deployment also has another important goal and that is to know exactly what is in production at all times and to know immediately if any unauthorized changes have been made. My primary goal in setting up any deployment process is that all changes are tracked and that promoting a release or rolling back is easy, reliable, and predictable.

1.4.7 Automation

Years ago, there was a common mantra that process was more important than tools, and that is certainly still true to a point. But the ALM is just about impossible to implement without effective tools *and* processes. Automation is fundamental in any useable ALM approach. The automation must include effective version control, automated application build, package, and deployment (including deployment frameworks). Automated code review is also important, along with unit and application testing. We discuss automation in Chapter 7, but suffice it to say that you just won't have a very effective and viable ALM unless you embrace and implement automation. We discuss how to do that in this book. Among the most important practices in automation is continuous integration, which is a fundamental requirement for any effective ALM.

1.4.8 Continuous Integration

Continuous integration (CI) is an essential practice that involves putting together code that has been created and ascertaining if the code components can compile and run together successfully. Continuous integration often involves merging together code that has been written by different developers and is essential for code quality. We discuss continuous integration in Chapter 8, "Continuous Integration," but want to note the fundamental value of this practice is that integrating a small amount of code as early as possible avoids much bigger issues later. It would be difficult to imagine an effective ALM that does not embrace integrating code frequently, although we also discuss a couple of situations where it is difficult or even impossible to achieve. This introduces risk, and just like any other risk, must be addressed. Similarly, continuous deployment is also a fundamental aspect of an effective ALM.

1.4.9 Continuous Deployment

Continuous deployment, much like continuous integration, involves handling the build, package, and deployment of a small amount of code instead of the much more risky approach of planning a big-bang deployment, many of which are infamous for taking everyone's weekend. I have been doing DevOps and continuous deployment since long before it became a popular term in the industry. There has been considerable confusion between the terms continuous delivery and continuous deployment. Continuous delivery is typically used to indicate that you have a code baseline that is kept in a state where it could potentially be promoted to production at any time. In continuous delivery we sometimes promote changes to production but hide them using a technique called *feature toggle* until such time as we want the user to become aware of the new features. In the strictest sense, continuous deployment means that you are promoting changes all the way through to production on a continuous basis. For most large firms, continuous deployment may, at times, be impractical and often not even desirable, as many users do not like surprises, which can be quite disruptive. We discuss continuous deployment and continuous delivery in Chapter 9. Throughout this book we will use the term *continuous deployment* to generally mean promoting code to production as often as desired. Once an application is deployed, the operations team takes over and works to maintain continuous service without interruption.

1.4.10 Change Management

The goal of change management in the ALM is to carefully manage all changes to the production (and usually QA) deployment processes. Part of this effort is just coordination as well as communication, and that is very important. But part of this is also managing changes to the ALM that will affect all of the stakeholders in the organization. We discuss how to use change management throughout the ALM in Chapter 10.

1.4.11 IT Operations

The software development lifecycle typically does not extend beyond the application deployment. The ITIL v3 framework has become one of the most popular frameworks for defining IT service management. We discuss many of these best practices in Chapter 11, "IT Operations." There is often a disconnect between operations and the development team, as each has a very different set of priorities. DevOps is emerging as a set of principles and practices intended to help improve communication and collaboration between development and operations.

1.4.12 DevOps

DevOps is a set of industry best practices that improve communication and cooperation between development and operations. We carefully examine the emergence of DevOps in Chapter 12, "DevOps," and help you get started with implementing DevOps in your organization. This book takes a very wide view of DevOps and discusses DevOps principles and practices throughout the entire agile ALM.

1.4.13 Retrospectives

Retrospectives help drive the entire process improvement effort, especially in terms of defining application lifecycle management. This may not seem apparent at first, but your ALM must define the steps required to evaluate and solve problems. Retrospectives are very effective at enabling the team to understand what went well, as well as what needs to be improved. ALM should itself be defined in an agile iterative way, and that includes implementing retrospectives. Process improvement is hard. Identifying the processes supporting the application lifecycle is critical for your success. So how exactly do you go about implementing these best practices?

The most basic retrospective involves an open and honest discussion on what went well and what still remains to be improved. We dive into retrospectives in Chapter 13, "Retrospectives in the ALM." Retrospectives also set the stage for determining what information should be communicated to senior-level management as part of IT governance.

1.4.14 IT Governance

IT governance provides transparency to senior management so that they can make the right decisions based upon accurate and up-to-date information. The ALM provides unique capabilities for ensuring that managers have the right information so that they can make reasoned decisions. From the CEO to the board of directors, information must often be compartmentalized due to the practical constraints of just how much information can be consumed at any point in time. Getting this right empowers your leadership to make the most well-informed decisions possible in order to steer the organization to success.

1.4.15 Audit and Regulatory Compliance

The goal of establishing IT controls is to support audit and compliance by implementing procedures that bring IT governance into alignment with corporate governance. The most classic case is to establish controls that ensure that financial reports are accurate. Compliance is usually implemented based upon an established standard or framework. This means that the IT controls established conform to the recommendations specified in the framework mandated by a regulatory agency or adopted by the organization. For example, most financial services firms are required to have a separation of duties between the physical control of assets, such as a payroll or banking system, and those who have responsibility for developing and maintaining these systems. They should also have appropriate security measures in place that prevent unauthorized access and, of course, modification. In the event of unauthorized access, detection and audit controls should make remediation possible. Audit and regulatory compliance help to identify and manage risk. Risk is not always negative, and many organizations thrive by taking calculated risks. But risk must always be identified with appropriate controls established to mitigate unavoidable risk. Regulatory compliance is most often associated with following specific federal laws, which actually often do provide effective guidance that helps reduce risk and safeguard the interests of all stakeholders.

1.4.16 ALM and the Cloud

Cloud-based computing promises—and often delivers—capabilities such as scalable, virtualized enterprise solutions, elastic infrastructures, robust services, and mature platforms. Cloud-based architecture presents the potential of limitless potential, but it also presents many challenges and risks. The scope of cloud-based computing ranges from cloud-based development tools to elastic infrastructures that make it possible for developers to use full-size test environments that are both inexpensive and easy to construct and tear down, as required. The first step is to understand how application lifecycle management functions within the cloud.

Technology professionals often use cloud-based tools at each stage of the development lifecycle to manage the workflow and all of its required tasks. Cloud-based ALM tools commonly include source code management, workflow automation (including defect and task tracking), knowledge management, and community-based forums. Cloud-based tools can be employed throughout the entire ALM. Many organizations make good use of the cloud by maintaining their own private cloud. Virtualized environments enable continuous delivery and robust testing environments. The real advantage of cloud-based computing is its ability to deliver enterprise architectures at low cost and then scale the architecture as demand increases. Companies that use cloud-based technologies can focus more on operating expenditures (OPEX) than on capital expenditures (CAPEX). Therefore, businesses can keep initial costs low and pay only for use of the resources as use of the system grows. Making the best possible choices requires that you understand the goals of the ALM in the cloud.

1.4.17 Mainframe

The mainframe is alive and well. Many corporations have been planning the deprecation of their mainframe infrastructure for years, and yet the mainframes continue to be in use. Application lifecycle management on the mainframe typically enjoys a very specific structure. The culture of the mainframe lends itself well to step-by-step defined procedures. Yet ALM on the mainframe often falls short of its potential. Sure, we can identify specific steps of a process, and everyone accepts that process tollgates are necessary on the mainframe. But that does not mean that our mainframe processes help improve productivity and quality. Even more essential, ALM on the mainframe must be agile and help the team reach their goals and the business achieve success.

1.4.18 Integration across the Enterprise

Understanding the ALM across the organization requires an understanding of the organization at a very broad level. It also requires that you understand how each structure within the company interfaces with the others. In DevOps, we call this *systems thinking* when we are examining an application from its inception to implementation, operation, and even its deprecation. DevOps principles and practices are essential in integrating the ALM across the organization.

1.4.19 Quality Assurance and Testing

Quality assurance and testing are essential to any software or systems lifecycle. Most technology professionals view the QA and testing process as simply executing test cases to verify and validate that requirements have been met and that the system functions as expected. But there is a lot more to QA and testing, and Chapter 21, "Personality and Agile ALM," helps you understand how to establish effective processes to help ensure that your systems function as needed. DevOps helps us build, package, and deploy software much more quickly. Unfortunately, too often, the QA and testing process cannot keep up with the accelerated deployment pipeline.

1.4.20 Role of Personality

Technology professionals have remarkable analytical and technical skills. But even the most skilled professionals often have great difficulty dealing with the interesting behaviors and personalities of their colleagues. Implementing an agile ALM requires that you are able to work with all of the stakeholders and navigate all of the people issues inherent in dealing with diverse groups of often very smart people.

1.5 Conclusion

Agile ALM provides the essential structure to the entire software and systems development lifecycle. This includes specific details on the tasks, roles, responsibilities, and essential milestones that help us track progress. ALM also helps us ascertain and communicate when we will be able to deliver the completed solution. There are many ways to create an effective ALM. You need to start by understanding all of the inputs required by the ALM ecosystem. The rest of this book helps you understand how to design and implement an effective ALM. This book will also help you understand how to drive the entire ALM using DevOps principles and practices.

References

[1] Aiello, Bob and Leslie Sachs (2011). *Configuration Management Best Practices: Practical Methods that Work in the Real World*. Boston, MA: Addison-Wesley Professional.

Chapter 2

Defining the Software Development Process

Defining the software development process always sounds straightforward until you actually start trying to do the work. Many tasks are involved with any software or systems lifecycle, and a well-defined process must provide guidance on exactly what needs to get done and who is responsible for completing each task. Years ago we focused entirely on the software development lifecycle (SDLC), and that was not a bad place to start. But today's systems have many more moving parts and take much more effort to manage than just sitting a business analyst down with the Cobol developer who needs to write the code. Before we dive into agile application lifecycle management in Chapter 3, it would be helpful to review how we used to design software development processes before all of the buzz around agile, scrum, and DevOps. Some of the process engineering techniques that we employed were actually quite good, and as the old adage says, "To know where you are going, you must first know where you have been." This chapter helps you understand the basic skills of how to define the software development process. This will make it much easier for you to define processes that meet your requirements while applying all of the principles in Lean and agile.

2.1 Goals of Defining the Software Development Process

The goal of defining a software development process is to clarify exactly what needs to get done in developing a new software system. Most software development processes are described in terms of phases, and we provide some examples of how to approach defining your software development process using this technique. In the past, traditional software development processes usually focused on requirements, design, programming, and testing. Back then we described deployment and operations in a runbook that specified all of the procedures required to operate and support the system. IT professionals by and large were quite good at producing documentation and tailoring processes to the needs of the organization. Your goal in defining a software development process is to provide just enough guidance to avoid costly mistakes. Another important goal is to ensure that there is clarity around the tasks that each stakeholder is responsible for completing throughout the entire software or systems lifecycle.

2.2 Why Is Defining the Software Development Process Important?

Defining the software development process is important because it helps clarify what each stakeholder needs to accomplish throughout the software or systems delivery lifecycle. The well-defined software development process helps avoid costly mistakes by clarifying the tasks that need to be completed and enhances communication between each stakeholder. In a time when so many technology professionals are specialists and many organizations suffer from silos that are insulated from each other, a well-defined software development process can be very helpful in providing clarity as to what is going on during the software development effort. Without a well-defined software development process, your team risks having a lack of clarity as to what they are expected to do on a daily basis. They also won't have a clear idea of what is coming down the road that may affect them.

We have heard IT operations directors describe just how difficult it is for them to anticipate the requests that come in at the very last minute from development managers trying to implement new features required by their customers. If the IT operations director has some visibility into the software development process, then there is more opportunity to clarify the upcoming requirements without the usual fire drill that affects so many IT organizations. We explain how to create a well-defined software development process that helps your team respond to change and avoid costly mistakes without having to be bogged down in unnecessary bureaucracy. Remember always that too much process is just as bad as not having enough. But a well-defined process also helps us avoid mistakes caused by missing steps or failing to communicate. The software development process helps us right-size the amount of ceremony that we have in our approach to getting the work done.

2.3 Where Do I Start?

Getting started with creating an effective software development process begins with defining the high-level tasks that need to be accomplished to get the job done. This typically begins with understanding the business goals of what you are trying to accomplish and the high-level requirements necessary to deliver the business value. You then identify the stakeholders who will need to be involved with delivering your system. From there, our approach is to interview each stakeholder and ascertain what tasks he or she needs to accomplish. The software development process identifies the work each stakeholder must complete and should always start with collaboratively defining exactly what needs to get done. You won't get all of the tasks defined the first time, and that's fine. In the beginning of a project, there are usually some initial activities to define goals and also evaluate the technologies that are to be part of the proposed solution. Technology professionals are usually in an exploratory mode at this point, and there may be little need for a formal software development lifecycle. Pretty soon the project goals and the solution strategy will begin to take shape and then you need to start introducing some structure into the software or systems development effort. My experience is that it is usually best to start with a very Lean process that grows with the project itself. Start by creating a draft task list with roles and responsibilities and then review and update your process as needed.

2.4 Explaining the Software Development Lifecycle

Years ago it was popular to create a software development lifecycle that defined all of the tasks involved with developing software, including requirements gathering, design, development, and testing the application code. This approach to an SDLC was often associated with the waterfall lifecycle and had a limited scope and focus. I remember working on a large team to create my first SDLC and all of the revelations that I had when I learned about the work that all of the other technology professionals were doing as part of this effort. I was a software development programmer back then, and I got the opportunity to work with a group of industrial psychologists interviewing a large group of technology professionals in order to document their jobs and look for opportunities to eliminate duplicate roles and positions. This was back in the era of downsizing, and I certainly had some mixed feelings about participating in an effort that we all knew up-front would result in a lot of people losing their jobs. In the end, most of the people who wanted to stay with the company were able to do so, and lots of other people took lucrative buyout packages and either retired or went on to their next opportunity. This company handled downsizing well and has stayed profitable to this day.

The software development lifecycle was certainly flawed back then. Most organizations wrote SDLCs that did little more than sit on a shelf and collect dust. The basic problem with the SDLC was that there was no way to actually execute the delivery other than a manager following up on each and every task on a day-to-day basis. This wasn't very efficient, and I recall thinking that as soon as I became a manager, I would find a way to handle managing an SDLC better. It wasn't long before I got the chance.

Bob's First Experience Managing the SDLC

As soon as I was in my first management position, I immediately decided to create a software development lifecycle to help guide the work that my team would accomplish. I engaged a consultant who happened to be my former boss (and mentor), and we set about defining all of the tasks that should be found in an SDLC. These included requirements gathering, design, programming, and testing. I was thrilled at having this guidance in my back pocket and felt ready to manage the upcoming software and systems development efforts for the company that I was working for. However, I never got the budget to hire the programmers to do the work, and once again the SDLC document we created sat on a shelf while I ran around troubleshooting my systems myself and wishing I had the resources to make things better. The lesson learned was that I needed to have a wide business focus instead of just focusing on the technical software development lifecycle.

The software development lifecycle does indeed provide clarity on what needs to get done by the technical team on a day-to-day basis. But trying to manage the execution of an SDLC without the right tools is simply impossible.

We will discuss automating the execution of the SDLC later in this chapter. It is also helpful to use industry standards and frameworks when defining the software development lifecycle. One of the most popular standards is the IEEE 12207, which describes software lifecycle processes (see Figure 2-1).

There are times when the standard must be followed very closely in order to ensure compliance with either regulatory requirements or contractual agreements. There are also other times when you can use the standards as simply guidance to ensure that you don't skip an important step in your process.

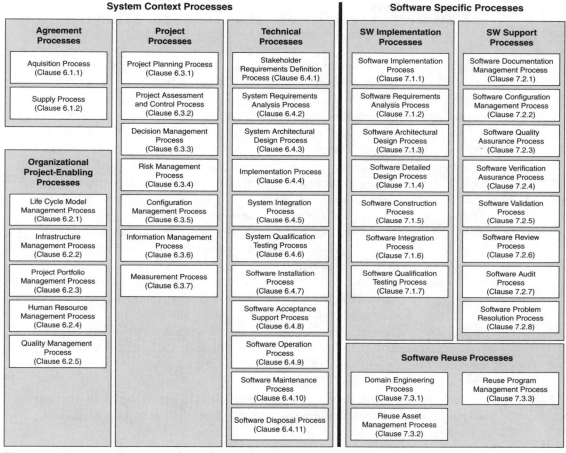

Figure 2-1 *ISO 12207:2008 Life Cycle Process Groups, page 14*

Whenever we read a standard, we always find some task or function that we realize we should have thought of, and the standard helps me avoid missing a key control. Even if you are not required to adhere closely to the comprehensive guidance provided by ISO 12207, you will find that the guidance contained therein will help you realize what you forgot to include in your software development process.

One of the issues that often comes up is how to handle a software development lifecycle when no software is being written. This is precisely where the SDLC focuses more on a system development lifecycle instead of a software development lifecycle.

2.5 Systems versus Software Development Lifecycle

Purchasing software that has been written by a vendor, or even reusing code written by another group within your organization, is a little different from developing the software yourself. We have seen many organizations stumble when they purchase commercial-off-the-shelf (COTS) software applications. Many organizations fail to realize that anything more complex than a word processing package requires a robust software or system lifecycle. Just because you buy the code doesn't mean that you are not responsible for ensuring its successful procurement and implementation. The systems development lifecycle should include requirements, evaluation, configuration, testing, implementation, and support. In addition, an essential aspect of vendor management is involved. You need to ensure that you have evaluated the vendor organization to confirm that they have the ability to deliver the functionality as promised. This is often called a vendor *risk* analysis. When procuring a system from a vendor, testing is very important, and often the configuration effort requires skilled software developers just as if you had actually written the code in-house. One of the biggest mistakes you can make is to trust the vendor to install, configure, and test the application, as their goal is to sell you the product, and ultimately you have the responsibility to ensure that the application delivers the functionality as promised and actually meets the needs of your business. ISO 15288 describes the common lifecycle processes that you should consider in your systems development lifecycle (see Figure 2-2).

Understanding and defining requirements is an essential aspect of any software or system lifecycle and often one of the most difficult aspects to manage.

2.6 Defining Requirements

Whether you are developing a software system or customizing a COTS product, understanding and defining requirements is essential. Much has been made of the fact that we often do not understand our requirements, and that is certainly true. Unfortunately, many technology professionals have taken the approach of not even trying to develop good requirements documents, and that is often a very serious mistake. Just because requirements are not well understood or may change does not change the fact that we should do our best to define the requirements that we do understand in a pragmatic and Lean way.

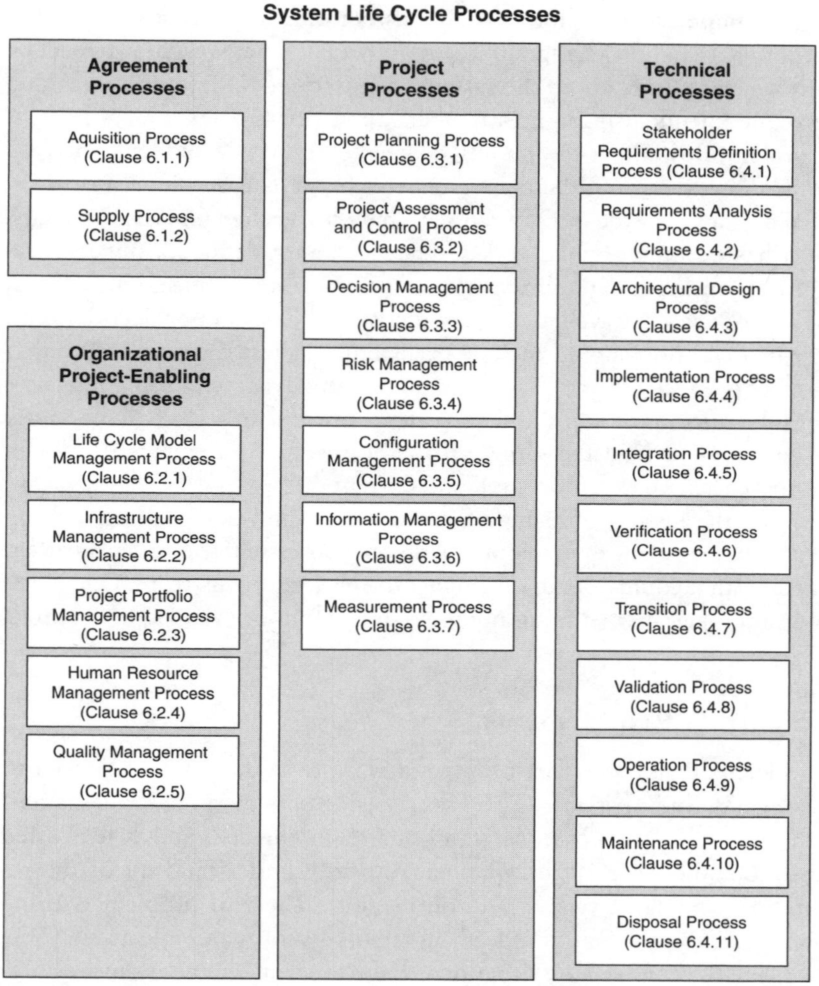

System Life Cycle Processes

Agreement Processes	Project Processes	Technical Processes
Aquisition Process (Clause 6.1.1)	Project Planning Process (Clause 6.3.1)	Stakeholder Requirements Definition Process (Clause 6.4.1)
Supply Process (Clause 6.1.2)	Project Assessment and Control Process (Clause 6.3.2)	Requirements Analysis Process (Clause 6.4.2)
	Decision Management Process (Clause 6.3.3)	Architectural Design Process (Clause 6.4.3)
Organizational Project-Enabling Processes	Risk Management Process (Clause 6.3.4)	Implementation Process (Clause 6.4.4)
Life Cycle Model Management Process (Clause 6.2.1)	Configuration Management Process (Clause 6.3.5)	Integration Process (Clause 6.4.5)
Infrastructure Management Process (Clause 6.2.2)	Information Management Process (Clause 6.3.6)	Verification Process (Clause 6.4.6)
Project Portfolio Management Process (Clause 6.2.3)	Measurement Process (Clause 6.3.7)	Transition Process (Clause 6.4.7)
Human Resource Management Process (Clause 6.2.4)		Validation Process (Clause 6.4.8)
Quality Management Process (Clause 6.2.5)		Operation Process (Clause 6.4.9)
		Maintenance Process (Clause 6.4.10)
		Disposal Process (Clause 6.4.11)

Figure 2-2 *ISO 15288 System Life Cycle Processes*

2.6.1 Managing Complexity and Change

Managing requirements as part of a software development lifecycle should focus on managing the complexity of what you are trying to design and implement. Well-defined requirements helps all of the stakeholders understand what we are trying to build (or procure and customize) and then respond effectively to changes as they occur. Defining requirements means that we also have version control to help handle changes to the requirements that we all know will be required as we learn more about the system we are trying to develop. Managing changing requirements also requires that the appropriate stakeholders be kept informed and be allowed to offer input when necessary. If you suddenly increase the rate of transactions, your database engineers or systems administrators may need to make changes to the infrastructure to handle the changing requirements. Although it has become popular to say that we cannot define all our requirements up front, mistakes in requirements definition can result in serious defects, including security risks as well as increased cost and delays in project delivery. Requirements definition should include traceability to test cases to ensure that the requirements have been met. I have long been an advocate of using test cases to augment the information in the requirements document. Clearly defined test cases can provide much of the same information as a requirements document and tends to be easier to keep updated and current.

Maintaining the history of changing requirements and documenting the approvals authorizing changes in requirements is also essential and can prevent many problems that could potentially impact the project downstream. One of the most important issues is whether or not the requirements are valid and verifiable.

2.6.2 Validity of Requirements

The requirements defined as part of any software or systems lifecycle need to be relevant, valid, and verifiable. This is precisely where many IT professionals exclaim that "we don't really understand our requirements" and that is often indeed true. But the issue is not whether you fully understand all of the requirements up front (and very often you cannot). The real problem is being honest and clear about what is indeed understood and what still needs to be determined. We have seen many situations where everyone in the room was pretending to understand what was required for the system to be developed and implemented. Based upon the high-level discussion and the lack of specific details, we would sometimes come to the conclusion that we were all *pretending* that we understood the requirements. Being honest about what we know and what we do not know is very important, and sometimes technology workers find themselves in the uncomfortable position of thinking that they cannot admit their ignorance. W. Edwards Deming said it best when he pointed out that we need to "drive out fear," and defining valid and verifiable requirements is one of the most important areas where everyone needs to be comfortable with what they do not fully understand. This is where we have often found that it can help to talk about testing requirements.

2.6.3 Testing Requirements

Every requirement should have a matching test case to ensure that the requirement is verifiable and that it has been met. It is sometimes difficult, and not entirely necessary, to have a one-to-one relationship between requirements and test cases, but every requirement should have at least one test case that verifies the requirement has been implemented as expected and as desired. This corresponds to verification and validation, which answers the questions: Does the feature meet the specification? and Is the specification correct? Whenever it is difficult to understand requirements, it is often a good idea to figure out how to test them by writing test cases with the relevant stakeholders. This is usually how we handle situations where we suspect that everyone in the room is pretending that they understand the requirements.

> #### Bob Writing NYSE Test Cases
>
> I asked the user representatives if they would spend one hour with me writing test cases. During that first hour in which we simply documented what we were going to test and what we expected the results to be, a strange thing happened. The business expert stopped the conversation and picked up the phone to call the head of software development. At that point I heard him say, "What I have asked for is not what I want and I only realized this when I started to think about how to test the system." I had effectively caused him to go into a more active cognitive state which helped him visualize his requirements in a clearer way. At that point, the folks responsible for defining requirements and test cases came back into the picture, and they proceeded to clarify how the system should really work. I had simply been the only person in the room willing to admit that I did not understand the requirements, and it turned out I was not alone.

Testing requirements is important. But there are many kinds of requirements, and creating a topology of requirements is very important. Let's take a brief look at some of the different types of requirements and how they fit into the software or systems lifecycle. The first type of requirement describes how the system should function.

2.6.4 Functional Requirements

Functional requirements describe the desired behavior of a system typically in the form of use cases that meet specific business needs. Use cases explain how the system should work and function on a day-to-day basis. Most requirements documents describe how the system should work including information that is to be input, behavior such as calculations, reporting, and other key features. Documenting functional requirements can be very challenging especially in terms of maintaining a consistent level of detail. While functional requirements explain how the system is used, non-functional requirements describe how the system should behave in a number of important ways.

2.6.5 Nonfunctional Requirements

Nonfunctional requirements may include performance and response time, capacity reliability, and security. Designing good functional requirements obviously affects many other stakeholders and is a key consideration in defining the software or systems lifecycle. There is a broad array of nonfunctional requirements, and almost anything outside of user functionality can be described in terms of nonfunctional requirements. In many organizations, it has become popular to describe use cases in terms of epics and stories.

2.6.6 Epics and Stories

In agile software development there is often less of a focus on developing comprehensive requirements documents, and instead user stories explain the desired functionality. Groups of user stories can be organized in terms of epics, which is a reference to the long poems that are commonly found in Greek mythology. Finding the right level of detail for documenting requirements can be experienced as a balancing act. If you are designing a complex trading system, then defining your requirements may need to be quite detailed and precise. Other times the agile approach of defining requirements in user stories can be quite sufficient. Either way, change is inevitable, and any requirements management process must contain a well-defined process for managing the change that is certain to be required.

2.6.7 Planning for Changing Requirements

Much has been written about the fact that requirements are almost certain to change over time. Change is not bad, but it does need to be managed. The fact that requirements cannot be completely understood up-front or that they will inevitably change over time is not a valid reason to skip documenting them. The decision to have an exhaustive effort to document and manage requirements should be decided based upon the risk of getting a requirement wrong or missing a key requirement all together. Designing the software for a life support or missile defense system requires well-defined requirements. You need to right-size your requirements definition effort based upon the needs of the business. You also need to consider the lifecycle of a requirement.

2.6.8 Workflow for Defining Requirements

Requirements management should be automated using an automated workflow tool. There are many good requirements tools on the market, and once again, it is a matter of finding the right fit for your project and your organization. Some requirements need to be reviewed by multiple stakeholders and perhaps even funded by a business unit willing to pay for the work required to implement a particular feature. Your software development lifecycle needs to strike the right balance in terms of the amount of process required for your requirements tracking lifecycle. Requirements tracking is very close to test case management, and many organizations prefer to focus on driving their development effort to a robust test-driven process.

2.7 Test-Driven Development

Test-driven development (TDD) is a methodology that has become popular in agile development, but actually could be used in any software development lifecycle. The basic premise is to define the test and automate the test case before even writing the application code. By definition, this means that the test case will initially fail because the code itself has not been written. Focusing on writing automated test scripts is a very effective way to develop self-validating quality code. In my work as a build and release engineer, I always focus on writing scripts that automate my own application build, package, and deployment. At least half of the code that I write tests the automation itself, because if any step fails, I want to know immediately so that I can quickly and easily address this issue. In manufacturing this is known as "stopping the line" and refers to a worker stopping the manufacturing process immediately when something is wrong, simplifying the effort to fix and resolve problems. Test-driven development should be a key consideration in creating any software development lifecycle. Ensuring that systems are testable is very important, as is also ensuring that they are designed properly.

2.8 Designing Systems

Systems design is a key function within the software and systems development lifecycle. Just like defining requirements, designing a system can range from a complex and exhaustive effort to one that is brief and agile. Defining the design for a system depends largely upon the architecture chosen and the related standards. Your software and systems lifecycle needs to ensure that you have sufficient coverage for systems design to mitigate risk and ensure that you can meet your users' requirements for performance, reliability, and security. The choices that you make in systems design will also directly affect your organization's ability to implement new features and scale to meet growing user demand. The design itself, just as every other feature, must be verifiable, which is where testing along with verification and validation become essential aspects of your software and systems lifecycle.

2.9 Software Development

Software and systems development is evolving to be largely influenced by the technology stack itself. Java J2EE developers work with integrated development environments (IDEs) and tools that largely facilitate their own productivity. This technology stack may be quite different than the approach used by C#/.NET developers or other technologies that come with a well-defined ecosystem such as Python or Ruby. Skilled software development professionals may try to achieve proficiency in multiple technologies, but there is so much to learn that they often specialize in one specific technical competency or another. Unfortunately, this can also lead to silos and hinder effective communication. Database analysts, systems administrators, and middleware administrators all have their specialized terminology and technical approaches, which can make development and support difficult to effectively manage. The DevOps approach of sharing technical knowledge, effective communication, and collaboration is essential for harnessing the knowledge within each of these technical areas.

2.10 Testing

The test phase of any software or systems lifecycle is normally viewed as a tollgate that must be passed before the application can be approved for promotion into production. The fact is that testing should occur throughout the entire software or systems lifecycle. But that does not remove the need for an official testing phase, usually performed by QA or another testing organization. The testing process has many phases, and your organization may handle testing in a very formal way, depending upon the risk of a defect being found in the application, along with compliance and related audit requirements. One of the areas where

I have seen testing handled in a very formal way is developing software for a nuclear power plant facility.

> ### *Nuclear Power Plants and Testing*
>
> Some time ago I had the pleasure of giving my CM Best Practices class to a group of software and quality engineers who were responsible for the development and support of systems used by nuclear power plants. I was pleased to learn that not only were they focused on quality and defect prevention, but also realized the value of enhancing productivity. The most striking observation that I noted was they had a culture of ensuring quality in every aspect of their work.

We discuss unit testing as part of build engineering in Chapter 6 and as part of continuous integration in Chapter 8. Systems integration testing is also an essential aspect of any software development lifecycle, along with QA and user acceptance testing. As with any part of the software development process, the amount of formality required in testing depends largely upon your requirements and the risk and impact of a defect found in production.

2.10.1 Testing the Application

Application testing is a key step in any software development process. Testing should be continuous through the entire development effort. Unit testing is only the beginning and often has very limited coverage. Functional testing is also essential, although limited by the application interface. In Chapter 20, "QA and Testing in the ALM," we cover testing in greater detail and explain how QA and testing should integrate with the application lifecycle. The entire SDLC should be integrated with the application testing process. This includes tracking requirements to test cases and automating as much of the application testing as possible. Although application testing is essential, testing the software development process is also an essential, although sometimes overlooked, aspect of establishing a robust ALM.

2.10.2 Testing the Process Itself

The software development process usually consists of many steps and considerable complexity. Although most folks are well aware that the application needs to be tested, care should also be taken to test the software development process itself. This would include testing the requirements, the architecture, and the infrastructure. It is also essential to test the application deployment pipeline, and this is a fundamental aspect of implementing DevOps to support the software development process. Testing is an important part of any software development process. Building quality in should obviously start at the beginning of the lifecycle, and continuous integration is one of the best ways to make that happen.

2.11 Continuous Integration

Continuous integration (CI) is discussed in more detail in Chapter 8. For the software development process, CI provides an important point at which code may be integrated during the development phase of the lifecycle. By integrating early and often, CI tames cognitive complexity by making it much easier to detect potential problems when integrating code, which often comes from two or more different developers. If you do not integrate early and often, it becomes very difficult to understand code issues and, more importantly, how to fix them. Continuous integration relies heavily upon compilers to identify code conflicts by assuming that the code will not compile if it not compatible. The fact is that code also needs to be reviewed by the engineers who are best equipped to identify any defects or other opportunities for improvement. This is discussed further in Chapter 8.

> ### Beware of Too Much Noise
>
> In one of my consulting assignments I came across a team that had effectively implemented a number of tools, including a continuous integration server. Although the system was set up correctly, there were so many failed builds that no one on the team actually paid attention to the results, and the CI server added no value whatsoever. I suggested that they trim down their continuous integration efforts to only build code on an integration branch and have specific engineers responsible for addressing any broken builds. Having a CI set up and just generating noise had conditioned the team to ignore continuous integration altogether.

Much of the value of continuous integration is also related to continuous deployment.

2.12 Continuous Delivery and Deployment

Continuous delivery and deployment are closely related to continuous integration. We will distinguish between continuous delivery and deployment in Chapter 9, but for now we refer to continuous deployment as a methodology that allows us to deploy to production as often as desired. By deploying more often, you implicitly reduce cognitive complexity in several important ways. The first reason is that smaller and simpler deployments are inherently less risky because there is much less that can go wrong. If something does go wrong, then the problem will be easier to diagnose and then fix. If necessary, it is much easier to back out the code. Deploying more often also allows you to get better at doing the deployments and automate each and every step.

When Bad Things Happen

I am often called in to help when companies have suffered a failed deployment, resulting in some serious impact. The first thing that I do is get them to deploy more often. Typically, taking them from deploying every other month to twice a week eliminates most of the problems immediately. Continuous deployment enhances reliability and eliminates the sources of many potential errors.

Continuous deployment is essential for ensuring that the customer receives all of the desired and required features and fixes successfully. We will discuss continuous deployment (and continuous delivery) in Chapter 9. It is also essential to define the phases of the software and systems lifecycle.

2.13 Defining Phases of the Lifecycle

Most technology professionals find it useful to define a software or systems lifecycle in terms of distinct phases. What is important is that you consider what phases make sense for you and your organization. I have seen lifecycles that were defined with many phases and others that were very brief. The first thing to consider is whether you can take an existing lifecycle that is used by others or if you have special needs and would be best served by creating your own custom software or systems development lifecycle.

Most SDLCs start with defining requirements and establishing a design architecture. Software is then developed and tested. Some lifecycles can be just that simple, and others may require far more rigor. Your goal is to find the right balance in defining a lifecycle that will actually be used to guide everyone in understanding their own commitments in the software or systems delivery lifecycle. Pragmatism is essential, as the best lifecycles are useable and can be tailored to guide everyone to understand their own tasks and deliverables.

My First SDLC

I still remember my first SDLC. I enjoyed working with a trusted consultant who helped me analyze the phases necessary for a comprehensive software development lifecycle. Sadly, the document sat on the shelf and was never really used to develop our software.

Process maturity is an important consideration when defining an SDLC. Typically in the beginning of a project, your process can be loosely defined. As the project progresses, process maturity becomes essential. Get close to a deadline, and your process needs to be very well defined, repeatable, and completely traceable. Process maturity is among the most important considerations when defining a software or systems lifecycle. Don't forget that the best processes are iterative in nature.

Whether your process is agile or waterfall or some other methodology, taking an iterative approach will greatly enhance your chances of success. Process maturity is essential, although sometimes not a prime focus in the agile world. Similarly documentation is also occasionally overlooked. You need to take a pragmatic approach to deciding just how much documentation is required.

2.14 Documentation Required

It has become popular to minimize the importance of comprehensive written documentation. The agile manifesto notes that working software is more important than comprehensive documentation. But sometimes documentation is absolutely required, including when there are regulatory requirements, as described further in Chapter 16. Our view is that documentation should be as complete and comprehensive as possible. I also always encourage draft documents to be circulated for comment as early as possible.

> ### *Working Sessions to Write Documentation*
>
> Getting developers to write documentation can be very difficult. Too often the author of the document fears criticism and keeps putting off delivery of the document, which creates a risk that you will finally receive the draft when it is too late to address issues with its contents. We have found it very effective to hold working sessions to review and improve written documentation. The key is to stipulate that we are working with an early draft and then get everyone to work together to get the job done. In some ways, this is applying "left-shift," discussed in Section 12.12.1, to documentation.

Some technology professionals find it very difficult to write documentation. The best approach that I have found is to get rough drafts completed as quickly as possible and engage a cross-functional team to review, edit, and improve the documentation. This approach exemplifies the principles and practices found in DevOps.

2.15 DevOps

DevOps is a set of principles and practices that help improve communication and collaboration that we discuss in more detail in Chapter 12. DevOps puts a strong focus on interactions between the development and operations teams, along with QA, testing, and information security; but really, DevOps has a much wider focus. The fact is that all stakeholders represented in the software development process need to have excellent communication and collaboration, and silos within the organization are the root cause of many problems and issues. DevOps practitioners need to ensure that all of the stakeholders within the organization are able to effectively communicate and collaborate together. This book focuses on DevOps throughout the entire ALM. DevOps best practices deliver the capability of ensuring that changes to systems can be implemented as often as desired while also ensuring that systems are reliable and secure. Much of the day-to-day work of DevOps is on creating fully automated deployment processes and tools. But DevOps has a much wider focus, and the DevOps approach can help the entire organization make better decisions.

> ### Cutting Corners
>
> I was once asked to promote a half-baked release into production that I knew was not ready for production usage. Fortunately, I was sitting next to the product manager at this company and had many opportunities to speak with him and gain a better understanding of our customer's requirements and the overall business perspective. I was surprised to learn that several of our best customers wanted an early peek at the release even if it was not really completely tested. This business perspective taught me the importance of including product managers in the DevOps relationship. We deployed the release to a production "beta test" environment, and orders from our customer base came flooding in. We had to babysit the initial users, but the results were greater profits for our company and a successful new product launch.

DevOps has a fundamental goal of promoting excellent communication and collaboration with all stakeholders.

2.16 Communicating with All Stakeholders

Whenever I assess an organization to baseline their existing practices, several common themes always seem to be apparent. The first is that too often corporate divisions begin to act as if they are separate companies. This creates a dysfunctional "siloed" mentality that can be very destructive. The organizational structures may be very much needed, but the teams must also be able to communicate and collaborate effectively.

Poor communication often manifests itself in teams and team members lacking a clear understanding of what they need to accomplish and, more importantly, how their work affects the other team members. Dysfunctional behavior can include groups working against each other, which is usually a consequence of a lack of trust between the most senior managers who may be competing with each other through corporate politics.

The biggest problem that we often see is a sense of fear where team members are afraid to speak the truth and engage in open and completely honest communication. Deming said it best when he coined the phrase, "Drive out fear."

An Old Joke . . .

There is an old story of a ship at sea being commanded by a very senior admiral in the Navy. The admiral is on deck when he happens to see a light in the distance and in keeping with protocol has his radio engineer demand the identity of the other approaching ship. The response comes back that the other seaman in the distance is a first class seaman—a relatively low rank in the Navy—who requests that the ship turn 45 degrees starboard (to the right). The admiral is furious that the first class seaman is giving him an order and has his radio engineer send the message they are a large naval battleship and the first class seaman should turn his ship instead. The response comes back meekly: "Admiral, sir, I would if I could, but this is a lighthouse."

Sometimes rank alone does not get you the results that you want.

One of the important functions that needs to have very effective communication is the forward-facing group that handles support of your production systems.

2.17 Production Support

Production support is an essential function that is often overlooked. Responsible for maintaining continuous service, the production support engineer is often also responsible for updating the software and systems. The challenge of supporting production systems is that there is often only a brief transfer of knowledge as the system comes online and is supported by the production support group. The DevOps function plays a key role in engaging developers early in the process by training and collaborating with their production support counterparts.

Production Support Outgunned

I have seen situations where the production support engineers had very little training and technical capability to support complex systems. Developers quickly lost confidence in the production support engineers, who needed to get developers involved every time there was a problem or incident. This created a self-fulfilling prophecy where the developers saw no point in teaching the production support engineers since they knew that they would be called in to fix production problems anyway.

Production support engineers should have strong technical backgrounds, including experience as software developers. One model for this role is to rotate developers into production support roles for six to nine months and then return them to development work.

Skilled production support engineers should play an active role in creating bugfixes in addition to supporting and maintaining production systems.

2.18 Maintenance and Bugfixes

Maintaining code and creating bugfixes require a creative balance between moving ahead and getting essential quick fixes deployed. Focusing too much on short-term fixes tends to create too much *technical debt*, which refers to making short-term choices that will need to be "paid back" in the near future.

The agile ALM can help put the right perspective on fixing short-term bugs that are affecting our customers. It is also essential to find the right balance between having too much ceremony and keeping your processes as Lean as possible. As any hands-on practitioner will tell you, the beginning of a software or systems development effort usually begins with very little process and few IT controls.

2.19 Lifecycle in the Beginning

The beginning of any project is a time when roles and responsibilities are forming. I believe in keeping the development process very loose in the beginning. It is almost impossible to figure out how structure is needed in your development lifecycle until you have a very well-defined idea of what you are building and who is involved with the software and systems delivery effort.

My own approach is to use agile principles when defining the agile ALM.

> ### Finding the Balance
>
> Creating the right-sized ALM is a matter of achieving balance and being willing to evolve the process over time. Having too much ceremony is just as bad as not having enough. My approach is to keep the process very light until I find a reason for establishing more controls—usually to avoid making the same mistake twice.

As the project progresses, the agile ALM must mature, which means that additional IT controls should be established and the lifecycle itself must evolve.

2.20 Maintenance of the Lifecycle

The lifecycle itself requires a considerable amount of care and feeding. You need to ensure that you have a change control process in place for evolving the lifecycle itself. Too often there is a lack of structure to support updating and evolving the software and systems lifecycle.

Remember the SEPG

The Capability Maturity Model (CMM) made popular the structure of the software engineering process group (SEPG), which is responsible for maintaining change control on the process itself. All process changes should be reviewed by the SEPG, which is also responsible for communicating these changes to all of the stakeholders who should be involved.

We discuss creating a mature agile ALM in Chapter 4, "Agile Process Maturity," and defining agile processes in the non-agile environment in Chapter 14.

Right-sizing your processes is fundamental, and another critical success factor is establishing the efficient exchange of knowledge.

2.21 Creating the Knowledge Base

One of my strongest goals is to create an environment and culture where learning and sharing are core values. Like many technology professionals, I love to keep learning and often try to pick my assignments based upon how much I can improve my own knowledge and skills. The most successful organizations have a strong learning culture and an actively improving knowledge base. But this doesn't happen by accident, and facilitating a good culture is exactly what strong technology leadership is all about. My approach is to facilitate cross-functional learning sessions where different stakeholders can share what they know and also learn from others.

Will the Operations Guys Show Up to the Party?

I recall one DevOps session that I organized where the developers were somewhat doubtful that operations would participate in learning about the new deployment technology. When I scheduled the first working

> session, we were all pleasantly surprised when the two development re-
> sources were joined by ten operations engineers, who were all eager to
> learn the new technology and actively participated in a great learning
> session, which was recorded for future reference.

The journey to being a knowledge organization takes considerable effort and what Deming called *consistency of purpose*. If you want to be successful, you need to realize that improving culture and behaviors takes time and effort. Continuously improving your process is likewise a long-term commitment and a journey that can take years to accomplish.

2.22 Continuous Improvement

Continuous process improvement requires a commitment to honest communication and a willingness to change and improve over time. I usually find that the best time to make improvements is right after an incident has occurred. Mistakes are not always bad, especially when they result in us learning and improving the way that we do things.

> ### Never Let a Good Crisis Go to Waste
>
> Many politicians have noted that a crisis is often an opportunity. When systems have serious outages, this is often the very time to gain consensus on improving and evolving our processes.

It is always a good idea to start by assessing your existing processes so that you first do not fix what isn't broken and so that you can demonstrate progress by improving on your baseline processes.

2.23 Conclusion

Defining the software development process is a balancing act. Having too much process is just as bad as not having enough process. This chapter introduces some of the issues you need to consider when defining the software development process. The rest of the book continues to describe strategies for creating an effective and pragmatic agile ALM.

Chapter 3

Agile Application Lifecycle Management

Agile application lifecycle management requires a flexible and creative approach to managing the software and system lifecycle that goes beyond the traditional software or systems development lifecycle (SDLC). Agile ALM builds upon the SDLC by empowering the team to customize their approach to meet the unique needs of the business and the project that is being undertaken. The agile ALM also typically takes an iterative approach. Unfortunately, agile ALM has suffered from a dark side of rigidity, with too many "experts" prescribing their view of the one true path to agility. This book presents a pragmatic approach to dealing with real-world challenges, which departs from the agile purist view. We are challenging the status quo in agile development by suggesting that many, if not most, companies choose to take a more hybrid approach than many agile purists would like. We take a very wide view of the agile ALM, including functions that many other authors overlook. We also believe that your colleagues are smart enough to create processes that are appropriate to their situation and the organizational culture in which they must operate. We also focus on taking a true DevOps view in defining our processes by including many stakeholders as we describe our own experience in defining the agile ALM. In this chapter we discuss the core strategies that will help you create a flexible and robust software and systems development lifecycle while ensuring that the values and principles of agility are understood and maintained.

3.1 Goals of Agile Application Lifecycle Management

The goal of establishing an agile ALM is to create a flexible and yet effective software and systems lifecycle that adheres to agile values and principles and ensures that you produce high-quality software within the budget and the agreed-upon timeframe. The agile ALM must ensure that your team knows precisely what to do at any point in time and maintains just enough process to avoid costly mistakes while achieving the desired goals. The agile ALM also has the essential goal of ensuring that you do not suffer from having so much ceremony that your team is bogged down in processes that hamper successful execution. Agile ALM has the essential goal of achieving a balance between process and flexibility. In this chapter, we also have the goal of helping you understand how to take a step back and define your own lifecycle.

3.2 Why Is Agile ALM Important?

Having too much process is just as bad as not having enough. But that said, the team needs to understand what to do on a daily basis. This includes providing a roadmap so that each member of the team understands exactly what they need to do on a daily basis. We take a very wide view by including all stakeholders who could potentially be affected, including the folks on the help desk and internal IT audit department who need to test and verify IT controls. The agile ALM is important because it gives you a methodology for scaling your controls up when necessary and keeping your processes light when it makes sense to do so. This is no easy task, and the agile ALM helps provide the guidelines for evaluating when a process step should be enforced to avoid costly mistakes and when extra ceremony is not only unnecessary, but could get in the way of accomplishing your goals.

3.3 Where Do I Start?

Achieving agility requires a cultural shift. You need to start by ensuring that your team understands what agility really means in very practical terms. You also need to ensure that agile principles become part of your organizational culture. The agile transformation is a journey that involves understanding and evolving behaviors and the basic assumptions inherent in the software and systems delivery process. This is precisely where each group in the organization may have a rather different experience and even a slightly different journey. Agility for the operations team may be a different experience from that of the developers—even in the same organization. You need to start by understanding the paradigm shift itself.

Agility in the Eye of the Beholder

The challenge of using common everyday words to refer to very uncommon constructs is that some folks actually start making up their own definitions. I have heard a number of colleagues refer to agility as just simply being "flexible." These same folks do not seem to understand very much about agile practices and just seem content to make up their own definitions of what it means to be truly agile. It is no surprise that these same folks have a fairly negative view of agile methodology and can be quite vocal in their opinion of a methodology that they know little to nothing about. Agility should not just be in the eye of the beholder, but a cohesive set of practices based upon the agile manifesto and its supporting principles.

Undergoing a paradigm shift can be difficult and disruptive for many organizations that attempt but fail to achieve the full benefits of agility. The agile transformation is not just a change in what you do on a day-to-day basis—it is truly a cultural change as well.

3.4 Understanding the Paradigm Shift

Implementing an agile ALM often involves a major shift in the way that most folks view the software and systems lifecycle. Understanding what this shift requires in terms of attitude and behavior requires both a cultural transformation and a change in the way that the work is organized, tracked, and completed. The key to understanding the paradigm shift is to embrace agile principles and practices within the culture of your organization. Implementing agile in a bank or other large financial services company is not the same as implementing agility in a smaller, privately owned startup. Yet it may actually be the bank that reaps the benefits despite the challenges of right-sizing agility in a large organization that must adhere to audit and regulatory requirements. You need to understand the organizational culture that will affect any process improvement initiative.

Organizational Culture

Understanding the culture of an organization involves studying both its history and the environment in which the company must operate. For example, a trading organization and a medical engineering firm each has its own cultural norms. Much of this culture involves how members of the organization communicate, in addition to understanding the basic assumptions that are commonly accepted and viewed as going with the organizational culture.

At the core of understanding this paradigm shift is adopting a rapid and iterative approach to software and systems development.

3.5 Rapid Iterative Development

Rapid iterative development has been around a long time, and its meaning and methodology have evolved over time. The basic premise of rapid iterative development is that it is much easier to develop applications in an iterative fashion than to attempt to build the entire system in one cycle. Iterative development helps by allowing the team to get a piece of the code working without trying to complete all of the features in one lifecycle. This approach helps tame technical complexity by allowing the team to understand the technology and what they are trying to develop through a series of iterations. Many organizations today approach iterative development using scrum, but iterative development has been around a lot longer than scrum. Closely related is rapid application development (RAD).

We will examine RAD as it is discussed by industry leaders, including Barry Boehm and James Martin, in the next section. In Chapter 5 we will discuss how to create your own approach to rapid iterative development. But for this chapter you need to understand how rapid iterative development affects the development of agile application lifecycle management.

Mistakes Are Good

Bob had the experience of serving as a volunteer cop in a very busy police station in Brooklyn. The commanding officer was a gentle Irishman who seemed to be everyone's grandfather. This police commander managed to create a culture in a police station where cops felt comfortable admitting their mistakes up-front and looking for creative solutions. This CO had magically created a culture, in a very high-stress environment, where mistakes were viewed as good—especially if you learned from them and worked to do better.

Understanding our mistakes is very important. It is equally important to learn from incidents and problems.

3.6 Remember RAD?

Rapid application development (RAD) became popular[1] in the late 1980s and 1990s as technology professionals began to look for faster approaches[2] to developing software. Industry experts, including James Martin and Barry Boehm, provided their views on how to develop software faster. Efforts to use computer-aided software engineering (CASE) were also intended to take us from the prevailing waterfall methodology to more efficient approaches to developing software. Getting the computer to write code for us was certainly ideal. But another approach was to take common everyday tasks such as report writing and make them easier to accomplish in less time. For this purpose we evolved from third-generation languages (e.g., Cobol, FORTRAN) to programming frameworks that promised more productivity without requiring as much training and expertise. Fourth-generation languages (4GL) were popular in the early eighties—often as report writers that did not require comprehensive software programming as was necessary with Cobol, FORTRAN, and PL/1. These efforts had some success, but more importantly, they provided a direction for thinking of better strategies to developing software and systems.

> ### RAD at the Insurance Company
>
> Bob recalls when he was at a large insurance company that decided to start using RAD for a few projects. Lots of folks were concerned that requirements would not be gathered in an accurate and comprehensive manner. RAD enjoyed moderate success, but the old waterfall methods were still regarded as the most reliable and effective approach.

Although RAD provided a path to thinking out of the box, agility provided a much more robust foundation that included effective principles and practices. As noted, DevOps consists of a set of principles and practices that help improve communication and collaboration. Although our practices may be different based upon the needs of the organization, the principles are always the same. We take the same approach to using agility to guide our approach to agile processes. This

---

1. Martin, James (1991). *Rapid Application Development*, New York: Macmillan Coll Division.
2. www.casemaker.com/download/products/totem/rad_wp.pdf

means that when we think through designing processes, we always keep in mind the agile manifesto and the agile principles. The next section explains how we use agile principles to guide our approach to application lifecycle management.

3.7 Focus on 12 Agile Principles

The agile ALM requires that we understand and apply agile principles. Let's review these principles[3] and suggest some ideas for how they can be applied in real-life situations:

1. Our highest priority is to satisfy the customer through early and continuous delivery of valuable software.

   We are always focused on meeting the customer needs, and the best way to accomplish this goal is to deliver working prototypes for review and verification during the software development process. This requires true partnership, but is not a blank check to modify any and all requirements. The best approach is fair and reasonable for both the customer and technology professionals creating the system.

2. Welcome changing requirements, even late in development. Agile processes harness change for the customer's competitive advantage.

   Changing requirements come from improving our understanding of what the system needs to do and from changes in the surrounding environment. The customer may not actually know how to ask for what he or she really needs up-front. During the development process, the requirements become clearer to both the end user and the professionals writing the code.

3. Deliver working software frequently, from every couple of weeks to every couple of months, with a preference for the shorter timescale.

   Delivering working software helps ensure that you fully validate and understand the requirements. Each iteration will bring you closer to creating a complete and comprehensive system. You will also discover what you forgot or did not completely understand with each iteration of the software.

4. Businesspeople and developers must work together daily throughout the project.

   Many perspectives must be considered during the software development process, but the most important view is that of the business and product

---

3. http://agilemanifesto.org/principles.html

users. Creating a technical masterpiece is of little use if it does not meet the needs of the end users.

5. Build projects around motivated individuals. Give them the environment and support they need, and trust them to get the job done.

   People are your greatest resources. Companies today often forget this lesson and fail to develop their most important assets, which are smart, motivated individuals who know how to work as part of a team.

6. The most efficient and effective method of conveying information to and within a development team is face-to-face conversation.

   Face-to-face conversation is indeed far superior to any other mode of communication. That said, many of us work remotely, and teams are often dispersed throughout the world. Successful endeavors place a premium on facilitating face-to-face conversations to build relationships and establish common understanding.

7. Working software is the primary measure of progress.

   The goal of any effort should be to create working software. Requirements and test documents that sit on the shelf do not make a complete system.

8. Agile processes promote sustainable development. The sponsors, developers, and users should be able to maintain a constant pace indefinitely.

   Working long hours can get old very quickly. The best working environments maintain a healthy work-life balance and can be sustained for a long time.

9. Continuous attention to technical excellence and good design enhances agility.

   Technology changes quickly, and maintaining technical excellence can be difficult to achieve. Choosing the right design and architecture is essential for successful agile iterative efforts.

10. Simplicity—the art of maximizing the amount of work not done—is essential.

    Technology professionals sometimes make things too complicated. Truly elegant design is simple and thereby much more capable of adapting to required change if necessary.

11. The best architectures, requirements, and designs emerge from self-organizing teams.

    Self-organizing teams are often the most high performing, which results in the best architectures, requirements, and designs.

12. At regular intervals, the team reflects on how to become more effective and then tunes and adjusts its behavior accordingly.

Process improvement is a journey that must be improved upon and adapted over time. Achieving excellence requires that the team regularly reflect on how they can improve and evolve.

Applying Principles

Being able to apply agile principles requires that we understand agility at a deeper level. There are many situations where organizations cannot just abandon their current processes. Having a deeper understanding of agile principles can help you iteratively improve your processes in a manner that aligns with the needs of your organization. We often find ourselves facilitating a discussion on how to apply agile principles in a practical way.

Agile principles help us understand and implement the guidance provided by the agile manifesto. Make sure that you understand the manifesto and can implement your processes in an effective way.

3.8 Agile Manifesto

Manifesto for Agile Software Development[4]
We are uncovering better ways of developing
software by doing it and helping others do it.
Through this work we have come to value:

Individuals and interactions over processes and tools
Working software over comprehensive documentation
Customer collaboration over contract negotiation
Responding to change over following a plan

That is, while there is value in the items on
the right, we value the items on the left more.

We discuss the agile manifesto and its practical usage throughout this book.

---

4. http://agilemanifesto.org

> ### Back to Basics
>
> I have noticed that many folks who say they are agile cannot actually recall the words in the agile manifesto and agile principles. We often take teams through a discussion of agile principles and how they can be applied in a pragmatic way. Make sure that your team has the right training and culture to really embrace agility at a level that ensures they can apply these principles on a daily basis.

Agile makes effective use of fixed timebox sprints.

3.9 Fixed Timebox Sprints

The notion of developing code in iterations is not new to agile. Waterfall was envisioned by Winston Royce as being an iterative process. What is relatively new is the idea that we should fix the length of each iteration. Scrum has made popular the notion of sprints with durations of two to four weeks. I have seen engineering firms where they could not develop any useful hardware chip in less than two to three months, and then their iterations matched the lifecycle of the hardware. The real point here is to pick a length of time that allows you to produce a useable piece of code that can be shown to the end user or his representative for feedback and the collaborative evaluation of requirements. Many teams do very well with sprints of two to four weeks as made popular by scrum. But there are also very good reasons to sometimes have longer or shorter sprint durations. There are several factors to consider when choosing the length of the sprint.

The first is to consider how long it will take to produce a useable piece of code as we have described. Perhaps a more subtle consideration is how long can members of the team stay focused. A six-month sprint would certainly not seem very useful or viable. But sometimes four weeks is not enough time to really get very much done. My view is that choosing the length of time for a sprint and whether or not the timeframe really has to be fixed is a decision best made by the team and reviewed as needed during the sprint. Another consideration is technical risk. Sometimes you really don't know how long a particular task will take. This occurs when you are working with a new technology and therefore there may be considerable technical risk that needs to be managed. Choosing the right length of the sprint and whether or not the timeframe should be fixed at all should be done in collaboration with the customer or end user.

> ### Circuit Chips in Three Months
>
> I worked with a medical engineering firm that was trying to embrace agile development practices. I suggested that we embrace a four-week fixed timebox sprint. The engineers explained that this would not work because they needed the circuit chips in order to load the firmware. Creating any useful circuit chip took at least three months to complete. Therefore, the best that we could do is to have three-month sprints.

Customer collaboration is also an important consideration.

3.10 Customer Collaboration

Customer collaboration is essential for any comprehensive and usable ALM. I always try to ask the customer or customer representative for their input on how often they can receive a release and the impact of software upgrades to the end user. It is my experience that successful DevOps-driven deployment pipelines are often able to generate changes much faster than customers can handle receiving the changes.

The customer is also the most important stakeholder to be involved with feedback loops by helping the team understand the priorities as well as risks that need to be mitigated. Customers often surprise me with their view of how we should approach the release and deployment of milestone releases. This input is essential and really helps the team stay on focus. Sometimes, I learn that it is worth taking risks in order to achieve time-to-market, and other times I am told that the end user cannot handle the constant flow of changes.

Customers are also the best resource for validating and clarifying requirements so that we focus on the right features to be delivered. Most importantly, customers have the best focus for guiding the quality assurance and testing efforts too. Collaboration and communication are essential for any successful organization. This is also why I believe that DevOps must include the end-user perspective. Customers should be collaborating directly with the developers, testers, and service desk personnel. DevOps is not just about development and operations, and customer collaboration is of paramount importance.

DevOps for Customers

DevOps is not just about operations and developers. DevOps also involves collaboration between the customer representatives and the technology professionals creating the system. The first question that I ask the customer representative is how quickly they can accept change because DevOps often speeds up the build, package, and deployment process where releases can be generated faster than they can be reasonably consumed.

The most important area of collaboration with customers is ensuring that we all understand exactly what needs to be built.

3.11 Requirements

Many good books explaining how to write requirements include guidance on how to create agile user stories. The process of defining requirements provides important information to the developers so that they know what needs to be coded. The process also helps the customers get a better idea of what they have asked for. Requirements change often due to the business landscape, including essential regulatory and audit controls. Far more common is our understanding of the requirements themselves, which evolve as the customers see the system and get to start testing it.

Understanding and specifying requirements must be an iterative process because users themselves often do not fully understand their own requirements up-front. The agile ALM helps clarify requirements, enabling the technology professionals to understand what they are building while also helping the end user understand what is required.

Writing Test Cases with a User

I once asked a user to write test cases with me. My suspicion was the technology professionals did not really understand what the users had asked for in the technology specification. What I learned was that the users actually did not understand their requirements to begin with. As we iteratively wrote test cases, the user began to realize and verbalize that "what they had asked for was not what they actually needed."

No one wants to have books of documentation sitting on the shelf, and agile development has famously deemphasized the importance of having written documentation. I view this as a case of right-sizing the documentation process.

3.12 Documentation

Understanding how much documentation is required can be challenging. The agile manifesto notes that working software is more important than comprehensive documentation. But the truth is that the amount of documentation required depends largely upon what the system is used for and the potential impact of inadequate documentation. For example, having requirements specified for a missile defense system or a life support system may be an absolute requirement. When comprehensive documentation is not practical, then sometimes it can be enough to use test cases to supplement the available information. In fact, it is common for test cases to contain the same information that might be documented in a requirements document.

Release notes are essential for understanding exactly what changes are included in a version of the code. User documents can also help with training and support. It is important to have sufficient documentation to avoid mistakes without creating books that are simply going to sit on the shelf.

3.13 Conclusion

The agile ALM helps put structure around the entire software and systems lifecycle. How much structure may depend upon the purpose of the system, the industry involved, and the culture of the organization itself.

Chapter 4

Agile Process Maturity

Agile process maturity is a very important consideration when implementing an agile ALM. But what exactly does process maturity really mean in an agile context? We know that agile is defined by specific values and principles,[1] so obviously the agile ALM must be—well—*agile*. To begin with, we know from the agile manifesto that agile ALM values individuals and interactions over processes and tools.[2] But this does not mean that we don't need to focus on processes and tools. Similarly, the agile ALM focuses on creating working software over comprehensive documentation and customer collaboration over contract negotiation. Still, documentation is often absolutely necessary, and signed contracts are rarely optional in the business world. It is equally true that successful professionals do not hide behind a contract and make every effort to delight their customers with excellent value and service.

The agile ALM also emphasizes responding to change over following a plan, although many of the places where we work will not fund any effort without a comprehensive plan. Those who provide the funds for a development project want to know exactly what they are getting into and when they will see results.

In this chapter, we will examine the factors that affect agile process maturity from a number of different perspectives. Many technology professionals find that they must implement agile processes in a large organizational context, including managing teams that are composed of many scrums, totaling scores or even hundreds of developers working from a variety of locations. Scalability is certainly an essential aspect of agile process maturity. Mature agile processes must be repeatable for each project in the organization and have sufficient support for project planning. We also need to understand how process maturity affects non-agile development methodologies, including waterfall and other

---

1. http://agilemanifesto.org/principles.html
2. http://agilemanifesto.org

process models. There are other important considerations as well and any discussion of ALM should start with a clear understanding of the goals involved.

4.1 Goals of Agile Process Maturity

This chapter focuses on helping you establish an agile development process that is light but effective and, most importantly, repeatable. This is not an easy goal to accomplish. In many ways, agile shifts the focus away from implementing processes that contain comprehensive controls, or as agile enthusiasts describe as being high in *ceremony*. Ceremony, in this context, really means bureaucracy or, more specifically, laden with excess controls and "red tape." The goal of this chapter is to help you implement agile processes that are Lean,[3] repeatable, clearly defined, measureable, and adhere to the principles defined in the agile manifesto.[4] We will also discuss how to coexist (or perhaps survive) in non-agile environments. The first step is to understand process maturity in an agile development environment.

4.2 Why Is Agile Process Improvement Important?

Any software or systems development process must continually evolve to meet the ever-changing challenges and requirements of the real world. Agile is no different in this respect. Agile practitioners also know that agile is not perfect and many agile projects have failed for a variety of reasons. Agile processes need to evolve and improve using the very same values and principles that are expected in any agile development effort.

> ### Getting Started with Agile Process Maturity
>
> - Assess your existing practices.
> - What works well?
> - What needs to be improved?
> - Process improvement must be inclusive.
> - Prioritize based upon risk.
> - Process improvement is a marathon—not a sprint.
> - Process improvement must be pragmatic, agile, and Lean.

---

3. www.poppendieck.com
4. http://agilemanifesto.org/principles.html

In some ways agile process maturity could be understood almost in terms of a purity measure. Agile processes that adhere closely to agile principles would, in these terms, be considered a more *agile* process and, obviously, processes that just embrace some agile processes would be more of a hybrid waterfall-agile process.

In order for this measure to be valid, we need to operationalize these principles by considering the extent to which processes embrace agile principles and practices. So how agile are you?

Many organizations want to embrace agile practices and may even recognize the value of agility. They also may find themselves unable to immediately shed their existing processes, especially in terms of corporate governance. This does not mean that they don't want to start the journey, and they may actually reach a very high level of agile process maturity eventually. So how do you start to adopt agile practices and begin the journey?

4.3 Where Do I Start?

The toughest part of implementing mature agile processes is figuring out where to start. I usually start by assessing existing practices and fully understand what works well and what needs to be improved. It is common for me to find that some practices work just fine in one organization that I would have expected were the source of problems. I find that sometimes less-than-perfect processes and procedures may not really be the pain point that one would expect—usually because of the organizational culture. Obviously, trying to fix something that isn't broken will not be very successful, and you will likely find that you do not have much credibility with the key stakeholders if they just don't feel that you are focused on solving the most important problems. In these situations, I communicate my concerns and then focus on what they want me to work on, although I know that they will come back to me and ask for help when things go wrong.

Cludgy Version Control

I recall working with a small software development team supporting an equities trading system. The developers used ClearCase and wanted my help with implementing some branching methods. While I was working with them, I discovered that they had integrated ClearCase with bugzilla in a very unreliable way. They had written the scripts (e.g., ClearCase triggers) themselves and were very proud of their achievement. I looked at the scripts and realized that these would not work if they had more than one or two developers on the project. I communicated my concerns to the development manager, who assured me that "his" scripts worked just fine. There was no point in trying to fix something that my colleague did not view as broken. The manager approached me a year later, right after he added two more developers to his team and he ran into the problems that I had explained could occur. This time he was more than willing to work with me and accept my help.

Getting started with agile process maturity is certainly an essential first step. Being successful with agile ALM requires that you understand what agile process maturity is all about.

4.4 Understanding Agile Process Maturity

Agile process maturity can be understood in many different ways. The most obvious measure of agile process maturity could be in terms of the degree to which the practices adhere to the agile manifesto and the agile principles.[5] I usually refer to this as a *purity* measure to indicate the degree to which the process follows authentic agile principles. As a consultant, I am usually called in to help with situations that are less than perfect. This pragmatic reality does change the fact that we want to approach implementing the agile ALM in a manner that adheres to and benefits from agile values and principles.

> ### *Agile Process Maturity*
>
> Agile process maturity may be understood in terms of
>
> - Adherence to agile principles
> - Repeatable process
> - Scalability (scrum of scrums)
> - Comprehensive (the items on the right)

---

5. Ibid.

- Transparency and traceability
- IT governance
- Coexistence with non-agile
- Harmonization with standards and frameworks
- Planning
- Continuous process improvement

These need to occur without compromising individuals and interactions, working software, customer collaboration, and responding to change.

In order for this measure to be valid, we need to operationalize these principles. So let's consider what following agile values and principles really means in practice and how we can strive for the most effective agile practices possible.

4.4.1 Adherence to the Principles

Mature agile requires that we adhere to the agile principles that we reviewed in Section 3.7. In this book we seek to educate you on software methodology in a way that empowers you to apply these principles and create a software lifecycle that is best for your project and your organization. One of the ironies that we often see is that some agile practitioners are the least "agile" people in the world, insisting on there being only one right way to become *truly* agile. I disagree, and we hope to share the best practices in creating an agile ALM that you can tailor to your own special requirements.

Dysfunctional Agile

In our consulting practice, we often see groups adopting agile practices and actually getting lost along the way. Becoming agile does not happen overnight and, in practice, maybe it shouldn't. Many groups have legacy processes in place that cannot be abandoned without affecting projects already underway. We view organically transitioning to agile as being more practical. In order to be successful, your team needs to understand agile principles and how to create a mature agile application lifecycle. Above all, right-sizing your processes is your most critical success factor.

4.4.2 Repeatable Process

Agile processes, just like any other process, must be repeatable. It does not help to have an agile ALM unless it can be used repeatedly to achieve the desired results. We have seen many agile teams struggle with repeatability because they depended upon the guidance of individual players rather than understanding that agile is still a process that should yield the same results, regardless of who is performing the task—assuming the proper level of skills and training.

> ### *Agile and Law Enforcement*
>
> Bob has long had a passion for serving as a volunteer in both law enforcement and emergency medical services. From responding to fires, to medical emergencies, and especially to crimes in progress, police and emergency personnel must provide a predictable consistent response while still maintaining the flexibility to deal with the situation at hand. When you call because a bad guy is breaking into your car in front of your house, you expect the same results regardless of which police officer happens to respond. You also realize that the situation can be dynamic, and police must be the very model of agility. Law enforcement, emergency medical, and fire response must provide repeatable processes while maintaining the flexibility to respond to the situation at hand.

Agile process maturity should be understood in terms of repeatability. Another important issue is scalability.

4.4.3 Scalability (Scrum of Scrums)

Organizations often pilot agile methodologies in one particular group with spectacular results. The truth is that the participants in the agile pilot are often hand-picked and among the best resources in the organization. But agile processes must be scalable so that other teams within the organization can also be successful. We discuss the critical success factors for scalability throughout this book and then tie them together in Chapter 19, "Integration across the Enterprise." If you want a scalable process, then you need to start by ensuring that your approach is comprehensive.

4.4.4 Comprehensive (Items on the Right)

Agile processes must be comprehensive so that everyone understands what needs to be accomplished, including interdependencies and deadlines. The agile manifesto aptly notes the following:

> We are uncovering better ways of developing software by doing it and helping others do it. Through this work we have come to value:
>
>> Individuals and interactions over processes and tools
>>
>> Working software over comprehensive documentation
>>
>> Customer collaboration over contract negotiation
>>
>> Responding to change over following a plan
>
> That is, while there is value in the items on the right, we value the items on the left more.[6]

Mature agile processes value the items on the right so that we can ensure our processes are comprehensive, including processes and tools, comprehensive documentation, contract negotiation, and following a plan.

Comprehensive processes are essential, as are transparency and traceability.

4.4.5 Transparency and Traceability

Mature agile processes are transparent and traceable. Transparency is fundamental because you want everyone to understand what is being done and how their work impacts (and is impacted by) the work of others. You also want to be able to verify that steps have been completed. Processes that are transparent are easier to understand and follow, ensuring that everyone understands the rules of the road. Being able to go back and verify that each step was completed successfully is also essential, particularly when regulatory compliance is required. In addition, you want to be able to provide transparency to senior management through effective IT governance.

4.4.6 IT Governance

IT governance provides visibility into the organizational processes and existing operations so that senior management can make accurate decisions based upon the information that is available. I always explain to my colleagues that IT governance is essential because this function enables senior management to make the right decisions based upon accurate and up-to-date information. You can even look at IT governance as managing the right information "up" to those who are in the position of making decisions. In some large organizations, agile projects may be in progress at the same time as non-agile projects.

---

6. http://agilemanifesto.org/

Mature agile processes must be able to successfully coexist in these real-world hybrid environments.

4.4.7 Coexistence with Non-agile Projects

The elephant in the room for agile is the number of non-agile projects that exist within an organization that is working to implement agile. We have seen many organizations where existing non-agile projects were already underway, or perhaps existing team members were just not comfortable with taking an agile approach. Mature agile application lifecycle management often requires coexistence with non-agile projects. Coexistence is a sign of maturity, as is aligning with industry standards and frameworks.

4.4.8 Harmonization with Standards and Frameworks

Many organizations must follow the guidance provided in industry standards, including ISO 9000 or frameworks such as ISACA COBIT or the ITIL v3 framework. Mature agile processes can easily align and harmonize with the guidelines provided by these well-respected industry standards and frameworks. This includes meeting the requirements of Section 404 of the Sarbanes-Oxley Act of 2002 or safety standards such as those commonly required by the automotive, medical engineering, or defense industries. Mature agile helps improve quality and can align well with IT controls that are reasonable and appropriate.

The agile manifesto notes that it is more important to be able to respond to change than to simply follow a plan. However, mature agile processes must still be able to create adequate plans that will help guide the development effort.

4.4.9 Following a Plan

Planning is essential for the success of any significant endeavor. Too many agile enthusiasts erroneously think that they don't need to create comprehensive plans to guide the software and systems development effort. The dark side of planning is that sometimes those creating the plan refuse to admit what they do not know. Mature agile processes plan as much as possible and communicate those plans effectively. Unknowns should be identified as risks, which are then mitigated as part of the risk management process. Many years ago W. Edwards Deming noted the importance of "driving out fear." Agility admits when it does not have enough information to specify the details of a plan. Decisions are made at the "last responsible moment." Mature agile processes embrace comprehensive plans but also do not attempt to plan out details that cannot yet be specified.

4.4.10 Continuous Process Improvement

Process improvement is a journey that must be continuously harnessed throughout the software and systems lifecycle. The mature agile process embraces continuous process improvement at both a deep technical level and at a pragmatic business level. Improving your technical processes is mostly focused on avoiding human error while maintaining a high level of productivity and quality. Improving your business processes can be a bit more complicated.

Do you make satisfying the customer through early and continuous delivery of valuable software your highest priority? Does your agile ALM process harness change for the customer's competitive advantage and welcome changing requirements, even late in development? Your delivery cycle should favor shorter iterations, with delivering working software frequently, from every couple of weeks to every couple of months. Developers and businesspeople should be working together daily throughout the project. Projects are built around motivated individuals, and they are provided the environment and support they need and are trusted to get the job done. Information is best conveyed face to face, and working software is the primary measure of progress.

The agile ALM should help all the stakeholders maintain a constant pace indefinitely in what is known as sustainable development. There is also continuous attention to technical excellence and good design, including a focus on simplicity—the art of maximizing the amount of work not done. Self-organizing teams produce the best architectures, requirements, and designs. At regular intervals, the team reflects on how to become more effective and then tunes and adjusts its behavior accordingly. These principles have formed the basis of agile development for many years now. In order to understand them, you need to consider how to operationalize and implement these principles in practice. Then we will show how they fit into and, of course, facilitate the agile ALM.

4.5 Applying the Principles

Implementing the agile ALM requires that you understand the agile values and principles and, more importantly, how to utilize them in practical terms. Technology projects require a deep understanding of exactly what the system should do and how it should work. These are important details that are typically expressed in terms of requirements. There are many different types of requirements, from system-level response time to functional usage, including navigation. Many professionals use epics[7] and stories[8] to describe requirements in high-level terms. Writing and maintaining a requirements document is often less than fruitful, with most requirements documents out of date even before they have been approved by the user. Agile takes a pragmatic approach to requirements management that focuses on working software instead of writing requirements documents that are often of limited value.

One very effective way to manage requirements is to supplement them with well-written test cases and test scripts. Test cases often contain exactly the same information that you might expect in a requirements document.

Test Cases for Trading Systems

Many years ago I requested that the testers work with me to write test cases for a major trading system in use on the floor of the New York Stock Exchange. The user representative was hesitant at first to focus on testing early in the software development process. I managed to persuade one of the senior representatives to give me one hour. During that session I simply asked him to say what he would test and what he expected the results to be. Within that first hour, this business expert actually picked up the phone and told the head of development that "what he had asked for was not what he needed." I had caused the business expert to start actively thinking about how he was really going to use the system. The requirements phase had been long and thorough, yet the real breakthrough occurred when we started writing test cases. Well-written tests can be very effective at supplementing, and even completing, requirements descriptions that are often incomplete because all of the usage details may not be initially understood.

4.6 Recognition by the Agile Community

Agile development is part of a large ecosystem with an active and involved community. Mature agile processes are aligned with agile principles and are recognized by the agile community. Much of my work involves taking innovative

---

7. Epics are a description of a group of features (e.g., stories) that help document requirements in agile development.
8. Stories are descriptions of features from an end-user perspective, which serve to document requirements in agile development.

and even risky approaches when I customize software methodology to meet the unique needs of often complex organizations. Although I always maintain confidentiality, I find it effective to write and publish articles that describe my approach to DevOps and agile process maturity. Sometimes, my views are well accepted by the agile community, and other times the reaction can be quite significant. I actually use my esteemed colleagues in the agile community as a feedback loop to continuously improve my own process methodologies.

Recognition within the agile community is a worthy goal. However, gaining consensus may be much more difficult to achieve.

4.7 Consensus within the Agile Community

The agile community can be both opinionated and very vocal. It can also be difficult to gain consensus. You need to expect that there will always be a diversity of views and opinions expressed in the agile community. Sometimes, views are expressed in rather emphatic terms. In fact, it is the great irony that some agile practitioners are the least agile people I have ever worked with, insisting that agility can be practiced in only one particular way. My view is to enjoy the plurality of opinions, looking for consensus when I can find it and also understand that sometimes experienced practitioners will have differing points of view. This is especially true when confronting some of the more thorny issues in understanding agility. One of these considerations is what agile process maturity is not.

4.8 What Agile Process Maturity Is Not

The agile process is not an excuse to skip documenting and tracking requirements, so agile process maturity is also not an excuse for failing to implement enough "ceremony" to get the job done. Although agile has boasted many fabulous successes, it is also not without its failures. One of the biggest problems with agile today is folks just going along with what they are told without questioning and reflecting upon the effectiveness of the agile process.

Emperor's Clothes

Hans Christian Andersen tells the age-old story of the Emperor's New Clothes in which a team of conmen come into a town and convince everyone there that they can create a set of clothes that can only be seen by those subjects who are truly loyal to the emperor and are invisible to those unfit for their positions, are stupid, or are incompetent. As the story goes, the emperor is sitting on his throne in his underwear while these two men pretend to be tailoring him a fine suit. Predictably, everyone is silent because they are afraid to speak up and have the emperor think that they are not loyal to him. Finally, a young child blurts out that the emperor is not wearing any clothes and the townspeople realize that they are being fooled.

Too often folks involved with the agile transformation are silent even though they may have well-founded misgivings. The young child in this fable innocently speaks up. We should all have the courage to express our own misgivings. Remember Deming teaches us to drive out fear.

Immature agile processes can create many challenges for the development team.

4.9 What Does an Immature Agile Process Look Like?

Immature agile processes can resemble software development in the Wild, Wild West. If your team delivers in an inconsistent way and lacks transparency and predictability, then you are likely dealing with a lack of process maturity. You might even be successful from time to time—but maturity involves a lot more than occasional heroics. There are many other potential problems with agile.

4.10 Problems with Agile

Too often agile has become an excuse to work in a very loose and ineffective way. We have seen agile teams use the agile manifesto as an excuse to not plan out their projects and also to not communicate their plans with others. Sometimes teams also fail to document and track requirements, which can lead to many problems, including a high incidence of defects. We have also seen teams that used agile as an excuse to not document their work. Mature agile processes provide the right balance of planning, requirements management, and documentation to avoid mistakes and get the job done. We recall one major incident in a large bank where a vendor claimed to be employing agile and shipped a release that was not really ready to be seen by the customer.

One CIO's View of Agile

During a configuration management (CM) assessment, which I conducted as a consultant, I had the opportunity to speak with the CIO of a large international bank, who described his recent experience with a software vendor who had represented their development practices as being agile. The vendor did a lot of development offshore with teams of only four or five developers using scrum and sprints that lasted only two or three weeks. Because the team adhered to fixed iterations, they were delivering code that was incomplete or, as the CIO described it, "half-baked." I spoke with the vendor's development manager, who essentially admitted that they did adhere strictly to fixed timebox iterations and, as a result, occasionally some features were not completely implemented. The vendor saw no problem with this and viewed their development methodology as quite excellent, completely ignoring the viewpoint of the customer.

Although agile has its challenges, let's not lose sight of the challenges often seen in waterfall.

4.11 Waterfall Pitfalls

Agile enthusiasts have long described the many pitfalls and problems inherent in following the waterfall software methodology. In Chapter 14, "Agile in a Non-Agile World," we will discuss these and other challenges as well, but also acknowledge that there are times when waterfall is the only choice. From the perspective of agile process maturity, we need to understand exactly where waterfall is problematic so that we do not make the same mistakes in our agile or hybrid agile processes.

Waterfall, as envisioned by Winston Royce,[9] was iterative in nature. But waterfall fails when you try to define requirements that are not yet understood. Many organizations go through exhaustive planning exercises that are essentially an effort to plan what is not yet known and understood. When creating a plan, you need to identify the things that are not yet well understood as project risks. Risk itself is not inherently bad. Many organizations, including trading

9. Royce, Winston W. (1970). "Managing the Development of Large Software Systems." In: Technical Papers of Western Electronic Show and Convention (WesCon) August 25–28, 1970, Los Angeles, USA.

firms, actually thrive on risk. It is also essential to create adequate documentation and to keep it updated as necessary. Many organizations spend so much time trying to track requirements and create exhaustive project plans that they leave no time to actually get to software development and have to rush to make project deadlines. This dysfunctional approach can result in defects and significant technical debt.

Mature agile processes take a pragmatic approach to requirements definition and tracking while also establishing enough of a project plan to communicate dates and deliverables to all stakeholders. There are times when documentation is not negotiable, whether your project is using agile or waterfall.

Essentials

- Planning the unknown
- Failing to manage risk
- Documentation outdated
- No time for coding since we spent our time planning

4.11.1 Mired in Process

We often see organizations that are simply mired in their waterfall processes. These groups typically take a very rigid approach to planning and requirements gathering. Although sometimes waterfall makes sense, it is essential to always be pragmatic and avoid getting mired in your own processes. When this happens, we have seen teams where it actually became part of the culture to pretend to be following the process.

4.11.2 Pretending to Follow the Process

One of the most dysfunctional behaviors we often see is organizations that require complete adherence to waterfall processes, which results in team members being forced to pretend to be following these rigid waterfall processes. In these circumstances we find people who feel pressured into creating and following plans even when they really do not have all of the necessary details, or creating requirements specifications that document features that are not yet well understood. If management forces employees to follow waterfall in a rigid and dysfunctional way, then they really have no choice but to smile and pretend to follow the process. The better way is to create mature agile processes that include both the items on the left of the agile manifesto and the items on the right.

4.12 The Items on the Right

The agile manifesto teaches us to value individuals and interactions over processes and tools, working software over comprehensive documentation, customer collaboration over contract negotiation, and responding to change over following a plan. But mature agile processes must have robust processes and tools, adequate documentation, and plans. You also don't want to try to engage with customers without well-written contracts and clear agreements. The items on the right side of the agile manifesto are actually very important. It is also important to adjust your ceremony for the environment and culture in which your organization is operating.

4.12.1 Adjusting Ceremony

Agile processes are said to be "light" in terms of ceremony, which means that they are not overly burdensome with rigid verbose rules and required procedures, which are inherent in creating IT controls. Mature agile processes are able to adjust the amount of ceremony required to avoid mistakes and still get the job done. Although right-sizing the amount of process is a must-have, so is coexisting with non-agile processes when necessary.

4.13 Agile Coexisting with Non-Agile

There are many times when agile simply *must* exist with non-agile processes. This is the real world that many agile practitioners find so difficult to accept. We work with many large banks and financial services firms where agile must coexist with non-agile processes. This is often the case when large organizations must have IT governance in place to ensure that senior management can make decisions based upon adequate information.

4.14 IT Governance

IT governance is all about providing information to senior management so that the right decisions can be made. Many agile processes suffer from failing to provide adequate information to senior managers. Mature agile processes provide enough information so that senior management can make the right decisions in support of the development effort. IT governance is closely aligned with providing transparency.

4.14.1 Providing Transparency

Mature agile processes provide the transparency that is essential to help all stakeholders understand the tasks that they have to complete and especially how their work affects the work of other members of the team. Processes, and especially workflows, help the entire team understand what needs to be done on a day-to-day basis. This is exactly where having just enough process can help you get the job done and avoid costly mistakes. Above all, you want to have an ALM that follows the agile principles.

4.15 ALM and the Agile Principles

Mature agile processes should obviously adhere to agile principles. The agile ALM is customer-centric and facilitates the early and continuous delivery of valuable software. We welcome changing requirements, even late in development, and harness change for the customer's competitive advantage. The agile ALM should help deliver working software by frequently facilitating daily collaboration between all stakeholders, including businesspeople and developers. Projects should be built around motivated individuals with the environment and support they need while encouraging face-to-face interactions. Working software is the primary measure of progress.

The agile ALM should promote sustainable development, including a constant pace throughout the duration of the project. There also should be continuous attention to technical excellence and good design enhancing agility, along with valuing simplicity instead of overly complex design and processes. The agile ALM empowers the cross-functional self-organizing team, resulting in the best architectures, requirements, and designs. The mature agile ALM also includes regular opportunities to reflect on how the process can become more effective, tuning and adjusting its processes and behavior. The mature agile process adheres to these agile principles on a constant and reliable basis. This is why you need to start off with processes that are repeatable and predictable.

4.16 Agile as a Repeatable Process

Mature agile processes must be repeatable above all else. Even the best process will be of little value if it cannot be used reliably across all of the projects and groups involved with completing the work. Closely related is the need for scalability.

4.16.1 Scalability

Scalability means that the mature agile process can be used reliably across the enterprise. We often find that this is exactly where organizations struggle the most. We will review some tactics to help ensure that your processes can scale to the enterprise in Chapter 19, "Integration across the Enterprise." Another key aspect of agile process maturity is ensuring that you deliver on time and within budget.

4.16.2 Delivering on Time and within Budget

We see many agile teams struggling with the reality that no one is going to give them a blank check and tell them to take their time on delivering results. Mature agile processes should provide enough planning and structure to help ensure that the software can be delivered on time and within budget. Unless your senior management team is clairvoyant and just anticipates your team's every whim, you will need to communicate what you need to get the job done. This should include a clear idea of the timeframe required and the budget that will help ensure success of the project. This is particularly essential when considering the quality of the software that you deliver.

4.16.3 Quality

Mature agile processes must ensure that quality is a top priority. This requires a strong focus on robust automated testing and benefits greatly from thorough test planning. Well-written test cases can help supplement even incomplete requirements documents. Mature agile processes cannot survive without a strong focus on quality and testing. W. Edwards Deming, regarded by many as the father of quality management, was well known for explaining that quality must be built in from the very beginning of the software and systems lifecycle. This is particularly true in mature agile processes.

4.17 Deming and Quality Management

Many of the lessons from Deming are a main focus of the agile ALM, and we will point them out throughout this book. Testing is essential, but there are many other ways to build quality into the agile ALM.

4.17.1 Testing versus Building Quality In

Application testing is a must-have. But quality has to be built in from the very beginning. Code reviews and inspections are among the tools that help ensure quality is built into the product from the very beginning. Ensuring that requirements are well defined is essential for ensuring high-quality systems. The agile ALM provides a comprehensive framework of best practices to help build quality into the product from the very beginning. It is also the best way to help improve productivity.

4.17.2 Productivity

Technology professionals often find themselves mired in the quagmire of trying to get work done efficiently. The mature agile ALM helps avoid mistakes and rework that is so often the reality of today's software and systems development effort. One of the most effective practices to improve productivity is rapid iterative development.

4.18 Agile Maturity in the Enterprise

Implementing processes across any large organization can be very challenging, and agile process maturity should be measured across the enterprise. While we are not advocating comparing groups to each other, which could actually be counterproductive, we do want to have common criteria to help each team plan their own process improvement efforts. It is best to understand processes within the group context itself. We have seen teams that had technical flaws in their processes, tools, or procedures and in one group these issues presented a significant challenge, but for another it was almost irrelevant. For example, we have seen teams lack strong version control procedures but somehow manage to avoid problems that we would have expected through sheer force of will or even manual controls. Obviously these situations are optimal, but still each team may have a very different view of their priorities and pain points. We implement agile processes consistently across the enterprise, while still understanding that each team may have a somewhat different culture, environment, and priorities. We can manage this balance by establishing the goals and objectives while understanding that there could be some difference in processes, tools, and procedures.

4.18.1 Consistency across the Enterprise

Process maturity models can be helpful in establishing common criteria to help ensure consistency across the enterprise. We also use industry standards and frameworks as a source of consistent best practices to implement across the enterprise. For example, we might ask a team to explain how they implement automated build, package, and deployment, including their procedures to verify and validate that the correct code has been deployed. Teams are often quite up-front about what they are doing well and what could be improved. Helping each team to focus on its own perceived priorities is essential for successful process improvement. But there is also room for ensuring that industry best practices are implemented consistently across the firm. This work requires excellent communication and even some good marketing of the new approach.

4.18.2 Marketing the New Approach

We never assume that teams will just automatically agree to implement the best practices that we advocate. Sometimes, it is best to help a team create its own plan. We balance this approach with enterprise process improvement efforts to essentially market industry best practices using the latest processes and tools. Throughout this effort it is essential to continuously focus on process improvement.

4.19 Continuous Process Improvement

The most effective way to implement mature agile processes is to take an agile and iterative approach to implementing the agile ALM itself. This means that you need to be continuously working toward excellence. Learning from mistakes is par for the course, and effective processes should also be self-correcting.

4.19.1 Self-Correcting

Process improvement is not without its challenges. The important thing is to ensure that your processes correct themselves and evolve. Being able to improve your processes is much easier if you are able to measure them and demonstrate progress over time.

4.20 Measuring the ALM

We tend to be wary of overengineering the measurement process, as some teams tend to try to game the measurement. With any measurement approach, it is important to consider validation up-front. This is especially true with regard to metrics.

4.20.1 Project Management Office (PMO) Metrics

Metrics, including those used in project management, can be very important. More importantly, selecting valid and verifiable metrics is key to ensuring a successful measurement approach leading to quantifiable process improvement. Our experience has been that less is more in this case, and the best approach is to select a few metrics that are valid and verifiable. Establishing an in-house metrics program is very important. It is also important to ensure that your vendors do the same.

4.21 Vendor Management

Vendors often have strong sales and marketing functions that sometimes include information on their processes, which can include metrics. It is important for you to review and understand your vendors' criteria. We have had many times when we were asked to review vendor programs and give our recommendations on ensuring that the vendor approach was aligned with our client's requirements. It has been our experience that many vendors welcome this input and where there are gaps, they should be understood as well. Although agile process maturity is typically focused on software, we often review processes around hardware development as well.

4.22 Hardware Development

Hardware development is often dependent upon a waterfall approach because half an incomplete circuit chip is often not very helpful. Our effort is to align the agile ALM with the engineering lifecycle required to design and implement hardware. This is often required when we consult with firms that create firmware.

4.22.1 Firmware

Firmware is software that must be created and embedded in the hardware that consists of the complete hardware-software component. We view agile process maturity as part of this alignment and have seen teams succeed quite well even when using a hybrid waterfall approach for the hardware and an agile approach for the firmware.

4.23 Conclusion

There are many factors to consider when creating a mature agile process. We have introduced and reviewed many of the issues involved with creating mature agile processes. The agile ALM needs to be aligned with the technology, environment, and culture of the team and the organization within which it will operate. Rarely do we see teams get this right the first time, and the most successful groups take an agile iterative approach to creating their agile ALM.

Chapter 5

Rapid Iterative Development

Long before agile was popular, technology professionals had proposed methodologies for rapid iterative development. These methodologies were often focused on the iterative nature of waterfall, but also attempted to address the challenges of developing software using traditional software development lifecycles. Another key differentiator was a focus on involving the end user throughout the development lifecycle, which previously was only accomplished by professional business analysts. Developers had little or no direct contact with the folks who were going to directly use the system. Back then, mainframe software development often took years from the point that requirements were defined to when the system was finally rolled out. Efforts to speed up the process met with mixed results. We discussed rapid application development (RAD) in Section 3.6, and much of the information aligns with the lessons we learned during that journey to improve our software development methodology. Many technology professionals looked for effective ways to quickly prototype and deliver applications more expeditiously. Although agility has many distinct advantages and capabilities, rapid iterative development is an approach that has merit even on its own.

5.1 Goals of Rapid Iterative Development

Rapid iterative development has a goal of quickly developing functionality that can be demonstrated and reviewed with all stakeholders. One reason why this approach has merit is that technology professionals often need to get up to speed when learning new technologies. Taking an iterative approach enables the developers to do this while simultaneously demonstrating functionality. Reducing the time-to-market is often an absolute necessity. Rapid iterative prototyping has long been a proven method to improve quality and productivity while often reducing costs and shortening timelines.

5.2 Why Is Rapid Iterative Development Important?

Rapid iterative development is important because it enables us to develop the code in an iterative fashion, improving our knowledge and technical capability much more quickly than would be possible using noniterative approaches. This is particularly important when learning new technologies and development frameworks that are being used by a team that has little or no prior experience with this approach. Gaining immediate input from the end user is also extremely valuable. Rapid iterative development is not necessarily agile in nature, and it was around a long time before agile became popular. We have seen situations where organizations had significant software processes in place, often due to audit and regulatory requirements specific to their industry. Trying to adopt agile development would have been disruptive and introduced far too much risk. Helping the teams adopt a rapid iterative approach was acceptable and aligned with their culture and existing processes.

> ### *Aligning Software to Firmware*
>
> We conducted a software assessment for a firm that was primarily focused on creating complex hardware components. The company was highly successful and had specific processes in place for creating their circuit chips. The company was resistant to implementing agile processes that they felt would not align well with their existing processes. Implementing rapid iterative development using simulation software was much easier to introduce and helped them improve their software quality and productivity.

Rapid iterative development reduces risk by allowing the team to build, package, and deploy in short timeframes—without necessarily having to use agile fixed timebox sprints.

5.3 Where Do I Start?

You need to start by understanding the value of embracing rapid iterative development and old-fashioned process engineering, which will enable you to tailor the methodology to your benefit. The following goals and objectives will help guide this effort. I usually begin by looking at the group's existing processes, identifying what works well and exactly what needs to be improved. Taking an iterative approach is especially helpful when we do not fully understand what needs to be built up-front. In this case, we often build a prototype, examine it, and then build the next iteration. This iterative approach helps from many different perspectives. The first view to consider is that of the developer's.

5.4 The Development View

Developers tackle many complex technical challenges, each of which can involve significant technical risk. Risk is not inherently bad, but must always be understood so that it can be mitigated. We have worked in many financial trading environments where some very smart folks thrived on accurately well-understood risk. However, technical risk can be a little different. Technical risk involves the use of a technology, usually for the first time, and may or may not be implemented successfully. As technology professionals, we all like to be at the forefront of the technology industry. However, being the first to tackle new ways of doing things also means that they might just not work as expected. If you have implemented a system using Java J2EE with a well-known relational database such as MySQL or Postgres, then you have a pretty good idea of how long the effort will take and some of the potential technical challenges that you might face. But if you want to implement the same system using node.js and a NoSQL database, then you might find yourself facing new and unexpected technical challenges. Tackling the unknown challenges is exactly what technical risk is all about. What you need to do is decide on a course of action that will accurately and reliably identify and mitigate technical risk.

If you are implementing a new technology, then building something very small is an excellent first step. It is wise to continuously add a few small features and verify frequently that the system works as expected. Taking an iterative approach significantly mitigates technical risk. Another way to mitigate technical risk is with efficient development practices such as controlled isolation.

5.5 Controlled Isolation

Controlled isolation helps developers be more productive and avoids costly mistakes by providing a private workspace to get work done without the distraction of changes from other developers engaged in the same development effort. In version control systems, controlled isolation is provided by workspaces that are periodically synced from the master version control system. Rapid iterative development also provides an approach that thrives on controlled isolation where developers can work on creating code to solve isolated problems without the distraction of trying to tackle too many moving parts. Rapid iterative development puts sufficient focus on getting a reasonable amount of work completed in a fast and productive way.

> ### Bob and His "Man-Cave"
>
> Much of this book was written in a private office in Bob's house that we call the "man-cave." This room contains multiple laptops, screens, and a TV constantly streaming the latest news, as well as a couch where Bob takes his power naps. This controlled isolation contributes to Bob's productivity while allowing him to balance solitude with interaction with the rest of his family.

Controlled isolation is closely related to managing complexity.

5.6 Managing Complexity

Complexity is one of the greatest challenges in any technology development effort. As software engineers, we manage increasingly complex (and exciting) systems. The only way that we can accomplish this work successfully is to tame this complexity. Rapid iterative development helps us manage complexity by completing one manageable piece of work and then tackling the next piece in an iterative way. This approach allows us to focus on just one challenging aspect of the system at a time without having to tackle the entire system—which for most professionals would be almost impossible. Trying to tackle overly complex systems results in human errors and software defects that can be difficult to find and resolve. Another important approach to managing complexity is continuous integration.

5.7 Continuous Integration

Continuous integration is a popular industry best practice that focuses on frequently merging and integrating changes from two or more developers. The more often that you integrate changes, the easier it is to address any problems or challenges that may arise. Continuous integration is usually managed by an automated merging of changes from developers using a version control system (VCS). Continuous integration servers generally take changes committed (e.g., checked in) into the VCS, automatically compiling the code, deploying the release baseline to a test environment, and then, most importantly, running a series of automated tests. Rapid iterative development benefits greatly from continuous integration, resulting in better code and improved programmer productivity. When implementing these industry best practices, it is always best to focus on effectively managing technology risk.

5.8 It's All About (Technology) Risk

Risk is not bad. Many organizations thrive on risk, but only if that risk is understood and managed successfully. Rapid iterative development provides an excellent approach for understanding and managing technology risk. With each iteration, specific features can be isolated, understood, and implemented successfully. What is key here is that risk must be identified and plans formed to mitigate the risk by determining the best course of action to accomplish goals. The rapid evolution of technology results in many challenges that must be addressed. This is especially important when adopting new, and often complex, technology approaches that implicitly involve technology risk.

5.9 Taming Technology

Rapid iterative development helps technology professionals implement a specific piece of technology, which helps development engineers tame what is so often bleeding-edge technology. This usually involves implementing a piece of the new technology, allowing engineering resources to get up to speed and understand how the new technology works. Taming technology also relies upon excellent architectural design.

5.10 Designing Architecture

Quality has to be built in from the beginning of the software and systems development effort. The only way to accomplish this goal is to design architectures that are fit for purpose and fit for use. The rapid iterative approach allows us to design architectures that are robust and scalable.

5.11 Conclusion

Rapid iterative development does not solve every problem and is not a substitute for more robust agile iterative approaches. But sometimes situations require a pragmatic approach that is less than ideal. Rapid iterative development provides a practical approach that should be part of your agile ALM arsenal.

Further Reading

Martin, James. (1991). *Rapid Application Development*. New York: Macmillan Publishing.

PART II

Automating the Process

Chapter 6

Build Engineering in the ALM

Build engineering is the discipline of efficiently turning source code into binary executables. Build engineering can be as simple as running a Makefile or Ant script and as complicated as writing a full build framework to support the underlying technology architecture. In our book on configuration management best practices we discuss build engineering in depth. In this chapter, we discuss build engineering within the context of the agile ALM. I love build engineering and have always found it to be among the most challenging and rewarding roles within configuration management.

This chapter helps you understand the build within the context of application lifecycle management. We discuss essential aspects of automating the application build with particular attention to techniques for creating the trusted application base. We also discuss baselining, compile dependencies, and embedding version IDs as required for version identification. We discuss the independent build and creating a fully automated build process. Building quality into the build through automated unit tests, code scans, and instrumenting the code is an important part of this effort. Finally, we will discuss the ever-challenging task of selecting and implementing the right build tools.

6.1 Goals of Build Engineering

The goal of build engineering is to be able to reliably compile and link your source code into a binary executable in the shortest possible time. Build engineering includes identifying the exact compile and runtime dependencies, as well as any other specific technical requirements, including compiler (linker and managed environment) switches and dependencies. Build engineering improves both quality and productivity for the entire team. We believe that the build engineering team should consider themselves to be a service function, with the development team as their primary *customers*. However, there are times when

91

build engineering must also have the authority to enforce organizational policies. As build engineers, we provide a service to support the development effort, but our primary goal is to help secure the assets of the firm that are built and released through the build engineering function.

6.2 Why Is Build Engineering Important?

Build engineering helps the development team by providing an accurate and repeatable way to compile and link the code in the fastest possible way. Being able to rapidly rebuild a release enhances productivity by facilitating software development. Fast builds are important for any software development methodology, a fact that agile and iterative development have highlighted for some time now. Getting the build right also avoids serious problems that could potentially have catastrophic impacts upon the development team as well as the entire organization.[1] Build engineering is important because it can improve both the quality of the application that you are developing and the productivity of the entire organization involved.

6.3 Where Do I Start?

We always start by looking at the existing development build procedures. Sometimes you will find that the development team already has existing build scripts, perhaps using Ant, Maven, or Make. Often, the existing build procedures will only handle deployment to the development test environment. It is pretty common for a build engineer to be required to take an existing build script and modify it to support QA and production environments. Legacy build scripts may also fail frequently and require developer expertise in order to support them. If you are the build engineer, then your job will be to make these scripts more reliable and supportable. We have often found that it is best to begin by understanding the application so that we understand what we are trying to build. Sometimes the architecture will be complicated enough that you may need to partner with the developer in order to write a suitable build system. Make sure that you start by evaluating the existing build tools and

---

1. Bob describes an incident in which New York Stock Exchange systems crashed, affecting the world economy, in Section 6.8.

processes before you attempt to improve them, implementing build-engineering best practices at every step.

Dangers of IDEs

Most developers rely heavily upon their integrated development environment (IDE), which is a tool that usually includes an "intelligent" code editor, a compiler, a debugger, and a graphical user interface (GUI) builder. IDEs help developers work more productively, but they also can pose a challenge for build engineering because developers typically forget the settings that they configured when they first got started with the development effort. In order to create a repeatable build, we usually have to help the developers figure out where they configured their compiler switches, classpath, and other environment settings. It is common to learn that many developers have different configurations, which are inherently not compatible. The build engineers' command-line procedures end up becoming the single authoritative configuration.

Done well, build engineering allows you to tackle the complexity of understanding the overall build and create safeguards to avoid common mistakes.

6.4 Understanding the Build

Application builds can be very complicated and often involve many components that each has its own dependencies, sometimes on multiple platforms. We have seen builds where the dependencies were so complicated that no one person actually understood the entire build. Sometimes this is because the build spans multiple technologies and even multiple platforms. But sometimes builds are just written in a ridiculously obtuse and overly complex way. To really understand the build, you need to understand the components from a complete ALM perspective. For me, this often means diving into Visual Studio, C#, and .NET one day and Eclipse, Java, and J2EE the next. A few hours later, we may be focusing on node.js and MongoDB. The next day, I may be focusing on mainframe JCL, Cobol, and Clists. Build engineering in the ALM can get very complicated very quickly, so the last thing that we need is a developer who makes any component of the build process more complicated than it needs to be.

> ### Bob's Build Nightmares
>
> As a build engineer, Bob has seen many really bad builds. One of the worst builds that he saw was written by a colleague who had his PhD in a field that had little to do with computer science. The approach and logic of his build scripts were so overly complicated that no other member of the development team actually understood the build. When it broke, he was usually on vacation and then, as Murphy would dictate he went on to another company—leaving this unwieldy mess to the rest of the group to rewrite.

Fundamentally, the code should only be built once and then configured for each of the environments. Build automation tools such as Ant, Maven, and Make are typically used for the compilation of source code to binary executable, which should only occur once. Subsequent automated procedures should be designed to simply configure the build for each of the environments and then deploy to the target location. Understanding the entire build is essential, but the next step is automating the process so that it is repeatable, verifiable, and traceable.

6.5 Automating the Application Build

We always automate every single step of the application build, package, and deployment across the entire ALM. Doing things manually results in mistakes and lots of time wasted due to rework. Even a one-line command is best done in a script to avoid any possible mistakes. Most of our code tests each step of the build so that any and all problems are detected immediately. We often refer to *failing fast* to indicate that a build script should identify a problem and stop the process immediately once an issue is detected. In manufacturing, we talk about "stopping the line," which is a reference to stopping the manufacturing process when a serious problem is discovered. Too often, automated scripts do not test themselves and the script goes ten lines down before the problem is discovered, and then it takes a lot more time to backtrack and figure out exactly what went wrong.

> ### Bob on Drugs
>
> I recall visiting my doctor when I was so sick that she considered having me admitted to a hospital. After the exam, my doctor agreed that I could

just go home, provided that I went straight to bed and stayed home from work for at least a few days. So I took the medication that the doctor prescribed and went straight to sleep as promised. Not surprisingly, I woke up to my cell phone ringing, only to hear my boss insist that it was urgent that I do a build, package, and deployment. Fortunately, I had automated every step of the build and each step tested itself. The scripts were numbered sequentially from 1 through 10, which was just about the limit of my cognitive ability that day. I did the build successfully and then went back to sleep. I never thought it would happen, but I had built and deployed a pretty complicated financial system while I was effectively under the influence of *drugs*.

Automating the build is essential, especially if you want to have a secure and verifiable build, which we refer to as the *secure trusted application base*.

6.6 Creating the Secure Trusted Base

There have been many high-profile cybersecurity breaches in recent memory, each of which landed on the front page of many newspapers. Organizations foolishly rely upon virus scans to identify malware that has been left on their servers by malicious hackers. This approach has very limited success because it relies upon knowing the signature of the malware in advance, which is obviously unrealistic and woefully insufficient. We usually only find out about an attack after a machine has been compromised and then forensically analyzed.

Inconsiderate Hackers

Hackers do not provide their code up-front to forensic engineers for analysis. We only discover the signature of an attack after the system has been compromised and the malware has been placed on the server. So virus detection, which assumes that a system has already been penetrated and the malware identified, is like locking the front door after the burglar has already entered the premises.

What works much better is to know exactly what was built and have an automated procedure to verify that the code was deployed correctly. In the next section, we will discuss how to baseline your code once it is built, packaged, and deployed. But first we have to ensure that we have a reliable way to verify that every single file has been successfully deployed. During the code build, we can embed immutable version IDs into each component and create cryptographic hashes (e.g., MAC SHA1, MD5) to use in verifying that the code has been successfully deployed. With every build of a package, you should also create a manifest that contains the complete list of configuration items included, the embedded version ID, and the cryptographic hash to be used for verification. This approach enables you to completely ensure that the correct configuration items (CIs) were successfully deployed. The next step is to automate the detection of any unauthorized changes, whether through malicious intent or human error. This ability requires that you establish baselines of the runtime environment itself.

6.7 Baselining

Once code has been successfully deployed, you need to be able to detect unauthorized changes, whether they be through malicious intent or simply human error. My approach is to create cryptographic hashes on the essential configuration items; these should be monitored and verified regularly, usually on a nightly basis.

Surprises in Production

Bob worked at a large bank that had repeated outages due to unauthorized changes, which were only detected after an outage occurred. Once the runtime environment was baselined and monitored, we began to learn that the middleware administrators were making changes that they thought would help the applications run more efficiently. Unfortunately, these admins were not communicating with other members of the teams and the changes that they were making not only violated change control policy, but also were causing production outages. Baselining provided us with an early detection system that allowed us to proactively identify the changes and work with the other members of the team to revert the changes before there was any adverse impact.

The challenge is that there are often too many files changing for legitimate reasons, resulting in what we will call *false positives*, so we need to ascertain which

CIs should be monitored and which ones can be safely ignored. In the real world, it is not so easy to tell which CIs are important and which ones can be safely ignored. The best approach is to start monitoring from the very beginning of the software or systems lifecycle by establishing baseline monitoring in the development test environment. The challenge in establishing these baselines is knowing what to monitor. Baselining often fails because there is no easy way to ascertain which configuration items really should be monitored. Once the project is completed, many developers move on to new projects and may not be available for consultation and troubleshooting. We need to engage with the developers early in the lifecycle while the code is being written and the deep technical knowledge is available to assist with implementing these procedures. DevOps provides us with the principles and practices to ensure that developers and operations folks can collaborate and communicate effectively to ensure that we know exactly which configuration items should be monitored and the best approach for doing so. Another important capability is to embed version IDs into these key configuration items, in a process that is known as version identification.

6.8 Version Identification

During the build, unique immutable version IDs must be embedded into each significant configuration item. This crucial step is often overlooked, but can be accomplished in several different ways. First, you can use build tools such as Ant, Maven, or Make to embed a unique version ID into the manifest of the build container and the configuration items themselves. You can also include some code that is designed to ascertain and display the version ID in your configuration items. Version identification allows you to verify that the essential components have been successfully deployed, and together with efficient use of cryptographic hashes such as MAC SHA1 or MD5, allows you to verify that all of your CIs have been successfully deployed and to detect unauthorized changes. Although many groups manage to create these automated procedures for individual code components, we really need to take a full ALM approach to ensuring that the complete codebase is secure across the entire system.

Stopping the World Economy

Bob was once told that he had made a mistake that led to the crash of a critical trading system on the floor of the New York Stock Exchange. The mistake involved deploying the wrong version of two shell scripts that were essential to starting up this critical system. Fortunately, the two scripts had embedded version IDs, and it took less than five minutes to investigate. Based upon the forensics, Bob and the other systems administrators were able to determine the actual cause of the problem, which was still online and risked causing another outage. Bob had in fact deployed the correct scripts and there was another unrelated miscommunication that led to the scripts being overwritten by one of the systems administrators. Embedding version IDs into the configuration items made it easy to determine the root cause of the problem and prevent another outage from occurring. This technique is known as a *physical configuration audit*.

Another common source of errors in the ALM is a lack of understanding of compile dependencies.

6.9 Compile Dependencies

Compile dependencies can be very complicated to ascertain and fully comprehend. While observing the build, reviewing build scripts, and tracking down the settings in the developers' IDE are essential, there are also some considerations unique to the agile ALM. Early in the lifecycle, developers are often learning new technologies and determining the best approach to building application components. Unfortunately, this information often becomes a distant memory and may even be lost when developers, perhaps even consultants, move on to their next project. You need to capture this information from the very beginning of the software and systems lifecycle. The agile ALM requires that we start thinking about production deployments from the very beginning of the lifecycle because this essential expertise simply may not be available later on. Creating an effective build is an ALM consideration.

6.10 Build in the ALM

Application lifecycle management takes a broad view, from collecting requirements to design, development, and even ongoing support after deployment. The build is an integral part of this process and needs to be considered throughout the entire ALM. What we often see is that developers have very elaborate build, continuous integration, and deployment procedures to test environments that do not match the approach that will be used to build, package, and deploy the code to production. Developers rarely think about verifying that the code has been successfully deployed using production-ready procedures. This is problematic for two important reasons. First, developers often get delayed by unexpected changes that were made due to human error or poor communication between the team members. Having sufficient IT controls in place from the very beginning of the process can avoid these types of mistakes.

Second, and even worse, changing the build, package, and deployment procedures in the middle of the software or systems development lifecycle is a common source of mistakes. DevOps best practices focus on using the same procedures and automation for deployments to every environment from development test to user acceptance testing (UAT) and production. Consistent approaches to builds are essential. Another best practice is the independent build.

6.11 The Independent Build

One of the most important best practices is the independent build. There is something about the process of trying to clearly communicate your build procedures to another person that almost always results in identifying the code that developers forgot to check into version control as well as build dependencies that were not well understood and documented. The ALM is the structure that can help identify and avoid these potential pitfalls. Organizationally, the build engineer should not report to the development manager so there is segregation of duties. Although, as a build engineer, I like to sit next to the developers so that we learn how the system works and we are plugged into the flow of the development effort. However, having the build engineer report to development frequently results in undue pressure to bypass established controls—a situation that can create a great deal of risk in the ALM. When regulatory compliance is not legally required, then another functional approach can be to use automation to create a "virtual" segregation of duties.

6.12 Creating a Build Robot

We see many teams creating fully automated application build, package, and deployment to test environments. Using a service account, this essentially comes down to creating an independent build-engineering robot. Although this is a best practice, it may not meet your organization's regulatory requirements for segregation of duties. More importantly, you need to ensure that the build procedures result in fully traceable procedures that can also be used to deploy code to all of the environments, including production. Another consideration is building quality into the process from the very beginning.

6.13 Building Quality In

Building quality into the process requires that you do the right thing from the very beginning of the software and systems lifecycle. The first reason for this is that these procedures can be very complicated, and starting from the beginning gives you a chance to learn and understand all of the essential technical details. The DevOps approach is to involve operations from the very beginning of the lifecycle. Getting DevOps involved in development has become known as "left-shift" and significantly improves the quality of the overall application build, package, and deployment effort. One aspect of this process to consider is implementing effective unit testing.

6.14 Implementing Unit Tests

Creating effective automated unit tests is a first step that is often overlooked in the software development process. It is very difficult, and often impossible, to create unit tests at the end of the lifecycle. The only effective approach is to begin creating unit tests from the very beginning of the effort. Many developers prefer to use test-driven development (TDD) so that the unit tests are actually created before the code itself. We view testing automation to be a must-have along with automating the code analysis.

6.15 Code Scans

The build process is the ideal time to automate code scans for a variety of purposes. We have worked with teams to automate code scanning to identify potential security and quality issues in the code. It has become common to also use code scanning to programmatically identify open-source components that need to be tracked for licensing compliance and potential downstream security vulnerabilities. Some of these code scans can be performed through static code analysis. However, sometimes it can be very useful to build a variant in the code suitable for instrumenting it.

6.16 Instrumenting the Code

Building the code for a specific purpose often involves instrumenting the code to contain libraries that enable dynamic analysis of the code during actual execution. This is used most often for performance, but also has applications in security and even quality. Excellent build engineering makes this approach viable and depends largely upon the quality of the build tools themselves.

6.17 Build Tools

The selection of build tools can be challenging. We are often deeply involved with evaluating and selecting build tools to automate the application build, package, and deployment. It is essential to always evaluate two or three leading tools based upon well-defined evaluation criteria. We are often involved in the proof-of-concept (POC) and final bake-off between the best two or three tools evaluated. It is wise to spend a fair amount of time on properly selecting build tools, as they will have a huge impact on your team's productivity and the quality of the system that you create.

6.18 Conclusion

Build engineering in the ALM depends upon both good processes and good tools. DevOps has driven many recent changes in the space, including the acknowledgment that DevOps should be involved from the very beginning of the software and systems lifecycle and also that having consistent procedures across the entire ALM is an absolute necessity.

Chapter 7

Automating the Agile ALM

Application lifecycle management (ALM) touches every aspect of the software and systems lifecycle. This includes requirements gathering, design, development, testing, application deployment, and operations support. Automation plays a major role in the agile ALM, which sets it apart in many ways from other software development methodologies. Since you simply cannot implement all of these practices at once, you will need to assess the scope and priorities for your team. That said, it is essential to appreciate the big picture at all times so that the functions you implement are in alignment with the overall goals and structure of your ALM.

7.1 Goals of Automating the Agile ALM

The goal in automating the application lifecycle management (ALM) is to ensure that processes are repeatable, error free, and executed as quickly as possible. There is also a goal of being able to run as many of these processes without human intervention as possible and appropriate. For some companies, the automation acts almost as a robot build engineer who never needs a vacation. Automation also provides a suitable framework for writing automated tests to support the ALM, improving quality and productivity and avoiding costly mistakes and rework. In Chapter 20, we discuss continuous testing which is a must-have for DevOps. In fact, many experienced professionals would say that you are likely to fail, if you do not automate.

7.2 Why Automating the ALM Is Important

Automating the ALM is important because tools, such as workflow automation, significantly ensure that your processes are repeatable and traceable. Workflow automation also helps facilitate teamwork because these tools enable each stake-holder to understand what they need to do on a daily basis, as well as the status of requests that depend upon others. When organizations use well-designed workflow automation, team members can easily ascertain the status of a request and employ formal or even informal channels to get tasks completed. ALM automation helps avoid costly mistakes and rework while providing a ready source of information on the status of requests. Even more importantly, these tools have the effect of forming a knowledge base so that everyone understands the processes, including requirements, steps for completion, and criteria for verification and validation.

7.3 Where Do I Start?

We always start by observing and learning as much as possible about the existing processes, making no assumptions about what may or may not be broken. It has always been our experience that most teams are doing some things very well, even though it may not be the approach that I would personally recommend. It rarely makes sense to fix things that are not perceived by the team as being a priority. Initially, we usually write scripts to automate processes with a strong focus on eliminating human error. My first scripts often require an operator read the screen and then hit Enter a few times. We call this approach *attended automation*, because the first generation of scripts often requires some operator intervention, or at least hand-holding. Although the long-term goal is to have scripts that can run without human intervention, beginning with this approach often goes a long way toward avoiding human error, improving productivity, and speeding up the overall deployment process. This is a great example of where 20 percent of the effort often gives you 80 percent of the value. Getting started in this manner is both pragmatic and, in my experience, very effective. We will discuss the importance of both process and tools.

7.4 Tools

Obviously, tools are essential to automation. But our discussion of tools still begins with the question of whether they matter. Then we consider whether process is more important than tools, tools in the scope of ALM, and commercial versus open-source tools

7.4.1 Do Tools Matter?

Application lifecycle management places a much stronger emphasis on tools than most other software and systems methodologies. Integrations between tools are especially important because the ALM has a very broad scope, from early requirements gathering to project management through the entire software and systems lifecycle. ALM tools should facilitate the completion of all required tasks, and this is exactly where workflow automation can be extremely valuable. Workflow automation provides much-needed structure to support the entire development effort. Determining the workflow that you need is not always easy, and sometimes it is necessary to model your process to determine the optimal flow of steps, including tasks, approvals, decision points, and milestones. A lot is required to successfully implement workflow automation and any other tool supporting the ALM as well. But what about those process improvement professionals who suggest that the process is more important than the tool? Are they wrong, or should we really just focus on the process?

7.4.2 Process over Tools

Process improvement experts have long maintained that getting the process right is a lot more important than picking the right tools. Many of my colleagues lecture me that I should be more concerned with the process than the tools. I used to believe that too. But after many years of implementing business and technical processes, I have come to the opinion that tools are just as important as getting the process right. In fact, both are must-haves if you are to be successful. Many tools come with well-thought-out process models that vendors have developed with input from their extensive customer base. If you select the right tools, then you also get world-class processes straight out of the box. The process of picking the right tools also helps you think through the processes that you want and need.

7.4.3 Understanding Tools in the Scope of ALM

Tools and automation are essential throughout the entire ALM, starting with workflow automation to ensure that processes are repeatable, traceable, and fully enforced. But that is not all. The agile ALM starts with requirements, typically described in user stories and often supplemented by test cases. We typically focus most of our energy on automating the application build, package, and deployment. But the true scope really is the full lifecycle, as we will explain throughout the rest of this chapter

7.4.4 Staying Tools Agnostic

We find that many teams can succeed with almost any toolset that aligns with their technical requirements and their culture. With a few exceptions, we are largely tools agnostic (caveat: bad tools do exist, including some that lose code and should never be used). You should always start by thoroughly understanding your requirements and conduct at least a proof-of-concept (POC) whereby you ensure that the tools can meet at least your basic requirements. Teams often fail with tools because they buy the first shiny toy that they see. Just as bad is the rigid view that open-source (essentially free or very low cost) tools are the only acceptable solution. Some commercial tools are worth paying for, and many vendors do indeed provide significant value, which justifies the purchase cost.

We strongly advocate a structured evaluation and bake-off between at least two or three leading tools vendors in whatever area is being considered. In large companies, we strive to ensure that there is transparency and an openness to input from different members of the team. Although this needs to be bounded because some team members can be very opinionated and rigid when it comes to tools and the technical direction for automation in general.

It has been our experience that large organizations are not always successful at getting down to only one toolset. There may be good technical reasons for why they need to support more than one set of tools. Even more importantly, the culture of different teams may demand different toolsets. If you force them to switch, these folks will typically spend an enormous amount of effort proving that you were wrong in taking away their preferred toolset and often blame every problem, delay, and challenge on the "bad" toolset that you forced on them.

7.4.5 Commercial versus Open Source

We have worked with technology professionals who had very strong opinions about whether or not open source is a better approach than using commercial tools. We have seen teams be very successful with open-source toolsets, and that is often because their culture really embraced open source. Some of these folks viewed open source as being essential for their future career aspirations. We have also seen folks who felt that as long as they got money to buy a particular tool then all of their problems would be solved.

The choice of whether to use commercial tools or open source often comes down to a balancing act between the budget that you have and the features that you need in order to get your work done. When commercial tools are deemed valuable, many organizations can come up with the budget to purchase them, although all too often they may lack the additional resources to properly implement and support the tools that they have chosen. We believe that it is essential to understand your requirements and the total cost of ownership before choosing a commercial tool or an open-source solution.

We also see some teams that start with open source but then quickly outgrow the limited features that they provide. This is not necessarily bad, as the experience of implementing low-cost or free tools can be very helpful in determining the necessary features that would otherwise not have been readily apparent. We see some teams where they use low-cost tools for developers but then purchase more robust solutions for their build and release engineers, a suitable solution for some companies. Regardless of the final decision, in all cases you need to start by understanding exactly what you are doing today.

7.5 What Do I Do Today?

The first step in any process improvement effort should be to assess what the organization is currently doing. Because it is almost certain that agile ALM will require you to make some changes to the way that you are doing things, it is essential to start by assessing your existing practices. We do many assessments for large and small organizations in order to help identify opportunities for improving their processes. The first step is to identify the stakeholders who will be interviewed in what we like to call the "dance card." We always warn that the dance card grows once word gets around about what we are doing. Typically, our meetings are with individuals or small groups, and we ask participants to explain what is going well and what could be improved. We then compare the responses to the guidance found in industry standards (e.g., IEEE, ISO, EIA/ANSI) and frameworks (e.g., ITIL v3, Cobit). Participants generally are very willing to volunteer what should be improved. Often they have been trying to express their ideas for years and, in larger organizations, we often find that individuals do not even realize that there are others with the same view in other parts of the organization. The assessment becomes the catalyst for change by identifying the important initiatives that need to be at the forefront of the process improvement initiative.

You can conduct the assessment yourself, although having an outside consultant has some strong advantages. First an outside consultant is free from organizational history that may give the appearance of bias or even political motivation. Participants are often more open to expressing their opinions to an outsider, especially if he (or she) is also regarded as an expert. Assessing to industry standards and frameworks is also essential because just relying upon one person's experience is obviously less than optimal. The results of the assessment help identify where to begin the process improvement effort. Usually this starts with automating the workflow.

7.6 Automating the Workflow

The workflow identifies the tasks to be completed, identifies who is responsible for completing them, and establishes decision points within the ALM. This approach eliminates many sources of common errors and helps reduce the inherent risk in any project. For example, workflows help ensure that you are not dependent upon one specific person, often a subject matter expert (SME), which is commonly known as *keyman risk*. When we automate workflows, we usually start by observing the overall activity within the group and then we interview each of the stakeholders. What is interesting is that sometimes experienced professionals cannot actually tell you what they have been doing in many complicated workflows because there are often many decision points and exceptions to the rules, which require judgment and considerable business knowledge. In doing this type of work, we are often helping these folks get some structure around what they have been doing via their own extensive tribal knowledge for years. Sometimes we discover mistakes that have been made, and obviously getting the process actually documented helps to eliminate keyman risk, while often allowing these colleagues to actually take a vacation without being interrupted for the first time in years.

Don't expect to be able to identify all of the steps in a workflow the first time that you try. This effort often takes a few iterations and generally requires a strong DevOps approach, including input from multiple stakeholders. In addition, processes often change—perhaps even on a seasonal basis. You may find that teams have special rules to handle emergency fixes when it is at the end of a financial quarter when deadlines must be met, although accuracy is an absolute must-have. The best way to handle this effort is to make use of process modeling software.

7.7 Process Modeling Automation

Modeling a process is almost impossible without the right tools. This is where visual modeling is essential, and the best tools allow you to create a model and then interactively update it as needed. Some tools create the visual model based upon a configuration file, whereas others allow you to visually model your workflow through a more intuitive visual interface.

Using automation to model your process helps communicate the steps to your workflow in a cognitively intuitive way. The agile ALM has many tools and approaches that you can use to manage the software and systems lifecycle.

7.8 Managing the Lifecycle with ALM

Managing the software and systems lifecycle can be challenging. The agile ALM provides the tools and processes necessary to manage the day-to-day activities within the lifecycle. Managing the lifecycle with the ALM begins with communicating the overall workflow, including a clear description of each of the required tasks, roles, and decision points to all stakeholders. There is no assumption that processes will not change within the ALM and, in reality, they often do change. But this approach puts structure around the workflow and helps us manage the required changes, including exceptions. Although we often focus mostly on application build, package, and deployment, the scope of the ALM is actually quite broad.

7.9 Broad Scope of ALM Tools

ALM tools should be used to manage the entire agile ALM, starting with requirements management, architecture design, and test case management, along with application build, package, and deployment. ALM tools have a broad scope and are essential for managing the software and systems development process. Each aspect of the ALM may involve different toolsets, or perhaps a complete ALM suite of tools from one specific vendor. Whether you are using a suite of tools from one vendor or different tools from an array of sources, it is essential to integrate toolsets into comprehensive toolchains. This is where creating seamless tools integration is a must-have.

7.10 Achieving Seamless Integration

Integrating tools is an essential, although often misunderstood, requirement. When we learn that a particular tool integrates with another tool, we generally ask what the integration actually does. Additionally, we need to understand what fields are linked and how that linkage is accomplished at a technical level. For example, many requirements tracking tools integrate with test case management solutions. The purpose of such integration is to ensure that each requirement is tracked to a test case, verifying and validating that the requirement was met in the features of the software. In an agile ALM, we should admit when the requirements are not fully understood, and with each iteration of the software, we partner with our business and product experts to understand exactly what the software should do. Tracking requirements to test case integration can help provide valuable information to developers who need to fully understand how a particular feature should function. Seamless integration in this context would involve being able to see the original requirement with the related test cases, which also describe expected behavior. We have seen many situations where the requirements description was completely correct, although less than clear and comprehensive. We often see that the test cases provide a valuable source of information describing the intended requirements, because well-written test cases describe user interactions and expected behavior in a clear and comprehensive way.

Defects that are found can also be linked to requirements and test cases, which can be very helpful to the analysts who are responsible for implementing changes to address defects found in the product, whether they be reported by your help desk or found within your own QA and testing process. Having seamless integration may also result in one consolidated defect-tracking system used throughout the ALM instead of the often-dysfunctional situation where there are multiple defect-tracking systems serving various systems—often with disparate descriptions, which can be confusing and less than helpful. Similarly, workflow automation tools can be integrated with other tools in the ALM to track pending tasks and completed work. This is especially important in the automation of the application build, package, and deployment, which we discuss in many chapters of this book. Integration is a particularly important aspect of requirements management.

7.11 Managing Requirements of the ALM

Requirements management has been largely maligned over the last few years by those who feel that these efforts simply result in large binders that sit on the shelf and are quickly outdated. The truth is that requirements management is best managed in modern systems that facilitate the thought process in working through exactly how the system should be designed and implemented. Documenting requirements is actually very important. Although the agile manifesto does indeed note that we value "working software over comprehensive documentation," a mature agile process, discussed in Chapter 4, should document requirements sufficiently. It has long been our recommendation that well-designed test cases be written to supplement existing requirements documentation. It is absolutely true that requirements will evolve over time, and the agile manifesto also notes that we value "responding to change over following a plan." As each iteration of the software is created and our product owners and business subject matter experts (SMEs) begin to more deeply understand how the system should ideally behave, our requirements understanding is likely to evolve. Outside industry forces, including competition from other firms, may also affect requirements. But modern requirements automation tools can help us understand and communicate these requirements. We also view test cases as being an ideal way to keep track of these details in a pragmatic and useful way. We also need to consider the best approach to documenting and clarifying the development work that needs to be completed.

7.12 Creating Epics and Stories

It has become popular to document requirements in terms of epics and stories. Writing good epics and stories can be challenging. We recommend that you have your user stories reviewed by SMEs for completeness and clarity. Well-written stories can help analysts understand the functionality that they need to support while providing a comprehensive design.

7.13 Systems and Application Design

Systems and application design depends upon a thorough understanding of the system requirements from not only a user functionality perspective, but also, more importantly, from a technical perspective. As architects, we need to be able to create comprehensive design documents that communicate both the system and the applications design and implementation details. Many great tools help to document and communicate comprehensive designs that can also be linked to requirements and test cases, which help ensure that the designs are fit for purpose and fit for use. This means that the system should behave as intended and as needed for practical use. Good design is a fundamental aspect of creating quality systems and applications. Another aspect of this effort is to create code of sufficient quality. Automation to inspect and analyze code quality often depends upon code quality instrumentation.

7.14 Code Quality Instrumentation

Code quality is essential, and many tools can be helpful in instrumenting and analyzing applications to identify opportunities to improve code quality. Instrumenting code means that you provide a runtime environment and possibly a separately compiled version of the code in order for the code quality tools to successfully provide useful information. Building variants of the code was discussed in Chapter 6. These capabilities are essential for automating the agile ALM. Testing the code is essential, but you should also remember that the software and systems lifecycle needs to be tested as well.

7.15 Testing the Lifecycle

Testing should not only focus on the application, but also the software and systems lifecycle itself. We have seen many situations where the lifecycle itself did not work as expected or needed. For example, all too often, each step is not completed or verified as required, or the process itself is not repeatable. One very common reason for these problems is when the workflow automation tools are hard to use and people become accustomed to working around them, which, instead of streamlining the process, can actually impede the success of the workflow. As users, we have seen many times when workflow automation tools require that the user select from a specific set of choices. This works fine until none of the choices make any sense or are just so hard to understand that it is too easy to make a mistake. When you implement a workflow automation tool, make sure that you test the automation itself, including the use cases and especially the user interface.

Similarly, we come across build engineering tools that are not working correctly, including continuous integration (CI) servers. This may be because the team responsible for supporting the CI server does not know enough about the application that is being built. When this happens, they run the tool, but the results may not be very useful. We have seen CI servers rendered useless because the team handling the support of the tool did not really understand its usage. Testing the CI server itself can help ensure that your continuous integration process and tools are aligned and can help ensure the success of the agile ALM. Closely related is the need for test case management to support the ALM.

7.16 Test Case Management

Managing test cases is an important aspect of automating the agile ALM. It is much easier to write and manage excellent test cases when you have the right automation in place. We have participated in helping teams develop effective test cases and test scripts for many years. This effort is often an iterative process itself, and feedback loops such as incidents and help desk calls should be embraced as sources of new tests cases—especially to ensure that problems do not recur.

Establishing the right approach to testing requires the right cognitive mindset. We have seen teams struggle with creating good test cases. There are many in the agile world who believe that QA and testing teams should be integrated into the scrum. We see value in having a separate QA and testing function that does not report to the development team, so as to avoid any undue influence or pressure to approve a release that, in fact, is not ready for production. However, colocating and embedding testers with developers is a great idea that facilitates knowledge sharing and communication.

There are two competing cognitive constructs here, and both are important. The first is that testers need some independence and should not be unduly pressured to approve a release that is not ready for promotion. The second is that testers need good technical knowledge, which they can acquire by interacting with the folks who wrote the code.

Keeping Them in the Dark

We have seen development managers purposely withhold information from QA and testing resources. Sadly, these folks are usually trying to make their deadline because their compensation is tied to delivering on time. But these folks will also blame the test teams for not catching mistakes that are found in production. Closely related is the inability of many developers to write release notes that are clear and facilitate the QA and testing process.

We all know that testing is everyone's job, but helping the team test effectively can be very challenging indeed. We find that reviewing test cases and test scripts as code can be very effective in improving the quality of testing. We run these sessions as we would any code or inspection and use a DevOps approach to having the cross-functional team review these artifacts. Developers in these sessions will volunteer technical information, and the QA and testing team will help developers think of edge cases that they would otherwise have not considered. Developers should be part of the QA and testing process. We also benefit from taking a test-centric approach during the construction phase, a practice that has become known as test-driven development (TDD).

7.17 Test-Driven Development

TDD has emerged as an effective best practice wherein developers write automated unit tests before they actually write the code itself. Because the code is created first, the initial test harness "fails"—which is expected. Then the actual code is written and the test cases should pass if the logic was clear. In practice, we like test-driven development, but have seen many teams struggle with getting beyond the most limited coverage using this approach. Once again, even though good tools can help, test-driven development seems to have some inherent limitations. Although TDD could be improved in the future, we also see environment management and control as an area that has much growth potential.

7.18 Environment Management

Runtime environments have many dependencies, which are often not well identified and understood. We believe that this is a key area that needs much more focus in the agile ALM. Automation is fundamental to understanding, monitoring, and controlling runtime dependencies. Most teams fail to get beyond monitoring memory, disk space, and CPU usage. But complex systems today have many essential runtime resources that need to be understood and managed. This is where the DevOps approach is once again extremely important. Your operations team likely knows how to establish effective IT controls, but it is the developers, who wrote the code, who really understand the application dependencies and what really needs to be monitored. When application problems occur, developers quickly begin checking technical dependencies in an effort to identify the source of these problems. You should try to capture these steps because they are often exactly the environment dependencies that need to be monitored. We like to encourage good environment management from the beginning of the software and systems lifecycle. We see developers expertly evaluating environment dependencies in the development test environments, but rarely sharing that knowledge with the operations team once the application is promoted to user acceptance testing (UAT) and production. We discuss change management in Chapter 10. DevOps encourages "left-shift," which means that operations should get involved early with managing the deployments to development test environments—long the sole domain of developers. When operations gets involved in the beginning, they begin to get the information that they need to automate the environment management process. Closely related is the need to baseline runtime dependencies, or as folks call it, creating *gold copies*.

7.18.1 Gold Copies

The term "gold copy" is reminiscent of a time when physical recordings were created by record companies. In IT, gold copy refers to the final release candidate that has passed tests and is approved for release to production. We use this term to refer to the code itself that has gone through an official build process and also the baseline runtime environment, which is essential to supporting the application. Gold copies should be maintained in a *definitive media library (DML)* and verified through an automated discovery process. We discuss the use of cryptography and embedding immutable version IDs into configuration items in Chapter 6, which is a requirement for any valid automated discovery process. The information that is discovered by the automation should be maintained in the configuration management database.

7.19 Supporting the CMDB

The configuration management database (CMDB) is a great tool that many companies have spent millions to implement, albeit often with very little return on investment. We see organizations purchase expensive database-driven CMDBs but then try to keep up the data through manual processes. If you don't automate the discovery process, then your CMDB will be useless. Truthfully, this is not that hard to do. You simply need to have a good build, package, and deployment process that embeds version IDs into configuration items and manifests in the release packages. The rest of the effort is simply to "discover" the version ID in the CIs that are running in production, UAT, or another environment in a process that is known as a *physical configuration audit*. We discuss these procedures in Chapter 6, "Build Engineering in the ALM." The CMDB is a valuable tool when it is designed well and kept up-to-date through automation. This is an excellent example of where development and operations must work together to ensure success. In fact, effective DevOps tools and processes are essential for driving the entire DevOps transformation.

7.20 Driving DevOps

DevOps depends heavily upon good tooling. Although many folks in the process improvement arena suggest that *process* is more important than tools, for those promoting DevOps, tools are first-class citizens. Automating the agile ALM is an essential aspect of driving successful DevOps. Without automation, DevOps would seriously fail to achieve its goals of improving communication between development and operations. Automation includes managing the workflow and, more importantly, the exchange of information between development and operations. Knowledge management and knowledge sharing are fundamental to driving DevOps adoption. We see far too many cases where development operates in a vacuum, excluding operations from decisions and the overall development process. This approach leads to dysfunctional behaviors that often adversely impact the company in many important ways. Automating the agile ALM directly improves the support of production operations and, of course, the operations team itself.

7.21 Supporting Operations

Workflow automation tools are fundamental to any successful operation function. Capturing and sharing knowledge is equally important and often overlooked during the development process. This dysfunctional behavior is bad for many reasons. First, the operations team is stuck with trying to play catch-up when they are brought into the learning process late in the game. This reinforces development's contention that operations lack expertise and creates a self-fulfilling process. In our work, we advocate hiring strong senior engineers into operations to take responsibility for running production applications and, most importantly, including them in the beginning of the software and systems development lifecycle.

Some folks in the DevOps community advocate that developers take responsibility for running their own code. We view this approach as a remarkably poor idea for several reasons. First, developers are often not of a mind-set to focus on creating repeatable processes and reliability. We see many senior software engineers who possess the necessary expertise, experience, and demeanor to handle production operations. More importantly, there is something about the transfer of knowledge that occurs when development does an effective hand-off to operations that results in improved quality. During this process, developers suddenly recall what they forgot to document or even code that was not checked into version control (sitting locally on their own private laptops). Having developers support their own code also often results in keyman risk where there is a lack of institutionalized knowledge. The IT Operations function serves an important and distinctive purpose; it should be staffed with strong technical resources and involved from the very beginning of the software and systems delivery process. We also need to support our frontline help desk engineers.

7.22 Help Desk

The help desk is usually on the front lines of ensuring that customers are kept happy and rely heavily upon automation of the agile ALM. Help desk staff are often not given enough training and support to ensure they can effectively address customer concerns. Keeping the help desk advised on system outages and issues and giving them a robust workflow tool to capture customer concerns and quickly feed information back to operations and other stakeholders is essential. We have worked with help desk managers to ensure that they get a constant flow of updated information and also that reported incidents are reviewed by QA, testing, and development managers as needed. Closely related is the service desk.

7.23 Service Desk

Many companies call their help desk a *service desk,* but they are really two distinct entities. The service desk manages, well, services. ITIL v3 defines the service desk as a primary IT service within the discipline of IT service management (ITSM), intended to provide a single point of contact (SPOC) to meet the communication needs of both users and IT employees. Typically, companies use the service desk function to handle the flow of frequent routine requests such as password resets or service requests upon which everyone depends. It is common to have specialized service desks and escalation points to help address and resolve issues. The service desk relies heavily upon excellent workflow automation and knowledge management. Closely related is the essential function of incident management.

7.24 Incident Management

Any large-scale production environment is going to be challenged with incidents, some may be routine; others extremely serious. Incident management done well can "catch the football before it hits the ground" or, if not handled well, can actually be responsible for making situations far worse than they need to be. Incident management also relies heavily upon workflow automation and knowledge management tools. When incident management recognizes a pattern, they can help save the day by getting the appropriate resources involved and addressing the issue to minimize, and often prevent, customer impact. Often incidents require root-cause analysis, and this is the point at which problem escalation becomes essential.

7.25 Problem Escalation

Routine incidents can often be handled by well-established procedures, but sometimes the root cause of the issue, particularly for recurring problems, must be analyzed, and often this means that a wider escalation of resources is necessary. Problem escalation is most often associated with system outages and can be extremely costly if not handled efficiently. The agile ALM relies heavily upon automation to manage problem escalation for proper communication, workflow automation, and knowledge management. Incident and problem management systems are essential for ensuring an effective response when issues occur. Fortunately, serious outages don't usually happen every day, but most large-scale projects do require daily coordination, and this is where project management is essential.

7.26 Project Management

The agile manifesto aptly notes that we value responding to change over following a plan, which is absolutely true. But large-scale projects will not be successful without good planning. The real difference is that agility admits when we do not fully understand all of our dependencies and therefore have to postpone some decisions until more information is available. Our Lean colleagues have coined the phrase "last responsible moment" to indicate that sometimes decisions should be postponed until enough information is available to make the best decision. We concur fully that responding effectively to change is far more important than following a plan, but the fact is that no one is going to give you a large budget without being assured that you have a comprehensive plan and can communicate both dependencies and goals in a clear and reliable way. Facilitating project management is the key concern of the organization that has become known as the project management office (PMO).

7.27 Planning the PMO

The project management office requires workflow automation and project management tools to successfully automate the project planning process. The right automation can alleviate the harsh workload that is often associated with project management and, more importantly, smoothly facilitate handling changes to the process when necessary. We see this as an area where many teams are failing miserably in implementing agility in large enterprise organizations. The PMO should facilitate the work between various stakeholders, accelerating DevOps principles and practices. We find ourselves constantly partnering with project managers to ensure that the right stakeholders are involved and that communication is Lean and effective. There is no place where this is more important than in planning for implementation.

7.28 Planning for Implementation

Implementation of a new release, or new system altogether, is the finish line that we are all working to cross together successfully. Like the conducting of an orchestra, implementation planning requires the coordination of an amazing number of actions from skilled resources. Getting everyone in tune and working together along the same cadence is no easy task. Like many aspects of the agile ALM, none of this coordination would be possible without the right tools.

7.29 Evaluating and Selecting the Right Tools

Tools selection is a sore point with us because we have observed too many organizations suffer from impulse buying after examining one shiny new tool, often shepherded along by a little slick salesmanship. Vendors are indeed often expert and do share best practices that have, in turn, been influenced by their customer base and years of experience. That said, we strongly encourage our colleagues to establish evaluation criteria up-front and then review at least two or three tools in the same functional space. When looking at products and vendors, you will absolutely find yourself updating your evaluation criteria, which is fine. But making decisions to purchase big-ticket items should be based upon due diligence—including a proof-of-concept (POC) and preferably a structured product bake-off. Another issue that we often see is a siloed approach to tools selection. Many companies purchase tools for individual teams without conducting an enterprise-wide evaluation, which would likely result in more thorough decisions along with better enterprise-wide pricing. Regardless of the direction you choose, it is essential to document how you will use your tools and train and support your team.

7.30 Defining the Use Case

We see many pragmatic situations where the best tools cannot realistically be implemented and used. Sometimes, this is because of a lack of budget. Often, it is because more powerful tools require much more training and ongoing support, which management refuses to pay for. When stuck with less-than-perfect tools, or even when implementing the best tools, it is essential to define how the tools will be used. This helps establish best practices and also the right processes, which may themselves evolve over time. We also find that training is the most important factor in successfully implementing tools.

7.31 Training Is Essential

We recognize the value of excellent vendor training, especially for those who will be responsible for supporting and maintaining the tools. But we also view training as a key corporate capability. You should develop your own training programs, tailored to your preferred way of using each specific tool. When training is done in-house by qualified resources, then the company benefits from not only spreading knowledge and best practices, but a preferred usage model as well. Successful tools implementation depends upon effective training. It also depends upon a strong relationship with vendors.

7.32 Vendor Relationships

Vendor relationships are essential. The right vendors understand that customer success and their own success are tightly coupled. We have had many long-term relationships with large (and small) vendors who value input from their customers and are committed to spreading industry best practices. This is a synergistic relationship that benefits both the customer and the vendor tool.

7.33 Keeping Tools Current

Tools must be kept updated to avoid common security issues and allow users to enjoy the latest features and fixes to key issues, including product defects. But large-scale tools used in the agile ALM automation may require a full systems lifecycle to manage the testing and upgrade process itself. We have seen situations where vendor-supplied updates cause major outages, so customers should always manage the process of keeping tools current with care.

7.34 Conclusion

There are many things to consider when automating the agile ALM. DevOps, along with most aspects of the software and systems delivery process, cannot succeed without excellent automation. Processes are very important in the agile ALM, but tools and automation are also first-class citizens that must be managed effectively. Get this right and you will have many competitive advantages and be a long way down the path of successfully implementing your agile ALM!

Chapter 8

Continuous Integration

Continuous integration (CI) is an essential practice that involves putting together code that has been created by different developers and ascertaining if the code components can compile and run together successfully. CI requires a robust automated testing framework, which we will discuss further in Chapter 20, and also provides the basis for ensuring code quality through both static and instrumented code scanning. Continuous integration often involves merging together code that has been written by different developers and is essential for code quality. The fundamental value of this practice is that integrating a small amount of code as early as possible can avoid much bigger issues later. It would be difficult to imagine an effective ALM that does not embrace integrating code frequently, although I will discuss a couple of situations where it is difficult or even impossible to achieve. When code cannot be integrated early and often, there is increased risk that must be identified and addressed. It is also important to understand that continuous integration relies upon many other practices, including continuous testing, effective build engineering, static and instrumented code analysis, and continuous deployment, discussed in Chapter 9.

8.1 Goals of Continuous Integration

The goal of continuous integration is to support parallel development while avoiding costly mistakes that often result in code defects. CI also provides better quality by identifying any potential collisions early in the process with merging code from two or more developers. Integrating code early and often makes it much easier to identify any potential problems during the merge process and, more importantly, remediate the code to include desired changes without defects.

Monolithic Merges

Bob supported a very large ClearCase system at a major New York City trading exchange. One of the main systems depended upon a system written in C++ and run on HP servers. A complicated user interface was written as a monolithic single program. Two or more developers would be working in this single program that was thousands of lines long. The developers would go off and write their code and then get together a week later and try to merge their changes together. The process was extremely painful, time consuming, and accounted for many defects in the code. Soon the developers learned that working together each day to frequently integrate their changes was much more efficient and effective. This was long before anyone coined the phrase continuous integration or XP-paired programming.

8.2 Why Is Continuous Integration Important?

Continuous integration is important because it reduces risk by identifying merge conflicts right away, while the changes are still fresh in everyone's mind. Without CI, developers would have a much more difficult time identifying potential code-merge problems and take much more time to fix them once identified.

Late-Binding Integration

You might ask why anyone would not want to integrate changes early and often. It turns out that sometimes there is indeed a need to develop features separately (often on separate branches). When the decision is made regarding which features to include in a release, the features are then merged together, which can be a very painful and error-prone process. Although not optimal, there are certainly situations when business or other technical constraints make late-binding integration necessary.

However, the general rule is, whenever possible, to integrate early and often. When this is not feasible, then late-binding integration should be identified as a risk that must be addressed. We will discuss strategies for dealing with this situation. It is tempting to call this approach "continuous everything," alluding to the fact that so many practices depend upon a well-designed continuous integration platform.

8.3 Where Do I Start?

Getting started with continuous integration requires that you have your build procedures completely automated, a task generally accomplished using a build scripting tool such as Apache Ant, Maven, or Make. You also need a continuous integration server such as Jenkins to start the build and record the results. Unit tests and code scanning should be part of the build process. Equally important is an automated procedure to deploy the code to a test environment and then start automated testing once the code has been deployed. We discuss build engineering in Chapter 6.

8.4 Principles in Continuous Integration

The basic principle behind continuous integration is that it is much easier to find and fix problems when code is integrated early and often. But much more can be achieved in continuous integration. Continuous integration provides a great opportunity to improve code quality while we have access to the code and we can so easily build not only the production baseline of the code, but also any variants to facilitate testing and quality assurance. This is analogous to a great automobile mechanic who, regardless of any specific complaints or repairs, also routinely checks one's oil, tires, and a few other important dependencies every time the car is brought in. CI servers could be viewed as the software equivalent of putting your car up on the lift in the mechanic's shop. So our principles should include taking a very broad view of code quality throughout the continuous integration process.

8.5 Challenges of Integration

The basic challenge of integration is that code developed on separate variants—often branches—tends to diverge. This means that two developers might be writing code that will have to run together using code baselines that are different from each other. The solution is to integrate code early and often, as in continuous integration, and also ensure that developers are coding from the same baseline. However, there are also times when it is necessary to keep code separate because the decision to include features has not yet been made. This is sometimes called "cherry picking," although a more descriptive term is *late-binding integration*. Integrating code late in the process is challenging because it is much more difficult to find and fix problems in code that was written days or even weeks ago.

Cherry Picking and Trading

Bob worked with quants at a hedge fund where each week formulas were developed that might or might not be useful in the next week's trading activity. Once a week—usually on a Thursday night—the decision was made regarding which formulas would be included in the next build. This worked well, except when it didn't. Unfortunately, there were many times when formulas (or the code to implement them) conflicted, and because the code was only merged at the last minute, it was always a painful fire drill to get the code compiled and running.

The more basic challenge comes when trying to get developers together to look at code conflicts discovered during the merge process. Obviously, this gets challenging when one developer commits his code on a Monday and then takes the rest of the week off to go camping, leaving his colleagues to try and deal with the merge difficulties. There are strategies for dealing with this situation, but the first approach is simply to commit changes to the repository on a frequent basis.

8.6 Commit Frequently

Committing code to the version control system frequently is an essential best practice. In continuous integration, it is common to trigger a build with each commit. However, when large teams are working together, this approach can be less than completely effective because the sheer volume of triggered builds can result in too much activity that is a burden for developers to monitor throughout the day. For example, with a team of ten developers committing code several times a day, you can end up with 40 or 50 builds to monitor. Many teams find that a nightly build is sufficient, especially in the beginning of the process.

However, when you get closer to release time, it is often common to have the CI server build on each commit so that problems are identified early enough without affecting the release date. This is a practical example of where you may need to have a little more muscle in your process as you get closer to the release date.

8.7 Rebase and Build Before Commit

Rebasing means that you update your local workspace with changes before you commit your latest changes back to the repository. In some version control systems, this means that you should *pull* the latest changes made by other developers before you *commit* your latest changes to the repository. This is important because while you were working in your own private sandbox, other people may have committed their changes to the version control system. If you commit your own changes without rebasing first, you may introduce changes that do not compile against the baseline, thereby affecting all of the other developers. To avoid this risk, you should proactively pull the latest changes to your sandbox, verify that your code builds, and then commit your changes, which I often refer to as **publishing** your changes back to the team. This procedure is known as rebasing and is closely related to another practice known as a preflight build, where you use the production build farm to test your build and ensure that it will not fail during the official build—this is often performed on a nightly basis. If you don't rebase and problems result, you will likely get blamed for breaking the build for everyone else. There are other merge challenges as well.

8.8 Merge Nightmares

We have seen several commonly used version control systems that did not handle merges well. We have also seen code that was so complicated it was very challenging to address the problem with merge conflicts. The more code involved, the longer the time required to resolve any merge conflicts found. Sometimes the changes made are complicated, and perhaps they cannot actually exist together in the same codebase. We have seen situations where developers reviewed their changes together only to realize that they had each adversely impacted the other's work. In these challenging situations, sometimes all they can do is drop the changes and start over again, this time with a deeper understanding of how their code is structured and interdependent. Complexity can be a factor, but size is often the more common challenge. In general, integrating smaller units is often much easier to accomplish than trying to manage a monolithic set of code changes, which may or may not be able to work together. Simplicity in this case comes directly from smaller units of integration.

8.9 Smaller Units of Integration

There is no doubt that dealing with a merge conflict of only five lines is much easier than a merge conflict with a hundred lines. Integrating smaller units is much simpler and often shows the value of the continuous integration process. The earlier that developers get feedback that they are touching the same code, the sooner they can collaborate and address any potential design and coding issues. The frequency of the integrations is essential for success.

8.10 Frequent Integration Is Better

Performing continuous integration more frequently is better for several reasons. The first, as we have discussed, is that dealing with a smaller set of code changes significantly reduces complexity. But there is much more to this than just the number of lines of code (LOC). By making continuous integration a daily activity, you introduce a cadence that can help you with testing, code scanning, and deployment. DevOps puts a strong value on feedback loops, and CI gives immediate feedback when your developers use this methodology on a daily basis. Your team also gets used to this practice and actually becomes quite good at using CI for daily benefit. For one thing, it is simply easier to find and deal with any issues found.

8.10.1 Easier to Find Issues

When your CI server is used daily, you get immediate feedback on whether the build succeeded or failed. But this is only the beginning. If you are practicing CI correctly, then you will also run code scans and unit tests, deploy the code to a test environment, and then run automated tests in a comprehensive practice that is becoming known as *continuous testing*, discussed further in Chapter 20. Finding issues is essential, but even more important is that it is much easier to fix problems once they are found.

8.10.2 Easier to Fix Problems

When you find a problem immediately, it is almost always easier to fix. When teams do not fully utilize continuous integration, they often do not find problems until later in the process, and consequently it can be much more difficult to understand and resolve these issues. We have seen many teams implement continuous integration but fail to realize its full benefits, usually because they fail to react quickly to broken builds.

8.10.3 Fix Broken Builds

When the CI server reports a broken build, it is essential that the problem be addressed in a timely manner, even if this requires that the team stops what they are doing and examines the problem. Ignoring broken builds is a symptom of much bigger problems and needs to be addressed as soon as possible. We have seen the same issues with ignoring failed unit tests, errors in the code scans, and other types of automated tests. The continuous integration process will only succeed if these issues are quickly recognized and addressed.

8.11 Code Reviews

Often overlooked, code review is a key area that is implemented within continuous integration. Many products perform code scans, reporting potential issues related to performance, failing to meet coding standards including security, and more. When the CI server reports that these problems exist, this is an excellent opportunity to take a DevOps approach and assemble a cross-functional team to review the code and recommend adjustments. We like to use the feedback from the CI process to foster better communication via working sessions that address any issues that are discovered. One common limitation that often undermines successful continuous integration is a lack of sufficient servers dedicated to the automated application build, package, and deployment.

8.12 Establishing a Build Farm

Continuous integration relies heavily upon having fast and reliable build servers. We usually refer to these machines as being a **build farm**. Ideally, you should have a build server and build agents to help manage the automation of the application build, package, and deployment. The build farm should be controlled and managed by a centralized build engineering team. Organizations that follow the itSMF ITIL v3 framework refer to this group as release and deployment management (RDM). The build farm is a key resource and should be protected from unauthorized changes. We do like to provide the ability for developers to run unofficial "production-like" builds, discussed in Section 8.13, on the build farm, but they should never be allowed to make changes to the build machines without working with the RDM team, whose members are responsible for en-suring that the build farm is working.

> ### The Build Platform that Could Not Be Rebuilt
>
> Bob worked with a team that had a build server that had been implemented by the developers who were building and deploying their own applications to production. They did not know how they had built this server. This was an international bank, so when the auditors caught up with them and cited the organization, management asked the release and deployment group to take responsibility for performing independent builds.

When resources are stretched thin, sometimes it is advisable to utilize virtual-ization and cloud-based resources.

8.12.1 Virtualization and Cloud Computing

We see many more companies embracing virtualization and cloud-based com-puting strategies. This has grown out of developers needing the speed and agil-ity of fast builds and test environments to facilitate continuous integration and especially continuous testing. Some companies are embracing on premises (ON-PREM) hypervisors, which are used to provide on-demand virtual ma-chines (VMs). With this strategy, developers can request a large virtual machine for a few hours to build, package, and deploy code in a half hour, when it used to take half a day. This approach can be combined with automated unit, functional, application programming interface (API), service virtualization, and performance testing, each of which will be discussed further in Chapter 20, "QA and Testing in the ALM." We will also discuss cloud-based computing strate-gies, including related DevOps strategies, in Chapter 17.

> ### Taming the Build
>
> We find that many companies are hampered by cludgy build, package, and deployment procedures that are not well understood and often sub-ject to failure. Much of our work involves helping companies review and iteratively improve their automated procedures to increase reliability of the application build, package, and deployment process. We commonly see companies dramatically improve their deployment automation, going

from two weeks to as little as two hours. Usually, this is accomplished by automating the simple steps (often the source of human error) and adding code to test each step of the process. By identifying errors quickly, one can save significant time and avoid errors. This is especially important in the continuous integration process so that we can make the best of automated procedures to build, package, and deploy to either on-premises private clouds or public vendor-provided clouds.

Do be aware that public vendor-provided, cloud-based resources come with significant risk. Not only have some cloud-based providers suffered from reliability issues, but information security continues to be a major concern. We do not see large companies such as banks and trading firms being very comfortable with using cloud-based public vendors for machines that contain customer information, but we do see many developers grabbing a couple of VMs for early development work, including support for continuous integration and related testing.

8.13 Preflight Builds

Preflight builds enable the developer to run the build privately on his or her machine before turning the code over to the build engineering team to verify that the code will compile on the build platform. Preflight builds save a lot of time by identifying anomalies without the volleyball game of tossing the build over the net to operations—only to have them toss the build back when it fails. While getting operations involved early in the build is a good example of the DevOps best practice of "left-shift," preflight builds are an example of what we have come to consider as "right-shift," where operations provides resources to developers early in the lifecycle so that the quality of the work can be verified, thus saving everyone time and effort.

8.14 Establishing the Build and Deploy Framework

Developers have a tough job. Understanding user requirements, designing scalable architectures, and implementing comprehensive solutions has always been challenging work. It is common, almost expected even, that the work to implement a comprehensive solution will take longer than expected. Add to this the fact that requirements are often a "moving target" that are not even fully understood when first specified. It is no wonder that technology professionals are often scrambling to get all of the technology pieces working together—not to mention actually writing the complex code itself that we have come to expect from enterprisewide solutions. Very often, creating a comprehensive build and deployment framework just doesn't rise to the top of the priority stack, and the result is builds are often not well understood and code that may build for one person may not even compile successfully for someone else—unfortunately, often the build engineer. There are many reasons for this problem.

Too often, developers do not fully understand their own build dependencies, especially when they are using powerful development frameworks that may abstract and effectively hide these complexities. Unfortunately, the result is that code may build successfully on one machine and actually yield different results on another machine. Consequently, it is essential to establish a consistent build framework, including all compile and runtime dependencies. In Java, this may mean that you need to establish the classpath and ensure that each developer uses the same environment settings. On the .Net framework, you may need to establish similar compile and runtime dependencies. We have seen many strong teams really struggle with this challenge. Some developers ask more senior colleagues to help them set up their development environments and then have no idea how to deal with these configuration details themselves. It is essential to establish a comprehensive build framework and then manage and communicate the changes that will surely be required over time.

We like to see the continuous integration framework be the reference architecture for all official application builds by ensuring that all builds are performed via automated scripts that establish and specify all dependencies from librarian search paths to compiler switches and other compile and runtime dependencies. This required focus on reliability should ensure that continuous integration provides traceability and transparency.

8.15 Establishing Traceability

Continuous integration helps provide much-needed traceability to the software development process by ensuring that there is a single source of information on important baseline builds, which sometimes become milestone releases. The agile ALM is often a long journey, spanning months or even years from project inception to delivery. The CI server, integrated with the version control system, becomes a fundamental resource for providing traceability throughout this journey. In practice, the CI server shows the work evolving from each of the teams, as well as the fundamental effort to actually integrate everyone's work in a timely manner. Sometimes the sheer volume of information can be daunting for even the most clever technology professionals.

The agile ALM inherently includes many complexities, and developers understandably struggle with compartmentalizing all of the information that they must process during the software and systems development effort. We find that information overload is a common source of mistakes, defects, and ultimately rework, among other forms of waste. Establishing timely and easy access to traceability can be a huge benefit by efficiently providing stakeholders with essential information that one might normally expect to be tracked manually. The continuous integration server actually becomes the central source of information about successful milestone releases or, as we will soon explain, *interesting* builds. Traceability, and for that matter, the entire continuous integration process, helps ensure effective communication, which is essential for productivity and quality.

Information Overload

We often see senior technology professionals struggling to manage all of the requisite information on a daily basis. Sometimes this becomes readily apparent when a senior technology expert will ask us to hand-hold him through simple tasks such as branching and merging in a simple version control system such as git or subversion. At such times, we see just how much our colleagues must compartmentalize information because of the inevitable information overload that has become so common in technology development efforts today. Establishing effective communication becomes a must-have in any enterprise agile ALM.

Managing information overload is essential for success in the agile ALM. Traceability helps a great deal in addressing this problem. It is critical to ensure that there is effective communication throughout the entire continuous integration process.

8.16 Better Communication

Communication is often overlooked in the technology development effort. The continuous integration process helps facilitate communication in many important ways. CI can be an effective information radiator helping to keep everyone advised of the status (including success and failure) of application build, package, and deployments. There is nowhere that this is more important than in the integration process itself.

CI provides a central point for the work of more than one developer to be integrated together, a juncture that often requires particularly good collaboration and communication between the developers who wrote the code. We see this as an area where many teams are really challenged. Sometimes it is because of the often-distributed working environments that many of us are operating within today. We may have one or more resources in the Northeast in the United States working closely with other resources based in Europe or India. Fortunately, we have good technologies that allow us to share a screen and collaborate on our work easily. But, we still see language and cultural barriers often resulting in situations where collaboration and communication can be challenging at best and sometimes almost impossible.

Offshore Support and Collaboration

Bob has spent a fair amount of time teaching in India and has worked with offshore resources actively for many years. One team in particular provided technical support for an enterprise version control system (VCS) used by more than 1,000 developers. This open-source VCS solution evidenced many challenges, and Bob was often up in the middle of the night working with the offshore team to get the system functioning again before U.S.-based developers came in the next day for work. Although the India-based support team was very capable, they were also extremely resistant to providing any information on how they went about troubleshooting and resolving problems. There was no doubt that they did a great job of figuring out the technical problems and getting them fixed. But it was almost impossible to get them to explain what they had done to diagnose and fix problems. This meant that there was no documentation on how to support the system, and in fact their expertise amounted to being tribal knowledge.

Communication and traceability are two very important areas for the agile ALM. But ultimately, the CI process must discover problems immediately and ensure that all relevant stakeholders are aware and able to respond. When something is broken, we need to immediately identify the right resource to address the problem in a timely manner. This process has become known as *fingering* and *blaming* the person who introduced the change that caused the problem, most often a "broken" build.

8.17 Finger and Blame

The terminology may seem a bit harsh, but identifying exactly who introduced a change that resulted in the CI server reporting a failed build, package, or deployment (including tests) is essential for the team to stay productive. It is especially true that the earlier we identify the person who broke the build—sometimes because he or she forgot to rebase or take advantage of the preflight build—the better. The "finger and blame" step of continuous integration refers to the important step of identifying who introduced the problem and who is presumably the right person to fix the issue. When teams choose to build and deploy on every commit of the code to the version control system, then fixing anomalies is much easier because the amount of code to review is relatively small compared with teams that have multiple developers committing code, but only performing integration builds on a weekly basis. Unfortunately, building on each commit can be impractical when there are ten or more developers committing code several times a day. Sometimes, the pragmatic choice is just to run a single integration build once each night.

8.18 Is the Nightly Build Enough?

We have known teams that relied upon an integration build executed each night long before it was popular to talk about continuous integration or even agile development. Sometimes, the nightly build is the best choice compared with trying to manage dozens of builds per day when teams decide to build, package, and deploy on each commit of changes to the version control system. There are several pragmatic reasons for this choice. First, setup for the build and resources required may be such that it is only practical to run one build per night. This works well when each member of the team ensures that their changes will integrate successfully by running a preflight build and, of course, rebasing their own sandbox before committing their changes to the enterprise version control system. The problem with the nightly build approach is that the more people who have committed changes to the system, the more difficult it can be to track down the cause of any integration problems. This may be acceptable early in the software and systems lifecycle, but may not be tolerable at all the week before your system is scheduled to be released.

We find that teams often need a little more structure in their processes when they are nearing the release date—especially if delays could cause the team to miss an important deliverable. We find that urgency is sometimes related to external dependencies such as the deadline for filing a tax return.

> ### Tax Nightmares
>
> Imagine working for a company that provides software that helps you prepare your taxes. Having a delay of even a few days close to that April 15 deadline could be disastrous for your firm. This is where it makes sense to check every single commit of the code to ensure that no defects are introduced into the system and to have immediate feedback if any defects are discovered.

Process in continuous integration is essential. Choosing and successfully implementing the right tools is also absolutely essential.

8.19 Selecting the Right Tools

It would be impossible to implement continuous integration without automation. Selecting the right tools can save a lot of time and make it much easier to successfully implement continuous integration. For years, many of us scripted these solutions, which truly became a labor of love. Sometimes, our home-grown build automation tools were more complicated than the applications we were building. The good news is that there are now many quality tools in this space, including popular open-source solutions and full-featured commercial solutions. The first step is picking the right continuous integration server.

8.19.1 Selecting the Right CI Server

Continuous integration servers come in all sizes and shapes. When selecting your CI server, you first need to establish your requirements for evaluation. We find that most teams focus on the features available, but may not adequately consider ease of use and time to administer and support. More basic continuous integration servers typically work from one configuration file, which can be difficult to administer. We ran into this situation when we first started working with CruiseControl. It was relatively easy to set up and get our first build to work, but then we discovered that supporting builds from multiple teams was difficult because we could introduce a change for one development team that might unintentionally affect another group. We found some commercial solutions that offered convenient menu-driven interfaces, making it easy to allow each team to configure and support their own builds with minimal risk of impacting other teams.

We have also seen organizations where each group simply set up and administered their own independent continuous integration server, which was limited to the development environment. As CI servers became easier to manage and support, this has turned out to be a perfectly viable approach. Some CI servers also integrate more easily with products in the software delivery lifecycle such as deployment frameworks. We have also found that reporting can be a differentiator between CI solutions. Successful continuous integration servers end up building many components. This has led to reuseability being another consideration in continuous integration. The demand for shared prebuilt components leads us to consider the requirements for shared repositories.

8.19.2 Selecting the Shared Repository

We first encountered shared repositories when supporting robust build frameworks, including Maven. As previously described, many companies find that open-source solutions give them all the functionality that they need, whereas others find that they really need the power, flexibility, and support of a commercial product solution. We believe that it is essential to once again consider your requirements and then conduct a bake-off between the leading vendors. All shared repos are not the same, and some have more advanced features, such as better reporting, which typically run counter to the time and effort to administer and ease of use. Choosing the right CI server and shared repository depends largely upon the requirements for your team and whether the solution will be for the specific needs of one group or be implemented as an enterprise solution.

8.20 Enterprise Continuous Integration

Enterprise continuous integration solutions need to consider what may be a variety of disparate requirements from each of the teams in the organization. We have worked with large financial services organizations where one team may be comprised of high-performance math wizards, known as quants, who come up with complex formulas for trading. Other teams may be handling mission-critical back-office batch processing that must be extremely reliable. Meeting the needs of different teams across a large enterprise can feel a lot like selling the same solution across different companies. Our focus is to share a minimum set of best practices to help teams implement continuous integration while allowing them the technical creativity to take things to the next level if so desired. The important thing is to have a consistent approach to training and support.

8.21 Training and Support

After 30 years in the trenches of IT, we are adamant that *training is the hill to die on*. We view training as being the most important investment that an organization can make to boost its success in implementing CI. Even if you must use a less-than-optimal continuous integration server, proper training can make the difference between success and failure. We provide a lot of training online, at conferences, and in corporate training rooms. Training team members to use each specific tool in an effective way is very important. In a corporate environment, we find that there is an even more essential goal of teaching one specific, consistent way to use the tool. Vendors often provide training in what their tool *can* do. Our training is often focused on what your team *should* do. We believe that enterprise deployment of tools and processes benefits from this approach. Picking the right approach to training and support is essential. It is equally important to realize that the tools implemented to support continuous integration must be deployed and tested successfully as well.

8.22 Deploy and Test

Implementing even the most basic continuous integration system can involve some complexity. It is very important to manage the deployment process of the tools, including planning for testing and ongoing support. We find that many teams fail to realize the importance of creating a repeatable process to install and configure the tools. We like to treat the implementation of continuous integration servers and shared repositories as we would any other systems development effort. This means that we start by understanding our dependencies, and then we create a checklist, and even scripts, to automate the installation and configuration of our tools. Having a repeatable process for installation and configuring our tools means that we can recover in the event of a significant outage by simply reinstalling our software and recovering any necessary data from the version control system or perhaps backups. We recognize that most folks don't take the installation of tools this seriously—we do, and we have repeatedly seen that this is the best approach for enterprise tools implementation. Getting things right the first time can be challenging, and thus we also take an iterative approach to both tools implementation and the processes they support.

8.23 Tuning the Process

You will not be able to implement a comprehensive continuous integration process perfectly the first time that you try. Tuning the process is a journey that is best approached in an agile iterative way.

Manager of Process

Bob once had a position where his title was literally the manager of process. This seemed like a perfect position for a guy who had spent his entire career in process improvement. Unfortunately, it soon became evident that Bob's colleagues thought that this title meant that Bob could just tell them what the process needed to be from the very beginning. There was very little understanding that designing a complex, error-free process can rarely be done up-front in a single effort; rather, it requires an agile iterative approach. In the real world, tuning and optimizing processes is a continual journey that is best approached as an agile iterative effort.

Sometimes processes are too informal to really help avoid mistakes. In this case, the steps of the process should be reviewed and updated. The only thing worse than a process that is missing a few steps, is a heavy process that involves too many time-consuming checkpoints. Lean processes are designed to incorporate just enough ceremony to be effective.

8.23.1 Getting Lean

Saying that a process is Lean indicates that it does not contain extra steps, which waste time and introduce unnecessary bureaucracy. Getting Lean requires its own journey. We typically find that processes early in the agile ALM can be relatively informal. But as the project progresses and deadlines approach, you will need more structure to avoid costly mistakes. Obviously, it is essential to ensure that you have enough "ceremony" in place to avoid errors, which are often prevented by well-designed and right-sized processes. For continuous integration, we often find that there are just too many builds being executed, and developers simply start ignoring the complaints of the CI server. Sure, we always insist that there be a designated resource responsible for dealing with broken builds, but in practice, too many builds often result in teams giving up entirely on continuous integration, which is obviously not the desired outcome. One approach of moderation is to identify "interesting" builds.

8.23.2 Interesting Builds

Builds that identify a milestone release are obviously of greater interest than builds that are mid-sprint. We never want to ignore any broken build, but in practice, it is often necessary to set priorities. This is where tagging a milestone build as being "interesting" helps identify specific builds that should be monitored more carefully. Getting continuous integration implemented successfully has many benefits. One of the most essential is that CI establishes the processes and technical procedures that will help lead to automated deployment.

8.24 CI Leads to Continuous Deployment

In Chapter 9, we will focus on continuous deployment, which although considerably more complicated than continuous integration, nonetheless benefits from many of the same principles and lessons learned. What you should understand in this section is that effective continuous integration establishes the required automated procedures that can then be used by the deployment framework to support continuous deployment.

8.25 Conclusion

Continuous integration is a well-established industry best practice that helps to deliver quality code and improve overall programmer productivity. Choosing the right tools and establishing right-sized processes are fundamental if you are going to succeed with CI. We emphasize that continuous integration is a journey that should be implemented using agile principles. Choosing the right tools is essential, as is providing training, administration, and ongoing support.

Chapter 9

Continuous Delivery and Deployment

Continuous deployment (CD) is a methodology for updating production systems as often as necessary and generally in very small increments on a continuous basis. It would be difficult to understand continuous deployment without discussing continuous integration and delivery. The terminology for CD has been confusing at best, with many thought leaders using the terms *continuous delivery* and *continuous deployment* interchangeably. We discussed continuous integration in Chapter 8. Continuous delivery focuses on ensuring that the code baseline is always in a state of readiness to be deployed at any time. With continuous delivery, we may choose to perform a "technical deployment" of code without actually exposing it to the end user, using a technique that has become known as *feature toggle*. Continuous deployment is different from continuous delivery in that the focus is on immediate promotion to a production environment, which may be disruptive and a poor choice from a business perspective. Throughout this book we will focus on deploying code as often as desired. The key to successfully implementing CD is focusing on specific goals.

9.1 Goals of Continuous Deployment

The goal of continuous deployment is to reduce human error by deploying code in small increments, thereby reducing risk and ensuring that the team has the capability to deploy code immediately—even in the middle of the workday. This may not be a desirable goal and may even be disruptive to the business. End users often do not want to see changes constantly, even if they are deployed flawlessly and deliver desirable features, because sometimes there is simply too much change, which can be disruptive. Continuous delivery takes a more pragmatic approach by ensuring that the baseline could potentially be deployed at any time and providing a means to deploy features that are not yet exposed to the user. We will discuss these techniques in more detail throughout the rest of this chapter. It is worth noting that continuous delivery and deployment are each focused on deploying to production environments and not just to development test environments, which is more the concern of continuous integration. The DevOps focus, as always, is to deploy using the same procedures to every environment and as early as possible to production-like environments. We also have a goal of ensuring that teams understand and use related terminology consistently.

> *Terminology Pollution*
>
> Many people are using the terms continuous delivery and continuous deployment interchangeably and also to mean other tasks such as build engineering. This confusion around terminology does not help with enterprise adoption of these industry best practices. Many other fields, including engineering, medicine, and law, require precise use of technical terms. We focus much of our training on ensuring that teams use these terms in a consistent way.

Next we will discuss why continuous deployment is important.

9.2 Why Is Continuous Deployment Important?

Continuous deployment (and continuous delivery) is important because it provides the framework for significantly improving reliability of application deployments by updating production systems more often and in smaller increments. Business often needs features or bugfixes delivered as soon as possible to stay competitive in today's demanding environment. By performing deployments more often, we get better at doing them and we make fewer mistakes with each successive effort. Having the capability to update a production system at any time is a huge competitive advantage. Automating the entire process and having a robust framework for deployments also helps improve reliability while ensuring that key business functions can be updated as often as necessary. Continuous deployment is important because it allows us to support the business more effectively by improving reliability while delivering essential features and bugfixes in a timely manner.

9.3 Where Do I Start?

Getting started with continuous deployment (and delivery) requires that you first understand your existing practices. We strongly recommend that you perform a comprehensive assessment of what works well and what could be improved. It is never a good idea to fix things that are not broken, although we have seen some well-meaning folks try to do exactly that when adhering blindly to following process improvement guidelines. When we do these assessments, we compare existing practices to the guidance provided in industry-relevant standards and frameworks, which we will discuss further in Chapter 16. The next step is to create a list of things that could be improved, in order of priority. Most importantly, we don't always start with the most important items to fix. It is helpful to pick a few easy items to address first, which helps your team realize how to make things change and helps especially to develop a culture that values process improvement and believes that it can happen!

Sadly, many teams are mired in the status quo, adopting a defeatist attitude that sabotages change.

> ### *Addressing the Culture*
>
> We take a very technical focus when understanding how the teams currently deploy application code. Although solid process is essential, the real goal is to help the team adopt a culture of process improvement, which helps them appreciate their own ability to overcome any obstacles. Once the team sees that things can get better, they often feel empowered to run with the ball, and the next step is to simply get out of their way.

Continuous deployment (and delivery) has an ultimate goal of establishing a fully automated deployment pipeline.

9.4 Establishing the Deployment Pipeline

Manual deployments all too often result in increased risk of human error. Continuous deployment places a strong focus on creating a fully automated deployment pipeline. Teams that cannot master this approach introduce significant risk in the deployment process, including the risk of human error. Further, the impact of delayed features and bugfixes can significantly disrupt the business agility of the firm. Imagine a team providing tax software that cannot roll out a feature on or before April 14 in response to a late-breaking IRS ruling!

Establishing the deployment pipeline is no easy task, and we prefer to take an agile iterative approach when creating the fully automated deployment pipeline. The first step is always to understand existing practices. We like to create checklists and start by scripting each and every step no matter how small or simple. At least half of our code is testing the actual deployment steps themselves.

Even copying a file should be handled with a script verifying and validating that the copy was made successfully.

Copying a File

Copying a file seems simple enough, but we have actually seen the simplest things cause serious mistakes. When we write a script to copy a file, we start by testing to see if the file is already there and, if it is, whether or not we can overwrite the existing file. Then we perform the copy and verify that the entire file was successfully copied. Finally, we log the results so that we have a record that the file was successfully copied. This approach makes it much easier to identify problems that may occur during the deployment. Our approach allows us to fail immediately if there is a problem instead of going three steps forward, which makes it much more difficult to identify any problems. Second, being able to verify that specific steps were successful helps your team focus on what actually broke the deployment. The added bonus is a record of the successful steps, which will help you when auditors come to review your deployment process.

Traceability to document, verify, and communicate that all tasks have been completed is essential.

Did You Do the Right Thing?

Bob served as an emergency medical technician (EMT). EMS protocols require that all medical procedures be documented. The requirement is so strict that EMTs will tell you that as far as EMS is concerned, you didn't give oxygen unless you wrote down that you did on the patient care form!

One very successful approach is rapid incremental deployments.

9.5 Rapid Incremental Deployment

Rapid incremental deployment is an approach where you quickly script and automate each step while performing your deployments. I usually start the first time by creating a checklist and then instead of trying to create a monolithic script that does everything, I create many smaller scripts that break the deployment into smaller chunks. For me, the train is always moving forward, and I rarely get much time to automate my deployments. I usually have to work with a team already in motion, meeting deadlines and ensuring that each release is deployed on time and without error. I take an iterative approach to writing my own deployment scripts, and I try to delivery very quickly. In the beginning, I am often pausing, reading the screen, and hitting Enter over and over again. With each subsequent release, the scripts get more mature and robust as we iteratively create the deployment pipeline.

Embracing change is normal when implementing rapid incremental deployment.

Hitting the Moving Target

Many of our colleagues suggest that they cannot automate the deployment because it is still changing. It is indeed common for deployments to be changing as new features and often new technologies are added. Bob worked on a banking system that added new interfaces each month. Still, automating each step in a rapid incremental way significantly reduced risk, including human error. Remember in an agile world we embrace change, even at the last minute; this flexibility applies to the deployment pipeline just as much as to the application being deployed.

Taking an incremental approach not only helps avoid risk, but it also helps avoid the defeatist attitude where folks believe that they cannot successfully embrace change, such as including automating application deployments of systems that are still under construction. Two key concepts should always be remembered. The first is that we want our deployment process to be the same across all environments, from deployment test to production. Too many teams create highly automated deployments to development test environments, but then jeopardize production by doing something completely different there. The second consideration is that it is extremely important to be deploying to production-like environments from the very beginning of the process. This is where container-based deployments have considerable potential, although some challenges remain to be addressed.

Container-Based Deployments

We are excited to be working with container-based deployments, but we also see some challenges. The first is that security around container-based deployments may be less than perfect for some time to come. This problem will likely be addressed successfully in the coming years, but there is a much more serious consideration that is actually behavioral in origin. We observe developers constructing containers without the due diligence that should accompany any effort to design a production environment. The attitude we see is that containers are shipped as is, so why should they worry about establishing baselines and communicating dependencies to operations? This is based on a naïve view that containers will be completely isolated, which, in practice, is unlikely to be completely true. We believe that containers should be first constructed from known baselines, including "fullstack," and developers should work only from known, approved existing container templates. Because container-based deployments are evolving quickly, please contact us on social media for our latest articles on this topic.

Make sure that you have a repeatable process for creating your containers, whether that be through a build of a declarative file or through an automated script. Using containers should never be an excuse for engaging in practices that lack traceability. Container-based deployments are an evolving capability and will mature and become a key practice within continuous deployment and delivery.

Much of this discussion has been at minimizing risk, which is a key consideration in continuous deployment.

9.6 Minimize Risk

Risk, often unavoidable, is not necessarily negative, especially if it is properly identified and accounted for. Continuous deployment reduces risk, but too often we see colleagues who fail to realize the importance of identifying and focusing on risk management. When we create automated deployment pipelines, we consider which steps have a high risk of human error. By following the manual process through the first time, we often notice that some steps are more error prone than others. Although picking some easy steps to automate is a great place to start, we also want to consider which steps have identifiable technical risk. These steps often involve environmental dependencies and interfaces to other parts of the system. Much of our code is intended to test, verify, and validate that any potential issues are quickly addressed. Technical risk should also be identified and reviewed during the change control process, as discussed in Chapter 10. When managing risk, we suggest that you initially script with the assumption that an operator will be running and reviewing each step. We call this approach *attended automation.*

> ### Attended Automation
>
> We know that many teams want to create single pushbutton deploys that automate the entire build, package, and deployment process from start to finish. This approach is often unrealistic. We usually start by writing some scripts that have to run and pause at specific key steps for the operator to review and then press Enter for the next step. This approach is often sufficient to significantly reduce or even eliminate the risk of human error.

The most important consideration in addressing risk is moving away from the monolithic deployment to a series of small steps. Many small deployments are inherently safer than a big-bang approach to application deployment.

9.7 Many Small Deployments Better than a Big Bang

The first thing that we do when addressing a troubled deployment process is to convince the team to break the deployment into smaller pieces that can each be deployed separately. Most often, we move from deploying every other month—usually through the weekend—to deploying twice a week in a much shorter deployment window. Obviously this won't always work, especially if the deployment involves a large infrastructure change, but, in practice, breaking monolithic deployments into many smaller deploys eliminates many sources of error and significantly reduces risk. Even if things do go wrong, it is much easier to identify the problem and either fix the issue or back out the change altogether. In general, many small deployments are much better than a big-bang approach.

Aside from being easier to accomplish, the team just gets better at deploying code and quickly adopts a new and much healthier attitude. Communication styles improve, and everyone gets more confident that they can be successful without making costly mistakes. The change in culture is often readily apparent as the team becomes a cohesive unit. These new capabilities can also help them handle larger deploys when they are unavoidable.

> ### Bimonthly Deployments at a Trading Firm
>
> Bob was hired to work with a large trading firm that had suffered several serious outages due to issues during the deployment process. The team had become accustomed to giving up their weekends and simply assumed that every deployment was too complicated to accomplish without some serious production outage. By getting the team to deploy twice a week, they came to the realization that simpler deploys were far less challenging, and they soon realized that they could deploy every day without making a mistake. Even when a larger infrastructure deployment came along that unavoidably took the entire weekend, their new communication skills and confidence helped them get through the entire deployment without a production outage.

Practicing the deployment procedures in a nonproduction environment is also essential for success.

9.8 Practice the Deploy

Developers frequently choose to handle their own application deployments in the lower environments, and this continues until the application is ready to be promoted to the upper environments. We will discuss a technique that is becoming known as "left-shift" in Chapter 12, whereby operations "shifts left" by getting involved with deployments to development and integration test environments in order to practice deploying the code in production-like environments earlier in the lifecycle. We also find that it is essential to practice the deployment procedures in order to get comfortable with all of the required steps and automation. Often technology professionals fail to realize the importance of practicing the deployment in order to train effectively and gain the confidence necessary to be successful. Imagine a pilot who never practiced on a flight simulator before taking you on your next six-hour flight! Similarly, we find that many groups only have one deployment engineer and then they are susceptible to keyman risk. We saw one team make huge progress with their application deployment capabilities, only to suffer a major outage when one member of the team went on vacation. It is essential to ensure that you have sufficient resources who are each very familiar and comfortable with the tools and procedures necessary for deployment. This is why ensuring that deployments are repeatable and traceable can be absolutely essential. One key consideration is whether or not your team has a culture of learning and teaching.

The Value of Teaching

Sometimes, we see colleagues who are uncomfortable sharing their experience and expertise. These folks have difficulty documenting their procedures for fear that their documents will be less than perfect. Generally, we find that getting our colleagues to share rough drafts for review helps fix this problem. Sometimes we just ask them to run through slides with us privately in preparation, during which time we offer some coaching on speaking and presenting. Once they feel a little more comfortable, we often see these folks enthusiastically sharing what they know with their colleagues. We then get others to respond by sharing their own best practices. Pretty soon the team transforms into a "learning organization," where teaching and learning are safe activities that improve iteratively over time.

Teaching and learning are fundamental skills required to create deployment processes that are repeatable and traceable.

9.9 Repeatable and Traceable

Too often, we see individuals who can perform tough technical tasks, including complex deployments, as one-off activities, but struggle when it comes to creating a repeatable process. We would prefer to have a slightly less fancy approach that is repeatable and fully traceable. We find that developers can do a great job of showing us the way through the deployment process the first time through, but it takes an operations view in order to make it a repeatable process. This is also true for creating the traceability that is often a requirement for compliance, as discussed in Chapter 16. Traceability comes into play during many aspects of the deployment process. Scripts should always be logging their results, including snapshotting environment settings. More importantly, processes will only be reliable and repeatable if they are implemented using a workflow automation tool.

9.10 Workflow Automation

Workflow automation tools help the entire team understand their roles and responsibilities, along with their own required tasks and dependencies, while being aware of the outstanding and completed tasks from others that may need to be completed throughout the ALM. We discussed automating the agile ALM in Chapter 7. Workflow automation is essential in the continuous deployment process. First, we need to track the steps of the deployment itself, but then we also need to establish feedback loops to report both successful steps and especially when exceptions occur. Processes themselves may sometimes necessarily be fluid to meet the dynamic requirements of the business and the team.

> ### *Managing a Changing Process*
>
> Bob worked on a project where the process seemed to be changing on a weekly basis. The team used a workflow automation tool with a visual interface, which made it much easier to review the existing workflow and then decide on changes, which were then communicated to each member of the team. When tasks were required, they either appeared in someone's e-mail or on their dashboard. Even though the process had to change fairly often, the team was able to communicate clearly what tasks had been completed and which tasks should be handled next. The team effectively managed their changing workflow requirements through the tool itself.

One key aspect of workflow automation is facilitating the orderly assignment of work, a function best accomplished using principles from Kanban.

9.10.1 Kanban—Push versus Pull

Managing the flow of work can be challenging. We acknowledge a tendency in our practice to welcome any assignment, no matter how large or small. Bob's grandmother washed down railroad trains by hand, so he inherited a work ethic to never turn down a reasonable task. Unfortunately, hardworking folks with this view often find themselves with more tasks than they can possibly complete in a timely manner. One key to success in these situations is correctly identifying the priorities and communicating status, especially if a task will not be completed on time.

Cops and Kanban

Bob learned about Kanban while patrolling the streets of a large city as an auxiliary police supervisor. As calls came in via 911, the central dispatcher would read out the pending jobs, and police officers would indicate that they were available to take specific assignments. The police auxiliary was unarmed and technically not allowed to take jobs. But when the number of pending jobs exceeded the ability of the available police officers, the precinct would go into "alert." This was not a good situation because the police were then pressured into rushing to complete assignments and could not take a meal break until the alert status was lifted. The auxiliary got very good at identifying low-priority jobs to handle that did not involve significant risk or danger to its members. (These calls explain how Bob's family ended up fostering several friendly lost dogs that people had nervously reported as being "vicious dogs.")

The truth is that there is a cost to having too many balls in the air at any point in time. Kanban enthusiasts call this work-in-progress (WIP). Kanban teaches us to limit WIP and then to pull tasks when we are ready to start them. Unassigned tasks aging in the queue also help us by identifying that we might need to hire more resources.

Bob's First Position as a Data Processing Director

Early in Bob's career, he worked as the director of data processing for a large radio network in New York City. With only two direct reports, tasks were coming in faster than they could possibly be completed. To communicate the work that the team was being assigned, Bob published a list of open requests, which was updated daily. This did not work very well because the list just simply grew and grew and took time to just maintain. Having too much work-in-progress can adversely impact the productivity of the team.

Many workflow automation tools make it easy to manage work using Kanban concepts. Managing incoming requests is essential, as is understanding the ergonomics of deployments.

9.11 Ergonomics of Deployments

Ergonomics is the study of how people work efficiently in their environments. Closely related is the study of human factors, especially in terms of identifying their source. The cockpit of a plane is a great example of ergonomics, as pilot controls are typically designed to reduce the chances of human error. The next time you board a plane, see if you can take a quick peek at the cockpit controls, which provide a considerable amount of information to the pilot and copilot, while their design is intended to ensure that the complex controls are read accurately without the risk of human error. Deployment automation can learn a lot from pilots and other aviation experts. The deployment pipeline should always be designed to avoid any chance of human error. This means that scripts and dashboards provide accurate and timely information in a way that is likely to be interpreted correctly, avoiding mistakes that can potentially lead to failed deployments.

There are many circumstances in which mistakes are simply not acceptable. Mission-critical systems from missile defense to life support systems are a good example of applications that must be updated without any chance of human error.

Nuclear Power Plants

Bob taught a configuration management (CM) best practices class to a group of engineers who supported nuclear power plants. It was readily apparent that these engineers shared a culture of ensuring that everything humanely possible was done to avoid any possible source of error.

Sometimes it can be difficult to test all aspects of complex deployments because there is no human interface readily available to facilitate testing. This is where verification and validation (V&V) can sometimes help fill the requirement that quality standards are met.

9.12 Verification and Validation of the Deployment

We see many situations where the usual testing approach can be impractical or even impossible to accomplish. This is where verification and validation can be a practical alternative—sometimes used with whatever testing approaches are available. For example, we may find that infrastructure configuration changes are difficult to test in production environments. In these circumstances, it may be helpful to use system tools, with ping being a simplistic example, to verify and validate that the machine is at least up and running. This approach usually requires the ability to think creatively about what aspects of the system can be checked using the available tools. Some technologies are built with a restful application programming interface (API) that can also be used for this work. Most often this approach is closely related to environment monitoring, which is often overlooked in many organizations. Monitoring the environment is discussed further in Chapter 11.

It is fundamentally essential for the application deployment to be fully verifiable via a methodology that we call the *secure trusted application base*.

9.13 Deployment and the Trusted Base

Deployments must be fully verifiable. Very often teams are haphazard with how they handle application deployment. We have seen many teams act as if they are unable to ensure that the deployment was completed successfully and also that any unauthorized changes can be quickly identified and remediated.

Deployments should actually be completely deterministic, with code written to ensure that we are completely certain that the right code has been deployed and that there have been no unauthorized changes due to human error or malicious intent. This is the goal of having a fully trusted application baseline. We approach this effort by starting with code that is correctly baselined in the version control system (identified with a tag, label, and often an immutable changeset). We strongly advocate that the code be independently built by a build-and-release engineer, based upon a locked version label as described in Chapter 6. The deployment pipeline then automates the application deployment and verifies version IDs built into the configuration items (CIs).[1] We also monitor the cryptographic hashes (e.g., MAC SHA1 or MD5) to detect unauthorized changes.

Monitoring baselines can be impractical because so many files, such as your message logs, will change constantly. Our approach is to start early identifying the files that should be monitored on a regular basis. This is a key part of our

---

1. Configuration items refer to any source code, binary, configuration file, or other artifact that is part of the system being built. Unfortunately, continuous integration adopted the same acronym of CI, which has caused some confusion, especially in organizations that need to use industry standards (e.g., ISO, IEEE) and frameworks (ITILv3) where the acronym CI most often refers to configuration item.

DevOps-focused approach to security that we call *continuous security*, which we will discuss further in Chapters 11 and 12. Securing the application baseline requires a great deal of technical knowledge, which must be gathered from the very beginning of the application development process. This is easier said than done, and we find that we have to employ some tactics to identify this technical information, which is often the basis of environment monitoring.

What Should We Monitor?

We often find that developers are completely unable to tell us what files should really be monitored for changes. We commonly hear that everything should just work fine. But as the old adage that "a chain is only as strong as its weakest link" implies, we must identify any potential points that affect system availability. We try to be involved from the beginning of the process to observe and participate in troubleshooting sessions. This is exactly when we learn which files and configuration settings are examined whenever things are not working right. Consistent with our view that no good crisis should ever go to waste, we use these troubleshooting sessions as a source of information to identify what configuration items and runtime dependencies should be monitored as part of our efforts to identify unauthorized changes.

Identifying dependencies can be very challenging, especially when development and QA testing environments may not match the target production environment. We sometimes hear that a feature worked fine on the developer's laptop or in the QA test environment, only to crash in production. Failure to identify potential points that could be problematic obviously introduces considerable risk. This is where deploying to environments that mirror production is essential.

9.14 Deploy to Environments that Mirror Production

Production environments often grow to be complex and robust platforms, which may not even closely resemble what are often limited test sandboxes. This not only creates a challenge for testing, but may also introduce considerable risks during the application deployment. We often see developers implement elaborate continuous integration procedures that completely automate the application build, package, and deployment to a test environment. But then the team does something different for production and things go badly wrong. We feel that the deployment procedures must be identical for each environment and that the environments should closely match production as much as possible. This is not always possible, and where discrepancies exist, they should be identified as risks, with appropriate procedures to ensure that service interruptions do not occur as a result.

> ### Apples to Apples
>
> All too often testing is done in limited environments that do not closely resemble the target production environment. This situation leads to defects being discovered in production that cannot even be reproduced in the test environment. Similarly, the deployment process itself may not proceed exactly as expected if there is any discrepancy between production and the test environments used for quality assurance.

Risk is not always bad, and continuous deployment has many points in which risk may need to be identified and appropriate plans created to mitigate it.

9.15 Assess and Manage Risk

Throughout the continuous deployment process, we need to always assess and manage risk, which may not always be avoidable. Risk may be present in the form of sources of human error, as we discussed, or there may be other types of risk based upon the architecture of the system and the technologies chosen for implementation. We find that technical risk is a common problem and goes hand in hand with using the newest technologies. Adopting the latest technology frameworks may give you many capabilities in terms of performance and usability, but being on the bleeding edge is also not without its own drawbacks. In continuous deployment, we may need to constantly adjust our procedures to match the new technology and its evolving requirements.

> ### Hibernate and Maven
>
> The first time that we used Maven with Hibernate was a challenging experience. Most of our build procedures simply stopped working, and since we were only notified of the change two weeks before the code had

> to go to production, we were left scrambling to fix the problems. We always try to stay up to date on the technologies and application architecture involved so that we don't get surprised as we did the first time we had to deploy Hibernate using Maven.

Managing technical risk often comes with any new technology. We find that it is essential to learn the new technologies. Next up is the dress rehearsal and walkthroughs.

9.16 Dress Rehearsal and Walkthroughs

We like to conduct deployment rehearsals and walkthroughs so that every stakeholder fully understands what we are doing and also so that we have an opportunity to review and verify all of our procedures before the actual rollout. The dress rehearsal is basically on-the-job training. But the walkthrough more closely resembles a code review or inspection.

During this effort, we reinforce everyone's role and responsibilities, along with a well-defined communication protocol. In very large deployments, we usually set up a command center and have designated escalation procedures so that all resources are available in case anything happens that is unexpected or more serious problems occur. We have seen very large banking systems implemented this way, often with a couple of hiccups, but with the right procedures in place to manage the overall process, including incident and problem resolution.

Many other fields also use dress rehearsals and walkthroughs.

Sarin Gas and DevOps

Bob was serving as the deputy director of a medical reserve unit that was directed by the Federal Emergency Management Agency (FEMA) to conduct realistic mass-casualty drills after 9/11. In one scenario, the dress rehearsal seemed to be going just fine. Volunteers acted as victims, and medical and logistics personnel practiced triaging hundreds of casualties. Although the team did a great job of identifying and coordinating the response, it was discovered halfway through the drill that no one had remembered to have a sarin gas decontamination checkpoint. Fortunately, this was a drill and not an actual event. Many of the participants actually lived in lower Manhattan during 9/11 and were very dedicated to ensuring that we had a well-trained medical reserve team using realistic dress rehearsals and walkthroughs to prepare and maintain readiness.

In the real world, we often cannot avoid risks and challenges during the deployment process. Dress rehearsals and walkthroughs are an effective methodology for addressing these challenges. In fact, handling the real-world scenario of imperfect deployments is exactly where continuous deployment has the most value.

9.17 Imperfect Deployments

Simple deployments are nice work when you can get them. But we more often find ourselves in demand when the deployment process has some unavoidable wrinkles and challenges. The imperfect deployment is exactly where our approach is most expeditiously applied and returns the most value. We commonly find ourselves dealing with scenarios that are quickly changing, making it difficult to fully automate our procedures. Test environments may not match fully, and manual testing procedures can greatly slow down the verification and validation of the system being deployed. The first time you deploy any technology may involve its own set of challenges, including learning the new technology or deployment procedures themselves.

Frequently we find teams with dysfunctional communication patterns, which must be addressed. Many organizations have poorly defined critical incident management procedures and an immature response to complex problem management. The imperfect world is actually where our approach has the most value and, truthfully, the real world is often an imperfect place. The key is always to assess where you are at the beginning of the process and then measure your success as you iteratively improve it.

Our most important lesson learned is always to have a plan B.

9.18 Always Have a Plan B

For every situation that is not perfect, which is basically every situation we find ourselves in, we always identify the risk as best we can. We try to understand what might go wrong and then we do some contingency planning. In continuous deployment, you cannot always control the runtime environment, technology risk, and related changes in the underlying technology platform. The key to your success is to always create a plan for dealing with any contingencies should they arise. This scenario is much more common than you might imagine. Successful teams establish a rhythm and a protocol, and approach each challenge with a can-do attitude. Having a plan—however brief—for dealing with unforeseen circumstances is essential for handling the real-world challenges that always seem to surface in complex production deployments.

Having a plan B is helpful, but the real key is leading the team to high performance.

Mission Impossible

We worked with a team in a large bank that was dealing with a huge legacy system. Very few people knew how to troubleshoot the system, and problems always seemed to arise. The best approach was to focus on the teamwork, communication, and effectiveness of the response process. This situation was far from perfect, but the team understood what they were up against and how they got there and made their best efforts to manage a difficult situation until we finally got the approval to reengineer the entire system.

One final consideration that deserves attention is the importance of continuous deployment, including a testing approach to verify that the deploy itself was successful. In a deployment context, we call this *smoke testing*.

9.19 Smoke Test

We find many deployment teams do not realize that smoke testing is part of the overall process. Deployments are part of the QA and testing process, and smoke testing is the last step of continuous deployment.

We find it valuable to actively participate in the smoke-testing process.

> ### *Smoke Testing in a Trading System*
>
> We always put in the first trade when upgrading complex trading systems. The technical knowledge of the architecture, time spent building each component from source code, and executing automated test scripts somehow is secondary to actually using the system and understanding how it should function in a true production scenario.

As noted, smoke testing is the last step in the deployment process. This underscores the reality that quality is everyone's job, and we view ourselves as playing a key role in the testing effort.

9.20 Conclusion

Continuous deployment and delivery are capabilities that are emerging as an industry best practice. In this book, we will push back against the notion of single pushbutton deploys in favor of completely reliable and secure deployments that can be executed as often as business needs dictate. Closely related is continuous delivery, with its focus on ensuring that we always have a deployable baseline and that features can be rolled out, but hidden, until the business decides that it is the right time to expose them.

PART III

Establishing Controls

Chapter 10

Change Management

Change management is a broad function that helps us plan, review, and communicate many different types of planned and emergency (unplanned) system modifications. Changes may be bugfixes or new features and can range from a trivial configuration modification to a huge infrastructure migration. The goal of change control is to manage all changes to the production (and usually QA) environments. Part of this effort is just coordination, and that is very important. But part of this effort is also managing changes to the environment that could potentially affect all of the systems in the environment. It is also essential to control which releases are promoted to quality assurance (QA) and production. Change control can act as the stimulus to all other configuration management–related functions as well. Throughout this chapter we will discuss how to apply change management in the application lifecycle management (ALM).

10.1 Goals of Change Management

The goal of change management is to identify and manage risk. Change management can help drive the entire build, package, and deployment process by identifying the potential downstream impact of making (or not making) a particular change. There are seven different types of change management, including managing changes to the software development process itself, which we will explain further in Section 10.17. Change management also has the essential goal of facilitating effective communication and traceability. Done well, change management can be an essential part of the software and systems delivery process, accelerating the rate of successful upgrades and bugfixes while avoiding costly mistakes. However, the lack of change management can lead to serious outages, lead to reduced productivity, and endanger the organization.

10.2 Why Is Change Management Important?

Change management is important because it helps drive the entire configuration management process while identifying technical risk inherent in making (or not making) a change. Risk is not always bad if it is identified and fully understood. An effective change management process helps identify, communicate, and then mitigate technical risks. Communication and traceability are key aspects of the effective change management process. In fact, change management can drive the entire ALM effort. When process changes occur, change management helps ensure that all stakeholders are aware of their new roles, responsibilities, and tasks. Organizations that lack effective change management are at increased risk for costly systems outages. Change management drives the ALM.

In some organizations, change management simply focuses on identifying potential scheduling conflicts that can adversely impact the application build, package, and deployment process. Managing the calendar is certainly important, but that is only the beginning. It is common for a particular deployment or configuration change to depend upon the same resource as another change. The effective change management process also identifies the affected assets and the experts who can best understand and communicate the potential downstream impact of a change. With complex technologies, many IT professionals are specialists in a particular area, resulting in organizational silos that may not fully understand how changes that they may make could potentially impact other systems. The change management process should identify all stakeholders who should be involved with evaluating a proposed change and then communicate the potential risk of making (or not making) a particular change.

> ### Change Management and Storage
>
> Bob worked with a large international bank, evaluating and working to improve their change management process. In one incident, the team had planned to upgrade a system over the weekend, only to discover when they started that needed storage devices were being upgraded and they had no access to the required disk drives for the deployment.

DevOps principles and practices are particularly effective in improving the change management process, which often fails to include all of the required stakeholders and subject matter experts.

10.3 Where Do I Start?

Getting started with change management usually begins with assessing the existing processes and identifying what is being done well and what could be improved. We find that many organizations focus narrowly on the calendar and then fail to adequately review and evaluate technical risk. This is usually because the technical experts associated with assets that are the subject of a particular change request have not been identified. We also find that many change management functions need to improve their approach to communicating planned (and unplanned emergency) changes.

It is common for the change management function to be conducted as a very long meeting, often lasting two hours or more, which is considered a painful bureaucratic experience of little actual value. We usually start by identifying routine change requests (CRs) that can be handled in a separate meeting, thereby shortening the change management meeting. Long painful meetings rarely motivate participants to implement effective change management.

We try to improve change management by having less of it.

Change Management Can Be a Painful Process

We often find that change management is a painful process that is viewed with disdain throughout the organization. Stakeholders often view the change management process as being ineffective and a complete waste of time. The first step in improving the change management process is to challenge these negative attitudes; making the meeting shorter is a visible positive incentive.

Identifying changes that are routine and can be designated as preapproved is an effective first step in improving the change management process. We are often able to separate out routine changes, which still need to be communicated but do not require the same assessment of technical risk as application deployments or configuration changes. Closely related is the practice of creating specialized change control boards (CCBs). We have seen organizations that had separate change control boards for information security, which focused on authorization, entitlements, and key infrastructure such as firewalls. The specialized change control board (CCB) may go into great detail, which could simply be a single line item in the centralized change management function. One key aspect of effective change management is ensuring traceability, which is actually a regulatory requirement in many organizations.

10.4 Traceability for Compliance

Change management provides a robust framework for documenting changes that are essential for successful operations as well as regulatory compliance. Publicly traded firms, including banks, trading firms, and many other companies, are required by federal law to provide accurate records of all changes to production, which helps to answer the question "what did we do last time" to solve a problem or to provide a new feature. The change management function provides this traceability through documentation, usually via a robust workflow automation tool. We discussed workflow automation tools in Chapter 7. Closely related are the functions of incident and problem management, which we will discuss later in this chapter. When bad things happen, it is not uncommon for outside agencies to ask for documentation to demonstrate that the company took prudent steps to avoid the risk associated with common mistakes. You may hear folks discussing what a "prudent" approach would be. Having your steps well documented, including approvals, tests, and steps taken to avoid human error, can go a long way to demonstrating that your team did everything possible to avoid a mistake. Change management plays a key role in providing that documentation and traceability. It also helps enable the assessment and management of risk.

10.5 Assess and Manage Risk

Risk is not intrinsically bad. But risk must always be evaluated and understood by all stakeholders. The first step is to understand the risk and communicate with all other stakeholders. The logical next step is to create a plan to mitigate and manage the risk. In practice, change management helps identify the risk of making a change versus the risk of not making a change. Large-scale systems actually have considerable inherent risk, often because of their complexity and decisions that have been made over time, which may have compounded the risk. Making pragmatic short-term decisions is sometimes referred to as creating *technical debt*. The idea here is that short-term decisions made for the sake of expediency build up a type of "IOU"—the technical debt. Too many short-term decisions increase risk and may eventually lead to the system being very brittle.

Technical debt is often unavoidable.

> ### Technical Debt
>
> We have seen many situations where technical debt built up over time. One example is a large clustered database that became so complex it was very difficult to maintain. To make matters worse, it could not be backed up and restored within any reasonable change window. This meant that we could not alter fields, and we had to make the very poor choice of always adding a new field in case we had to drop back, once again, creating more technical debt.

The most important aspect of managing risk is ensuring that there is excellent communication.

10.6 Communication

The greatest risk that we see in most organizations is poor communication. Large organizations in particular are often siloed, and many technology professionals may not even know who to reach out to for help or who should be informed when there are incidents and problems. This is precisely where DevOps principles and practices can be most valuable. We often find ourselves acting as a catalyst for better communication and collaboration by ascertaining who should be involved with a particular call. Organizational dynamics can sometimes be challenging—especially when managers model dysfunctional behavior by allowing their subordinates to view themselves as being in competition with another group. In this context, change management has the goal of keeping everyone informed and reducing the noise that is often associated with dysfunctional—and poorly implemented—change management. Change management is a valuable function, but unfortunately, we often observe ineffective or even counterproductive efforts.

Sometimes we even see behavior that somewhat resembles job actions as if IT professionals were part of a union. We also see situations where managers play politics to the detriment of the organization.

> ### Spiteful Retaliation
>
> Bob worked for a large international bank that had a considerable amount of tricky organizational dynamics. The test team was a critical

> resource, and each project manager jockeyed for testing resources so that they could make their deadlines. At one point, Bob's manager called him into his office and explained that one of the other managers had disagreed with him at an important meeting. Bob was then instructed to withhold testing resources to intentionally cause this manager to miss his deadline.

Managing changes is essential. Unfortunately, there is often a lack of coordination in change management within the ALM itself.

10.7 Change in Application Lifecycle Management

Change management, within the context of the ALM, must evolve and adapt in order to be effective. The ALM also should evolve as part of continuous process improvement. This effort is often managed by a software engineering process group (SEPG), a group that is responsible for managing changes to the process itself. We first learned about the value of the SEPG from the Software Engineering Institute's (SEI) Capability Maturity Model (CMM), which later evolved into the Capability Maturity Model Integrated (CMMI). Many folks found the full CMM to be difficult to implement, but the value of having a dedicated group manage changes to the software development process cannot be underestimated. This is particularly true when organizations themselves undergo significant changes, which could happen due to mergers and acquisitions.

> *Banking Mergers*
>
> Bob was in a large international bank that acquired a U.S.-based bank in an attempt to expand into the lucrative U.S. banking movement. The international bank had a very well-defined culture, which was part of that organization's deep history. The U.S.-based bank had a very different culture, and the two clashed. Merging these two entities was difficult to accomplish, and many employees of the U.S. entity left the organization.

Managing change must be handled in a holistic way. It is essential to consider the entire ecosystem.

10.8 The Change Ecosystem

Change management must always be understood within the context of an ecosystem. Developers have their priorities—generally to deliver new features and bugfixes at a rapid pace. We usually hear developers discuss what might happen if a particular change does not occur. Operations has a difficult perspective and should always be focused on maintaining reliable systems. The information security (InfoSec) group helps keep our systems secure, and QA and testing guide us along the path to producing code that is as free of defects as possible. End users and the business have their own perspectives, which may include dealing with strong competitive pressures, which in turn, puts pressure on the ecosystem to evolve and meet business demands. The change management function benefits greatly from DevOps by ensuring that we have effective communication and collaboration. We need to always consider the risk of making a change versus the risk of not making that change, and each of these stakeholders has an essential role in making these decisions. Only when you consider change management in a holistic way can you make the right decisions to ensure that your systems are reliable, secure, and effectively supporting the business.

Understanding change management in a holistic way is essential. Ensuring quality is also a fundamental requirement for effective change management.

10.9 QA and Testing

Change management benefits greatly from integration with the QA and testing process. Unfortunately, far too many folks fail to consider the requirements of QA and testing in the change management function. When we participate in change management, we often ask how we can verify that the change request was completed successfully. Equally important is establishing criteria for QA and testing should the change need to be backed out. The change request should document these steps and establish acceptance criteria, both for the successful implementation of a change and in the case of a change needing to be backed out.

We see many circumstances where QA and testing are limited, but other verification and validation criteria can still be successfully implemented. For example, you might want to ensure that systems have rebooted successfully before the testing process begins.

> *Cry for Help*
>
> Bob once had a QA director ask for help on a change management conference call. The problem turned out to be that the QA team would often find out, after an hour of testing, that one or more of the systems had not successfully started up. The DevOps team would then reboot the servers again, and then the testing would have to be restarted from the beginning. The QA director was frustrated that the team wasted hours each week, only to have to begin the testing process from the beginning. The solution was to run scripts to verify and validate that all of the machines had successfully started up and that all services were running. These scripts were already available and used as part of environment monitoring, but no one had realized that they would be useful to establish entry criteria before testing.

Environment monitoring helps maintain reliable systems by providing an early warning that an incident may be about to occur.

10.10 Monitoring Events

Event monitoring is an essential capability that is often overlooked in many organizations. Many types of events could potentially be monitored in large enterprise systems. The ITIL v3 framework describes events as a "change of state" that may require some action and could be indicating that an incident is about to or has already occurred. The most common events are alerts or notifications regarding thresholds such as disk and memory limits. These constraints must be defined and monitored, providing sufficient time to address any potential problems before they result in a systems outage. The change management process should always identify events that should be monitored and that might be potentially affected by the change request. One problem is that we often do not know what to monitor, and this is exactly where DevOps can help us.

Runtime dependencies can be complicated and difficult to monitor, as well as to interpret. Too often, the operations team starts to identify events that should be monitored late in the software and system development lifecycle. This approach often does not work because the experts who wrote the code and are most knowledgeable about dependencies may have moved on to other projects by the time that the operations team is starting to create runbooks and establish support procedures. The best approach is to begin to identify events that should be monitored early in the process and establish automated monitoring for test environments as part of the deployment pipeline.

> ### *Learning from Troubleshooting*
>
> We often find that technology professionals cannot explain up-front which events should be monitored. But once there is a problem, these same professionals start checking available memory, disk space, running processes, and other runtime dependencies, which could potentially be events that should be monitored. Our approach is to get involved from the beginning to capture these technical details, communicating them to operations and documenting them in the runtime operational procedures.

Monitoring events is essential. When major incidents occur, it is essential to establish an organizational structure to facilitate communications and collaboration. This is usually called the *command center*.

10.11 Establishing the Command Center

Large-scale technology systems always have challenges. Outages can occur due to hardware failure thought to be reliable, third-party products, or any number of other dependencies. What matters most is how the support team responds to and deals with any challenges that occur. We have discussed how monitoring events can sometimes help by providing an early warning system. We have sometimes identified serious issues about to occur and quickly scrambled to address problems, communicating with our users as needed. We find that fast and effective response is essential, but excellent communication is far and away the most important factor when it comes to ensuring that our customers and end users are satisfied with our service and support. When serious outages occur, communication must be managed from an incident command center (ICC).

The command center provides a structure to coordinate the response and especially the communication between all of the stakeholders engaged in addressing the incident. We view the command center from a DevOps perspective; resources from different teams must be able to communicate and collaborate effectively. In practice, we find these teams are often highly structured and accustomed to operating from what actually may be a very rigid interface. Other team members may experience these teams as being highly siloed. We often see dysfunctional behavior, which hampers the response and resolution. Establishing a command center provides an independent structure to ensure that the required groups are each represented and working together effectively. The measure of success is how effectively the team addresses and resolves incidents when they occur.

> ### *Managing a Globally Distributed Incident Response*
>
> It is always best to have team members colocated, but in large companies this is rarely a practical requirement. Some companies put out-of-town employees up in hotels and cater meals to try to make it easier for team members to work from a centralized location. But we often see teams that are distributed across multiple time zones and different locations, making coordination that much more difficult. Sometimes the incident command center has to be virtual and online to be able to coordinate resources across different locations. Although not an optimal situation, it is very common in many large organizations.

The command center is essential for establishing effective communications. Yet, most teams are judged based upon their initial response and escalation when incidents occur.

10.12 When Incidents Occur

When incidents occur, the team's success is often measured by their initial response. Identifying the scope of the incident—and especially all of the stakeholders who should be involved—is a fundamental requirement. Too often, the scope of the problem is not well understood and the necessary resources are not successfully identified and engaged. Sometimes this is because technology professionals are either afraid to speak up or they give their input but are ignored by those in positions of power when they do. In practice, we see professionals who want to do the right thing, but their cognitive processes may be impaired by the stress and shock experienced when they fear that they may be blamed for a catastrophic outage.

Mainframe Outage

Bob was working at a large financial services firm with an extensive mainframe system. One member of the team made a mistake, which took down the entire production environment. This individual had a well-deserved reputation for being extremely conscientious, but he executed a command while on the wrong mainframe LPAR,[1] which resulted in the entire system being brought down. Determining exactly what had occurred was the first step in restoring the production system. The problem was that the person who had made the mistake kept giving a different description of the steps leading up to the mistake. We all knew this person to be reliable and dependable, but the stress and anxiety resulted in misleading and inaccurate information, which complicated the efforts to restore the production environment.

Incidents are sometimes unavoidable, but once their negative aspects have been addressed, they should be used to improve our processes. From a DevOps perspective, incidents are *feedback loops* that serve to help us identify where we need to establish, or at least modify, IT controls intended to avoid mistakes. Incidents can also help identify test cases that should be created to avoid defects in future releases. Smart technology leaders embrace every opportunity for the team to continuously improve existing processes. The way in which you manage incidents will determine how your team responds to any future incidents that occur.

Constructive Feedback

One particular team struggled to successfully implement a new cash management system. It seemed that every week there was a new challenge, and the vendor-written system had quite a few weaknesses that resulted in outages with practically each configuration change. On one of the calls, the senior director joined us and reminded everyone that although he wanted these problems solved as soon as possible, he also noticed that the team was working together. He reminded everyone on the

---

1. An LPAR is a logical partition on a mainframe and is similar to a virtual machine (VM) on distributed systems.

> call that he valued good teamwork above all else and that he was very proud of the way that we were all supporting the efforts to identify and resolve these issues. Obviously, we all felt good about our performance and redoubled our efforts—working once more late into the night.

When incidents occur, we often have the opportunity to identify new test cases and events that should be monitored. Incidents may identify defects in the code or sources of human error, which could occur again in the future. DevOps teaches us to view these challenges as feedback loops and opportunities for improvement. This is also where we may need to establish IT controls, which we discuss in Chapter 16, "Audit and Regulatory Compliance." Sometimes, incidents may be difficult to diagnose, especially in terms of their root causes. It is common for serious issues to require escalation, a process known as *problem management*.

10.13 Problems and Escalation

Problems are generally distinguished from incidents by the need for root-cause analysis and often an escalation to include additional resources. We see many situations where the incident response team just does not have sufficient expertise and resources to address serious problems. Escalation may require that the developers who wrote the code participate in the problem resolution process, assuming they are still available. There are also many situations where third-party providers might need to be involved as well. Generally, we like to record problem investigation sessions so that we can review steps taken and consider ways to improve our processes later.

Significant outages may identify serious defects that need to be addressed, as well as new features and tools that should be developed to help prevent future problems. It is important to identify events that should be monitored in the future to avoid similar situations. Problem management and escalation also require effective communication to all stakeholders. We find that in the middle of a serious problem, stress and fatigue can impair the performance of many team members. This is where incident and problem management teams can help improve the effectiveness of the overall escalation effort.

In IT, no less than in politics, remember always that "no good crisis should ever go to waste."

> ### Never Let a Good Crisis Go to Waste
>
> When things are going well, teams often resist process improvement efforts. When things go wrong, it is often the only time the team is open to changing the way that they do things. We confess to actually waiting for teams to fail when all prior efforts to encourage process improvement have been disregarded. Although we would never want to cause a serious outage, we also never let a good crisis go to waste.

Problem management and escalation are essential processes that can harness the opportunity to minimize the impact of a serious outage. Generally, we find that the change management process itself must be continuously reviewed and improved.

10.14 The Change Management Process

The biggest impediment to effective change management is often the change management process itself. Too often, change management is a verbose bureaucratic process that wastes everyone's time while doing little to avoid human errors, along with other types of risk associated with implementing changes. The key to success is to choose the best tools to support the change management process.

> ### The Change Management Automation System
>
> Change management systems are often difficult to use, wasting everyone's time and providing motivation to simply bypass the process. One particular system in a large bank, which had specific options that had to be chosen in a specific order, comes to mind. The choices available often did not match the situation, and the descriptions themselves were confusing and misleading. The worst part was that any mistake meant that you actually had to start over again from the beginning. The organization was excited when funds were allocated to purchase a new system. Unfortunately, the new system was just as poorly designed as the legacy system, and the organization ended up with a new system that was just as bad as the old one.

The first thing that we usually do is work to get the change management sessions to be shorter and better organized. Creating an agenda and ensuring that subject matter experts (SMEs) are only required to join in when change requests (CRs) they are involved with are being discussed streamlines meetings and minimizes resistance. Routine changes should be identified and handled separately as "pre-approved" change requests.

The ITILv3 framework describes a change advisory board (CAB), which acts as an expert resource to the change management function. We have frequently seen confusion regarding the difference between the CAB and the CCB. Some organizations combine these two groups, often maintaining the name of CAB, which sounds more official to many. We believe that the CCB and the CAB should be kept separate, inviting CAB members into the CCB meeting when they are needed to act in an advisory capacity. The CCB should be more narrowly focused on the change process and traceability, whereas the CAB helps understand the downstream impact of a change. CAB members are the SMEs associated with specific assets that they know well. CCBs members are often willing to sit through the entire change management meeting. The SMEs in the CAB should only be consulted for the CRs for which they are involved. CAB members are certainly welcome to stick around for the entire change control meeting, but are not mandated to do so. We see CAB members self-select to leave as soon as the CR they are involved is discussed and approved (or not).

We also find that creating specialized change request boards can be helpful to streamline the process. For example, we had one specialized change management meeting focused on storage and capacity planning across Unix, mainframe, and Windows. This meeting took over an hour and covered technical details of interest only to those deeply involved with managing the complex storage devices, including storage-attached networks (SANs) and network-attached storage (NAS). The main change management meeting covered this item in a one-line summary, which advised everyone regarding which weekends would be focused on upgrading storage, effectively prohibiting any application upgrades on the same day. No one objected to getting a weekend off, and we avoided the scheduling conflict of trying to upgrade a system on the same day that the storage systems would be offline, effectively rendering the underlying systems inaccessible. One effective way to optimize the change management process is to establish entry and exit criteria up-front.

10.14.1 Entry/Exit Criteria

When changes are complicated and require a technical review, we have found that providing documentation of the change up-front can help make the change management process much more efficient. We have had considerable success with this approach, and shortening the time for the change management meeting can be reinforcing. Most importantly, we want to identify assets that may be impacted by a change and the subject matter experts who should be consulted for each change.

Similarly, establishing exit criteria up-front, including test cases and criteria for verification and validation, can also help make the process more effective. This is one area where having a post-implementation review can help improve the change management process.

10.14.2 Post-Implementation

Post-implementation reviews help us understand what went well and what could be improved in the change management process. In Chapter 13, we discuss retrospectives, which have a broader scope than post-implementation reviews. What is common to both is the need to get honest and open feedback on what went well and what could be improved. One clear way to improve the change management process is to preapprove routine changes.

10.15 Preapproved Changes

Some changes are well understood and may occur on a frequent basis. ITIL v3 refers to these changes as *standard* changes, and they are generally separated out to allow more time to focus on *normal* changes, which require full review by the change advisory board. Unfortunately, we see organizations where the change management function simply groups all changes together. This is usually because the folks running the change control process lack the technical expertise to really understand the nature of the changes. Mixing all of the changes together into one long meeting tends to be highly dysfunctional and really undermines the effectiveness of the change control process. Taking preapproved changes out of the formal change control meeting is a good first start to help make your change management function more efficient and effective. Pre-approved changes still need to be communicated, but should be handled separately, leaving the actual change control meeting to focus on assessing and managing the technical risk inherent in any complex software upgrade, configuration modification, or even bugfixes.

Focusing on the changes and the process is important. But establishing an effective change management function is even more essential for successfully managing changes.

10.16 Establishing the Change Management Function

Establishing an effective organizational structure to champion change management is a critical success factor for any agile ALM. Change management must work successfully within the culture of the organization, while ensuring compliance with any required regulatory and compliance requirements. The CM group facilitates and drives the process, but in many ways, they must align with the corporate structure in order to be successful. Change management ensures effective communication, collaboration, and documentation for traceability. Change management must be continuously reviewed and improved, while also ensuring that processes are well understood, followed, and work effectively to identify and manage risk. Change management should also effectively help change to occur. We find that the structure of the change management process is essential.

10.16.1 Change Control Board

As discussed previously, we view the change control board (CCB) as being the process-oriented representatives from each of the essential organizational functions. In practice, we see representatives from development, operations, the business, information security, and QA and testing being included. The CCB must ensure that all affected parties are informed and, when necessary, brought in for consultation. This is where we view the change advisory board as being quite helpful.

10.16.2 Change Advisory Board

The change advisory board provides expertise on the potential downstream impact of a change. It has become common practice to combine the change control board with the change advisory board, calling the resulting group the "CAB." However, we believe that these two entities are best kept separate, with the CCB focusing on process and the CAB advising on the potential downstream impact of a change.

10.17 Change Control Topology

There are many different types of change control, and you will likely need to have two or more different CCBs, with each handling one or more of the following seven types of change control. I am not suggesting that you need to implement all of these change control functions. It has been our experience that change control usually involves a combination of these functions.

Implementing change management usually just begins with a couple of these functions.

> ### Getting Started
>
> Most organizations get started with change management by focusing on controlling changes to the production environment, including new releases and configuration changes. Establishing a change advisory board and a group to manage changes to the process should be next on your priority list.

Controlling changes to production is a key place to start.

10.17.1 A Priori

Some organizations establish a disciplined process whereby permission for a change is requested before any actual change to the code is made. I have seen defense contractors who had to describe the changes that they wanted to make and then await approval from a government agency before actually writing the code that implemented the change. In this process, requests for change (RFCs) are usually created and reviewed by the respective change control board. A priori change control usually refers to changes in the code and most often consists of defining requirements followed by the actual designing of the system. The role of configuration management in this case is to track requirements throughout the lifecycle and confirm that all requirements were included in a specific release. Many organizations have a regulatory requirement for tracking requirements, and that often includes a change control function. Tracking source code changes to requirements is important, but changes are often related to environment configuration as well.

10.17.2 Gatekeeping

The most common type of change control, and usually the first to be implemented, is "gatekeeping" change control where the CCB reviews RFCs that will impact production or QA. Usually this involves giving authority to promote a new release of the code into production or QA. Similarly, patches to existing releases are also reviewed by the CCB. This function generally evaluates whether or not there is a risk that the RFC could potentially affect the production or QA environments (which is common for the members of the CCB to have questions about). The CCB is responsible for reviewing the RFC and approving or rejecting it. Traditionally, the CCB will require that all necessary technical experts be present at the CCB meeting, although, in practice, this is often not practical. The ITIL framework has made popular the use of a CAB that consists of experts who can advise on the downstream impact of a particular change. I will discuss how to set up a CAB and why it may need to be separate from the CCB in a later section of this chapter. Closely related are configuration changes, which will be discussed in the next section.

10.17.3 Configuration Control

When the request for change involves a configuration change, the CCB reviews and considers its downstream impact. Configuration changes can have the same impact as a new release. In practice, understanding the interface dependencies often requires specialized knowledge, and these should be reviewed by a board that contains members who possess this expertise. In this case, I believe that the governing body should be called a configuration control board. However, there is some confusion in the terminology commonly used today. Many of the industry standards describe the configuration control board as governing the configuration of a system in terms of the configuration of the source code itself instead of environment configuration. In these standards, a configuration of the code refers to a specific *set of versions of the source code*. I believe that this usage is confusing and a relic of days past when configuration control referred to controlling the version of a Cobol program that was being promoted on a large IBM mainframe computer. Today, most organizations promote a packaged release that may contain thousands of configuration items, including binaries, XML, and many other artifacts. I believe that it makes more sense to use configuration to refer to environment configuration and to use terms like "baseline" or "release" to refer to a specific set of code versions that are promoted as a release. There are many reasons for this. Most releases are packaged, and the entire release package is deployed as a complete package. The last thing that the administrator deploying the release wants to know about is the specific versions of each of the configuration items that make up the packaged release. However, in these same situations, environment configurations such as interprocess communication ports are still managed through the change control process, as they should be. So, if you want port 9444 opened on an application server, then you need to complete a change request and, once approved by the configuration control board, the data security team will modify the iptables to allow interprocess communication on port 9444. In my opinion, true configuration control should refer to interface (runtime) dependencies only.

10.17.4 Emergency Change Control

There will always be times when emergencies require immediate changes. It is likely that the CCB cannot meet at any hour of the day or night to authorize needed emergency changes, and focusing on strict adherence to the regular approval process may result in the company production system being down for an extended period. Any successful change control function must include a well-defined process for managing emergency changes. I recommend that a very senior manager's approval be required for emergency changes and that there be discussion after the event to understand why an emergency change was required in the first place. I have seen situations in which technology professionals abused the emergency change control process to bypass the regular change control process. In such cases, you will be more successful if you have the support of senior management to ensure that everyone follows the process in the best way possible.

10.17.5 Process Change Control

Organizations establish processes to run their operations on a day-to-day basis. These processes are established, and the teams affected are expected to comply. When circumstances require that the processes need to be adjusted and the changes can have wide-ranging impacts upon the entire organization, these changes should be reviewed by a specialized CCB, often called a software engineering process group (SEPG). In this case, the process engineering should be placed in the hands of a change control board that is responsible for reviewing requests for changes to the process. The CCB for process engineering is also tasked with communicating process changes to all affected parties and stakeholders. I believe that the best response to a mistake is to reexamine existing processes and ascertain whether or not additional process steps are warranted. Process improvement should be an organized continuing collaborative effort, and the process CCB can help manage the process engineering effort on an ongoing basis.

10.17.6 E-change Control

E-change control refers to using e-mail or a change control management system to electronically authorize changes. This approach is often used for emergency changes, as described in Section 10.17.4, or in routine changes that do not require review.

10.17.7 Preapproved

We strongly recommend separating out preapproved, or what ITILv3 refers to as *standard*, changes. These changes typically occur on a regular basis and are well understood by the organization. They still need to be traced and communicated, but should ideally be separated from the rest of the *normal* changes.

We often see a management oversight function, which may be its own change control board. This group, responsible for ensuring that the change control process is being followed, performs an important function; it is equally important to ensure that change management is handled consistently across each of the platforms in use throughout the organization.

10.18 Coordinating across the Platform

It is common for change control to focus on one or more platforms and, in many ways, that is actually quite appropriate. Change control for a mainframe follows a particular pattern and certainly a particular culture. Change control in a Linux or Unix environment may be quite different. We prefer to create change management functions that align with the culture of the organization, and often that requires that we align with multiple platforms as well. But the truth is that many releases affect one or more of the organizational tiers. You may have changes on the mainframe that are a dependency for corresponding changes on the Linux or Unix environment. Similarly, changes on the Windows platform may be dependent upon changes on the mainframe, Unix, or Linux machines. Sometimes, you will need to coordinate changes across, as well as within, each of the platforms.

Equally important is coordinating changes across the entire enterprise.

10.19 Coordinating across the Enterprise

Many large organizations have divisions that act as if they are separate companies. In fact, sometimes they are the result of mergers and acquisitions and functionally remain separate for all practical purposes. In banking and other highly regulated industries, there may actually be a requirement to keep specific divisions completely separate. We find that sometimes we are creating change management functions in one division of the company that operates significantly differently from another completely separate division. Typically, we set the same goals for communication and traceability, while establishing procedures that work in alignment with the culture and goals of each specific group. When working across a large organization, you may feel very much like you are working for one or more separate companies. One occupational hazard is trying to operate across organizational structures that have become accustomed to working as separate entities. This can sometimes be challenging, and often we struggle to work within the separate silos, which effectively act like fiefdoms.

10.20 Beware of Fiefdoms

Fiefdoms refer to the feudal lords who acted in a totalitarian fashion in medieval England. We apply this term to organizational structures that operate in a similarly totalitarian fashion. We are all too familiar with this dysfunctional structure and keep a suit of armor to don for just such occasions. Fiefdoms in business settings tend to self-destruct, and you may need to be there to help pick up the pieces and repair the damage. We find that these groups are so well entrenched that you may have little success dealing with them directly. Generally, everyone else is fed up with them, too, and may actually help you bypass them so that you can get things done. Sadly, we have seen fiefdoms in our work with government agencies, groups that put more effort into maintaining their authority than into accomplishing the objectives for which they are responsible.

> #### Change Control in a Government Agency
>
> Some government agencies operate in a remarkably dysfunctional fashion. We have consulted with a few on establishing effective change control. At times, we found individual groups that were completely dedicated to not collaborating and communicating with others. Honestly, we do not pretend to win every battle, and sometimes you have to know when you are outgunned and unlikely to be effective because of a turf war.

Fiefdoms present a strong defense when trying to establish effective communication and collaboration. Fortunately, such dysfunctional behavior is usually the exception and not the rule. We do find that sometimes we need to establish specialized change control.

10.21 Specialized Change Control

We have come across technical functions that required specialized change control in order to operate effectively. One example is within the security realm around firewalls and other security appliances. Sometimes, there is a limit to transparency to ensure that information around existing intrusion detection practices stays within the information security function. When appropriate, we work with stakeholders to establish specialized change control functions with enough interface to the main change control board to ensure sufficient transparency where it is warranted and necessary.

10.22 Vendor Change Control

There are times when you may need to visit vendor sites to ensure that they have sufficient software methodology and IT controls in place to avoid errors and meet your own regulatory compliance requirements. Banks and financial institutions often have to be reminded that using a vendor does not absolve them from having to ensure that their software is written in compliance with all regulatory and audit requirements. Health insurance vendors, for example, must be reviewed to ensure that their controls meet the requirements for Health Insurance Portability and Accountability Act (HIPAA) and Code of Federal Regulations (CFR) 21. We have attended and audited change control meetings at vendor sites to assess existing practices. It is not uncommon to include such compliance as a contractual obligation. Government contractors are often required to achieve and maintain CMMI level 2 (and some level 3) process capabilities. This is often referred to as subcontractor maintenance. Always bear in mind that outsourcing your work does not necessarily outsource your obligations.

Ensuring vendor compliance is essential. We also find ourselves needing to be very aware of service providers' change control policies and procedures.

10.23 SaaS Change Control

Software, Platform, and Infrastructure as Service providers all should maintain clear and transparent change control procedures, especially with regard to backwards capability. We have seen considerable bad behavior in this area with service providers forcing upgrades that caused downstream impact and yet provided no backwards capability.

> ### *Service Providers*
>
> We had an exasperating experience with an Internet service provider (ISP) that we originally used to host the website for our book on CM best practices. We constantly found ourselves being forced to take upgrades, which resulted in problems that we then had to spend time fixing. The ISP rarely planned for backwards compatibility, and the solution to every problem always turned out to be upselling us on more expensive services. The solution to our problem was ultimately to move our website to another service provider.

Beware of service providers who do not provide transparency into their change control processes. You need to identify this as a risk and plan accordingly. We have run into the same issue with upgrading software on electronic devices such as a GPS.

> ### *Upgrading a GPS*
>
> Bob is notoriously challenged with directions and always drives with a GPS. On one occasion, Bob's GPS kept showing a message that the firmware needed to be upgraded. Following the supplier's directions actually broke the GPS. Once again, we found that a well-known company did not have proper upgrade procedures in place. Their suggested solution was to buy a new GPS. Bob has been using the maps application on his iPhone ever since.

Change management requires a consistent focus on continuous process improvement.

10.24 Continuous Process Improvement

Change management is an organizational function that should, and usually does, evolve over time. We try to start with a very light approach to managing change and then only add more controls as necessary. The process itself should be managed, and effective communication is essential for its successful evolution. Try to avoid too much rigidity, which always motivates the team to bypass the process. Constantly evaluate your own effectiveness and focus on identifying, communicating, and mitigating risk.

10.25 Conclusion

Change management is an essential part of the agile ALM. Too often, this function is associated with verbose, painful, and ineffective processes. To foster colleague buy-in and increase compliance, focus your change management approach on both agile and Lean, maximizing its value as a feedback loop and a key driving force for an effective ALM.

Chapter 11

IT Operations

The IT operations organization is responsible for maintaining a secure and reliable production environment. In large organizations, operations often resembles a small army with too many divisions to navigate that is also often held responsible when things go wrong. Developers, working on the bleeding edge of technology, often regard their colleagues in operations as lacking technical skills and ability, which is true in so far as operations resources tend to focus more on the day-to-day running of the systems. In this chapter, we will discuss how to create an effective IT operations group that is aligned with your agile ALM.

11.1 Goals of IT Operations

The goal of IT operations is to ensure that your production systems are secure and reliable. Obviously, service interruptions can adversely affect the organization. If your business is to be successful, then your IT operations must be staffed with skilled resources and your processes must be able to handle the business demands while avoiding errors. We view IT operations to be a strong partner with development, which should also be aligned with agile principles and practices. Although IT operations often has its own terminology, usually based upon the ITIL v3 framework, we have found it helpful to encourage our colleagues in operations to learn agile concepts and terminology. There is much synergy between ITIL and agile and also much value in the operations group being able to share in the journey to agile development. As we have been discussing, DevOps teaches us that IT operations should embrace the goal of effective communication and collaboration with developers and other stakeholders within the organization.

> ### The Agile Service Catalog
>
> Many IT operations groups are heavily focused on practices described in the ITIL v3 framework One of the concepts in ITIL is to offer services through a catalog. We have been encouraging operations to consider providing a service catalog based upon agile principles and described in agile terms. Finding a common language is essential if the organization is to embrace and benefit from DevOps principles and practices.

11.2 Why Is IT Operations Important?

Without effective IT operations, your organization will suffer from service interruptions that will adversely affect your business and profitability. Effective IT operations will empower your organization to be able to meet and exceed your customers' expectations while maintaining a high level of security and reliability. Too many people view IT operations as being an afterthought in the agile ALM. We view operations as being an essential part of an effective and mature agile ALM, especially in organizations that want to embrace DevOps. It is also important for you to decide which of these functions and practices are needed by your organization. You will find that many of them go onto a list to be implemented later as the project matures. Make note of that because the time will come faster than you think, and you want to be prepared to enable the structure you need when you need it.

11.3 Where Do I Start?

Industry standards (e.g., IEEE, ISO) and frameworks (e.g., ITIL, Cobit, CMMI) provide an excellent blueprint for a comprehensive and efficient approach to IT operations. As always, we like to start by assessing existing practices. Start by getting input from key stakeholders on what is being done well and what could be improved. Your assessment should compare current practices to the guidance that you find in the well-respected ITIL v3 framework. Standards from the IEEE and ISO may be important as well, depending upon the industry that your organization falls within. We always start by documenting the existing practices "as-is," then use industry standards and frameworks to define "to-be," and finally create the plan to improve (or establish) the IT operations processes. One other key point should be mentioned here; we always start small. By picking a few easy-to-achieve items to improve first, your team will realize that change is not only possible, but within reach. Once your team realizes that change is attainable, the organizational culture will improve, and you will likely see real progress.

> ### Assessment Tip: Don't Fix What Isn't Broken
>
> I have seen team members who jumped on the process improvement bandwagon a little too quickly, identifying issues and problems that really weren't important to the current team or project. Sometimes, we all have a tendency to focus on challenges and barriers that we experienced on the last project. The most successful process improvement efforts must be relevant, timely, and pragmatic.

There have been many dramatic incidents in the news recently demonstrating the catastrophic results of operations errors, especially in terms of failed upgrades to complex trading systems.

> ### It Happened at Knight
>
> The Knight Capital Group (KCG) was a financial services firm that was engaged in high-frequency trading. KCG suffered a devastating trading loss in August 2012 after an application upgrade mistakenly caused the firm to purchase stock that it did not want, ultimately leading to a trading loss that grew to 460 million dollars. The firm was ultimately acquired by KCG holdings. This was a dramatic example of how an operation upgrade error could literally lead to a company going out of business.

Operations plays a key role in identifying and mitigating sources of risk. Establishing a robust environment monitoring system can provide a much-needed early warning system that makes the difference between detecting and addressing potential problems and suffering a catastrophic outage such as what happened at Knight Capital Group.

As you read through each of these practices, consider whether you will need them now, as the project nears delivery, or when the system is fully in production. You cannot implement every one of these functions overnight. You cannot even fix them all at once, but you can get a comprehensive list of process improvement initiatives and implement them in alignment with your project and organizational needs.

11.4 Monitoring the Environment

Environment monitoring is often a function that is overlooked in many organizations. Understanding runtime dependencies and associated events is actually a key requirement to ensure that your systems do not suffer serious issues that could result in outages. Event monitoring can be an essential first step to preventing such mishaps.

11.4.1 Events

Events can be as simple as alerts associated with finite resources such as memory or as complex as application or operating system resources, often only really understood by the programmer writing the code. We have seen many situations where even senior developers did not fully understand the development frameworks within which they are working. If developers themselves struggle to understand dependencies, then obviously operations must get involved from the beginning of the development process to capture the information needed to support complex IT systems and ensure reliable service.

> ### *Hedge Fund Trading Systems*
>
> We have seen complex trading systems written using frameworks such as Microsoft .Net that have so much complexity that even the developers writing the code did not fully understand the underlying dependencies. When these systems operate under extreme situations, involving millions of transactions, it is often difficult to really understand all of the underlying dependencies. In practice, we identify what we know in advance and then continuously improve our knowledge base, sometimes as the result of an incident or problem.

We find ourselves defining which events need to be monitored based upon what we see developers using to diagnose problems. What is interesting about this knowledge management challenge is that most technology professionals cannot define these constraints up-front, but immediately point them out when troubleshooting—for example, shutting down a Tomcat web application, followed by checking processes to verify that they have in fact terminated as expected, or noting a job that normally takes 20 minutes suddenly is completing in seconds, which may indicate that the job did not actually process successfully. Obviously, identified exceptions should be monitored, but we are more often dealing with the as-yet-undefined events to be monitored. Event monitoring requires an effective DevOps approach in which the operations team works closely with the developers who wrote the code to identify exactly what *can* be monitored versus what should actually be reported in the form of alerts or exceptions.

Two closely related monitoring capabilities are filtering events and correlating events across systems.

> ### *Troubleshooting Disk Space Shortage*
>
> We were troubleshooting an Atlassian system that was showing disk space errors in the logs. A quick check of the application server showed that we had plenty of space, which led us to contact the DBAs, who initially denied that there was any problem with the Oracle database. The problem turned out to be a storage volume on the Oracle database server. We would not have thought to even check on this if we had not first seen errors in the logs. Event monitoring can be a key strategy in identifying problems that must be addressed before more serious problems occur.

Monitoring events is crucial for ensuring reliable systems and avoiding costly service interruption, but sometimes incidents do occur. What matters most is how you identify and address these challenges when they occur.

11.4.2 Incidents

Bad things happen. Organizations succeed or fail based upon their ability to recognize, assess, and respond to unexpected and unplanned outcomes. Successful organizations pull together and really show what they are made of when incidents occur and everyone on the team responds to the call for "all hands on deck." You should always have a dedicated team responsible for organizing the response and communicating with all stakeholders for when incidents inevitably occur. This team is usually called the critical incidence response team (CIRT). The CIRT prepares for incident response by identifying stakeholders who should be notified and those who are on call to immediately address the response itself.

Intimidation and Incident Response

Bob participated in the incident response team for a large New York City–based trading firm. When bad things happened, a very senior manager would chair the incident response team, which consisted of representatives from each of the affected areas. This manager had a strong command-and-control demeanor, often bordering on extreme abruptness. Members of the team were afraid to speak up and offer their views for fear that they would be publicly criticized and even blamed for the outage.

Some incidents can be addressed and resolved in a timely manner. This is usually when the cause of the incident is well understood and the steps required to address the issue are easily identified and assignable to team members to complete. However, sometimes the underlying cause of a problem is not immediately evident. When root-cause analysis is required, a wider and more in-depth process, usually known as *problem management*, is needed.

11.4.3 Problems

Problem management is most often associated with the need for root-cause analysis. Sometimes, the immediate issue has already been addressed and systems are back online, but perhaps there is a concern that the issue could occur again. Sometimes, this is due to faulty hardware that needs to be examined by the vendor—and may even require plans for future upgrades in response to increased capacity demand.

We also see situations where problems with the application occur and there needs to be further investigation to avoid similar problems in the future.

Reboot or Not?

Although trivial, we often see situations where a system is malfunctioning and we suspect that rebooting the machine will solve the problem—and it often does. However, rebooting the machine may also make it harder to evaluate the root cause of the problem and means that we will be back on the CIRT next week again. There is always a judgment call to be made on whether we continue triaging and investigating or we "punt," reboot the machine, and get our users back online. There are no easy answers in these situations. Make sure to capture any available logs, renaming them to avoid confusion. With vendor products, we usually have a script that we run to capture the state of the machine before the reboot, and we send that information to the vendor for evaluation. You may want to create a similar support tool for your application and systems investigation.

Incident and problem support are closely related and usually involve many of the same stakeholders. In some organizations, there is a dedicated production support function which consists of developers who take responsibility for the maintenance and hands-on support for legacy applications, whereas other developers may be engaged in writing the next generation of applications.

11.5 Production Support

Some organizations have a separate function called production support, which is responsible for maintaining and supporting applications that are in use. These systems are often legacy applications requiring specialized skill sets that might be difficult to acquire. Whereas some technology professionals are glad to stay within their comfort zone, even if the legacy technology is older and not as much in demand, many developers avoid working with these older applications. Production support is often responsible for managing application patches and even system upgrades. We have worked with production support engineers who were highly skilled technology professionals with strong technical backgrounds, including software and systems development. It could be argued that production support is inherently a DevOps function because it is usually placed in the operations organization, but staffed with technology professionals who have the skills and expertise to maintain production systems.

We see production support sometimes being outsourced, or even offshored, sometimes with mixed results. Organizations need to make prudent decisions about the value of their legacy applications and the cost of a service interruption.

Who Needs Mainframe Programmers?

We recall one organization that decided there was very little mainframe development going on and therefore decided to eliminate their mainframe programmers, offshoring the entire production support function to a vendor in India. Managers congratulated themselves on their wise decision to save money by eliminating their expensive onshore support analysts who had been with the company for 20+ years. Most of these colleagues took their exit packages and "cried" all the way to the bank. But the real tears were shed the next time an outage occurred and it became evident that the offshore team lacked the skills and expertise to resolve the problems in a timely manner.

Production support should be focused on maintaining the necessary institutionalized knowledge essential for maintaining legacy applications. This information is often highly specialized and difficult to come by. The production support function should also be focused on developing support tools, including environment monitoring, to ensure uninterrupted service. It is not uncommon for the production support team to take responsibility for the creating and maintaining of the deployment pipeline (which we discuss throughout this book, including Chapter 9). Production support relies heavily upon the information that they receive either in terms of enhancement requirements or reports of defects. The help desk is often the first line of defense in gathering this information and reporting problems to the production support team.

11.6 Help Desk

As mentioned, the help desk is often your first line of defense and the difference between your customers having a positive impression of your organization and becoming totally annoyed and determined to take their business elsewhere. Customers and end users can often be a tolerant group of people. Even nontechnical end users understand that sometimes systems go "bump in the night." When bad things happen, the response from the help desk will directly preserve customer satisfaction or conversely lead to frustration and anger. Think about your own experiences contacting a help desk. When you feel that information is gathered professionally and you are being kept well informed, you are much more likely to form a positive impression and tolerate even significant service interruptions. We have seen help desks save the day with their professionalism and customer service.

Help Desks that Satisfy Customers

We have seen help desks that ruled the day by gathering information and quickly informing the customer that they would be compensated for the outage. Most people realize that the complexity of today's technology means that unforeseen things happen; being told that your business is appreciated and that the company will do something to compensate you for your inconvenience can make a huge difference in how people perceive an outage.

It is common for service centers to have a centralized office for the help desk, and there is certainly much value in being able to train and manage your help desk team in a collocated environment. But we also see a growing trend toward virtual help desks, which may be spread across many locations, often taking a follow-the-sun approach, handing off open tickets from one group to another.

11.6.1 Virtual Help Desks

Many organizations create help desks that are physically located in different locations and effectively follow the sun. Sometimes, these help desks are also organized by function. So your DBAs may be located in India, whereas your network operations team is in Europe. Virtual help desks should always provide a common interface and consistent communication, regardless of where they are physically located.

Following the Sun from Jerusalem

Bob likes to work from various locations, especially in the Middle East. On one recent trip, he discovered the advantages of being located in that time zone. Mornings were a convenient time to coordinate with both European and India-based resources, and evenings were dedicated to working with U.S.-based teams. Thanks to afternoon naps, Bob found himself well rested and able to facilitate communication more productively than when he was in the United States. More than a few people commented that it seemed as if he were online around the clock.

Closely related to virtual help desks is remote work. We see that many companies hold on to highly skilled employees by offering them flexible work-from-home arrangements.

11.6.2 Remote Work

Many technology professionals, including help desk analysts, are finding that working from home on a part-time or full-time basis helps them maintain a quality of life that would be inaccessible if they needed to be in the office every day. Working mothers (and dads), too, are among those who often appreciate flexible work arrangements. Salaries are typically lower for remote positions, and we have seen situations where highly skilled employees were given more flexibility to work from home in lieu of more compensation. One colleague sold his home and moved into his vacation home year-round. Obviously, there is some saving on commuting costs and perhaps some other incidentals. There is also, however, the risk of isolation and a lack of face-to-face interactions. There also may be a lack of upward mobility relative to that afforded to colleagues who are in the office and interacting with senior management on a daily basis. We have also heard some folks complain that working remotely on a help desk can get boring and repetitive. Although not yet a widespread practice, we have heard of some organizations experimenting with gaming and virtual worlds to address this challenge.

11.6.3 Virtual World Help Desk

We have reviewed some clever help desk interfaces that transform the monotonous help desk function into participating in a cool virtual world interface and others that simulate games. We see this approach becoming more prevalent in the coming years.

> ### *Avatars Filling In*
>
> Bob had to attend some meetings with a team that was developing standards for virtual worlds. Unfortunately, scheduling made attending the entire session impossible, so sometimes Bob would insert his avatar, who would faithfully attend the meeting, creating a record of the discussions and activities, which could be reviewed later.

There are times when help desk resources do not have the required expertise or perhaps intimate familiarity with the application to solve the problem. At times like these, it may be necessary to have developers participate in the help desk activities.

11.6.4 Developers on the Help Desk

We will discuss help desk escalation later in this chapter. For now, we will note that sometimes help desk staff must reach out to and pull developers into the help desk to provide their intimate knowledge of the system in order to assess, evaluate, and resolve issues. Getting experts involved is important, but ensuring that their expertise becomes part of the permanent knowledge base is where IT process automation becomes a valuable asset.

11.7 IT Process Automation

IT process automation helps capture specific steps to assess, evaluate, and respond to specific help desk requests. This approach helps by capturing and automating the necessary technical steps that are typically performed by skilled specialists who may not always be available to assist with responding to help desk issues and also routine requests. IT process automation is often used to handle common access requests such as unlocking user accounts, but also is useful in dealing with more complicated challenges. Some of these requests can be handled by help desk engineers, but most often IT process automation shows its real value when issues have to be escalated to specialized experts who are not always available. Closely related is knowledge management.

11.7.1 Knowledge Management

With the right experts available, almost any problem can be diagnosed and addressed. The real challenge is that skilled resources may be busy with other tasks or may have gone on to other projects. Help desk personnel need to constantly capture and store the steps necessary to identify issues and then fix them.

> ### The Accidental AIX Admin
>
> Bob was working at an international bank when the entire AIX administration team all decided to resign on the same day. AIX is IBM's robust and complicated open-standards-based Unix operating system, and the AIX environment was rather complicated when it came to supporting

the particularly complex DFS[1] storage systems. Bob had no prior experience with AIX, but was able to perform this function successfully using both the group's internal knowledge base and IBM's extensive knowledge resources, along with their online support services.

IT process automation captures technical steps. Equally important is a workflow automation tool to ensure that processes are repeatable and fully traceable.

11.8 Workflow Automation

Workflow automation can be used to identify the required steps and then guide the full lifecycle of a request, ensuring that all issues are handled in a timely manner while implicitly capturing important information about how issues are evaluated, diagnosed, and addressed.

What Process Do We Need?

We come across situations where even the subject matter experts are not completely certain how the process should be specified. They may also have difficulty verbalizing the steps, including checkpoints, in a specific sequence. This is where workflow automation tools that allow you to visualize the steps and then iteratively improve the process are worth their weight in gold. When in doubt about the exact sequence required, we put up a draft process, as we have learned that many people find it easier to tell us what is wrong with the proposed process than to tell us the required steps up-front.

Workflow automation tools also help by ensuring that issues and requests do not fall through the cracks and are automatically escalated if not acted upon within a specific timeframe. Most importantly, they facilitate traceability and communicating status to all stakeholders.

---

1. Often called the DCE Distributed File System (DFS).

11.9 Communication Planning

Communications planning is a fundamental function within any organization and one that is often not handled effectively. All too often, incidents occur and then we scramble to figure out who should be notified. It is essential to create a comprehensive communications plan to notify key stakeholders affected by specific incidents.

> ### When the Centralized Version Control System Goes Down
>
> We are often consulted when the centralized version control system is impacted by required maintenance or actually has a serious issue that interrupts service. Planned maintenance can often be handled by communicating with project managers, who disseminate information as they see fit, along with similar notifications for other systems. But when systems affecting one or two thousand developers go down, we often have to make an immediate e-mail notification to all impacted stakeholders. Most important is notifying our colleagues as to current status, ETA for problem resolution, and any steps that they may be able to take in the meantime to minimize disruption. Communication is always essential.

Although effective communication is very important, poor communication can be particularly disruptive. In organizations that suffer from dysfunctional communication patterns, immediate powerful interventions need to be taken to address and deal with these behaviors.

11.9.1 Silos within the Organization

The most common problem we come across is groups that have formed a dysfunctional, insular culture where they feel all information should stay within the group. Siloed behavior causes significant disruptions, builds resentment, and represents the antithesis of DevOps principles and practices. Unfortunately, siloed behavior is also very common in many organizations. The key is to understand the root cause of this dysfunctional culture.

> ### DBAs *in Secret*
>
> We have come across database administrators who act as if they are working for a separate company, refusing to communicate and collaborate with their colleagues and insisting that their databases are just fine. We dealt with a systems outage that pointed back at the DB2 database and noticed a couple of files that had mysteriously been modified. We consulted with a couple of the DBAs, who insisted that nothing had been changed. Curiously enough, soon after these discussions, the files were again modified and the database started working again. The problem was fixed as mysteriously as it had occurred. Make sure that you implement our best practices around watching and being notified of unauthorized changes. We knew who had dropped the ball, but our colleague was too embarrassed to admit his mistake.

We come across groups that seem completely unable to communicate with anyone outside of their team. In some cases, the team is in a different location, as is common with offshore support groups. Sometimes, we find that team members are sensitive about their language skills, so they effectively shut down and do not try to communicate. Far worse, we also see teams that have stopped communicating because of an overdomineering manager who is quick to criticize and insists on micromanaging all activities of the team. In these cases, you have two choices. You can either reduce the team's influence or have them focus only on specific well-known tasks (communicating through a workflow automation tool), or you can get the team a new manager.

Effective communication is essential, especially when situations have to be escalated to involve a wider group to help address a problem.

11.10 Escalation

When incidents and problems are not being resolved in a timely manner, then you need to have a plan to escalate the response from the team. Obviously you want to start with the first line of defense, which is typically called level 1.

11.10.1 Level 1

As mentioned, the first line of defense is normally called level 1 and consists of help desk engineers who are capable of quickly assessing challenges and coming up with quick fixes. These professionals are usually quite capable at determining what type of problem has occurred and might even know the solution (often by consulting an internal knowledge base). When a particular issue cannot be resolved immediately, then the level 1 engineer typically packages up the available information and refers to more experienced (and specialized) engineers, who are typically known as level 2 engineers.

11.10.2 Level 2

Aside from being highly skilled, these folks typically have specialized resources available to them, including consulting with the developers who wrote the code, who otherwise may be kept isolated from the end user so that they can focus on developing new features and products. Level 2 engineers are typically specialists and develop a deep level of expertise within a specific area. When the level 2 engineer cannot resolve the issue with all of his or her available resources, then this person typically seeks input from the developers who wrote the code.

11.10.3 Level 3

Level 3 usually refers to the developers who wrote the code and have the most specialized knowledge. They also typically know backdoor techniques to diagnose and resolve problems, often in the form of undocumented RESTful API calls, which produce information that can help diagnose and resolve problems. If nothing else, these folks are usually empowered to identify an issue as being a defect that must be addressed in a future release.

House Calls and Level 3

Bob was an early adopter of a large-scale robust enterprise version control system. But shortly after implementation, a defect was discovered, which went through the vendor's escalation process. Once the problem was identified, the vendor actually flew the developer out to the customer site. The developer explained the exact cause of the issue and handed over a CD-ROM with a fix. Bob was then Cc'd on all correspondence related to fixing this defect in a future release of the product. That was excellent customer service, and a day with the developer resulted in a deep dive into exactly how the product worked, which was valuable for future support. No one was angry that the product had a defect. In fact, everyone was thrilled to discover just how responsive and committed to providing excellent service the vendor was.

Escalation is, by its very nature, an excellent example of taking a DevOps approach. In fact, IT operations needs to adopt DevOps best practices even within the IT operations group itself.

11.11 DevOps

DevOps is discussed in detail in Chapter 12 and is a common theme throughout this book. That said, DevOps within the IT operations bears some specific consideration. We find that many enterprise IT operations groups are so siloed that they really need to focus specifically on improving collaboration and communication within the IT operations organization itself. We also find that operations sometimes goes off and builds infrastructure without involving the development team in the effort. It has been our experience that this usually occurs when the IT operations wants to build up their own expertise before bringing in the development team, often after being criticized by the developers for not being technical enough. We recently saw this lack of communication when the operations team picked one workflow orchestration tool and the developers picked a different tool for deployment automation. Each organization spent time and money implementing a solution without involving the other. Our only recourse was to define one part of the deployment process that would be handled by the operations tool and the other part using the tool chosen by the developers.

11.12 Continuous Process Improvement

IT operations processes must be continuously reviewed and improved. The best approach is to adopt a culture of continuous process improvement. Although many operations organizations will survey the business and end user for feedback, we rarely see them asking the developers for their input, which is most unfortunate. Developers are indeed "customers" of IT operations and should be part of the continuous process improvement initiatives.

We like to encourage assessments of existing practices before trying to improve the way that we do things. As discussed previously, we like to survey stakeholders, asking what is being done well and what could be improved. The assessment should take the form of documenting "as-is" practices and then planning for improvements or "to-be" practices based upon industry best practices. One excellent way to guide this effort is by using industry standards and frameworks.

11.13 Utilizing Standards and Frameworks

Industry standards and frameworks provide an excellent starting point for determining best practices. ITIL v3 has become well regarded by both corporations and government agencies. Depending upon your industry, the ISACA Cobit framework may also be valuable (especially for showing compliance with Section 404 of the Sarbanes-Oxley Act of 2002). Although less popular in business, there are still some areas where the CMMI is well accepted. We acknowledge our preference for using the guidance in the IEEE and ISO standards. (In full disclosure, it should be noted that Bob has had a long-time involvement with the IEEE Software Standards board).

> ### *Who Needs Standards Anyway?*
>
> Too often, our colleagues decide that industry standards and frameworks are not practical. With a little probing, we usually find out that our friends have not spent much time really reading and understanding these documents. Although we agree that sometimes industry standards and frameworks must be tailored for specific situations, we usually find that they are a great starting point, and their use helps to avoid missing key steps that might otherwise be overlooked. They also have the powerful value of being very credible in terms of showing compliance with common regulatory and audit requirements.

The ITIL v3 framework contains comprehensive guidance on establishing all of the functions and processes required for an effective IT operations organization. In the next section we will briefly review the ITIL v3 processes that are most relevant for establishing DevOps practices for application deployment.

11.13.1 ITIL v3

The ITIL v3 release control and validation (RCV) framework describes service management processes. It begins with the need to establish an effective service strategy that leads to a detailed service design, which is described in the service design package. The ITIL v3 framework describes the following RCV processes that transition new services from design into operation:

- Change management
- Service asset and configuration management

- Release and deployment management

- Service testing and validation

- Change evaluation

- Request fulfillment

- Knowledge management

As discussed in Chapter 10, change management processes evaluate, authorize, and implement changes to services that typically occur when you implement new components or change existing components. Change management processes are designed to

- Evaluate potential downstream effects from a change

- Reduce risk

- Improve communication to all stakeholders

The change advisory board (CAB) is the governing body that reviews each proposed change. Change management drives the entire release control and validation process. Effective change management balances risk with the need to implement new changes that deliver value to a business and make it competitive. Change management relies on workflow automation and accurate, up-to-date information on assets and configuration management baselines.

Service asset and configuration management (SACM) processes manage the software assets and maintain accurate information about configuration items. These processes create and manage baselines that track the status of changes to each configuration item. SACM processes provide all of the other processes and functions, such as the CMDB and the CMS, with accurate and up-to-date information on the status of configuration baselines.

Each software asset needs an owner who is responsible for the asset and can identify the subject matter experts who can accurately assess and evaluate the potential downstream effect of a change.

It is important to understand the interfaces between configuration items. SACM tracks changes to baselines. This tracking ability is essential for traceability. For many organizations, the tracking is required by compliance with federal regulatory and audit controls. With up-to-date information, it is much easier to operate the business, to ensure agility to implement desired changes, to conduct change planning, and to respond to incidents when they occur.

In many ways, SACM is the "glue" that holds together the other release control and validation functions. The activities in SACM include the following:

- Management and planning
- Configuration identification
- Configuration change control
- Status accounting
- Verification and audit

The software configuration management plan (SCMP) provides the strategy for how to handle all of the activities required for successful application build, package, and deployment phases of code development. The planning section can simply specify the schedule for the release iterations, or it can specify every aspect of the release and deployment process. The SCMP traditionally consists of four classic functions: configuration identification, status accounting, configuration change control, and configuration audit. Specify the following information for each of these four functions:

- *Configuration identification:* Specifies a naming convention for each configuration item and helps ensure that you select the correct configuration items for each release.

- *Configuration change control:* Includes specific procedures to manage changes to configuration items, to manage new releases, and to retire configuration items.

- *Status accounting:* Documents the path of a configuration item from its initial creation to end of life. Status accounting includes the status of configuration baselines and configuration items as they are developed.

- *Verification and audit:* Helps ensure that the correct configuration items are deployed. The audit information can be independently verified. Organizations depend on well-defined processes to manage release and deployment.

RDM processes focus on the activities required to build, package, deploy, and test the new services. RDM creates detailed plans that help ensure that configuration items can be successfully built and tested. The plans emphasize automated procedures that are repeatable and verifiable. RDM makes it easier for stakeholders to understand what is being done and increases the likelihood that they are satisfied with the results as the service transitions from design to operations.

RDM prepares the build, including automated procedures, and helps ensure that testing is conducted and that the test environments are coordinated. RDM processes include tasks related to the initial pilot and early life support of the service that is being transitioned into operation. After the RDM verifies these steps, it reviews and closes the transition effort.

Service validation and testing helps ensure the IT service is fit for purpose in that it matches the requirements included in the design and also that it is fit for use in that it meets the requirements that are needed for its intended use.

The service validation and testing process also helps ensure that the service design package correctly specifies the requirements. In addition, it helps ensure that the service provides value to the business, that it performs well in production, and that it meets the target level of quality.

This process focuses on the activities required to

- Create and validate test plans
- Manage the test plans and test environments
- Conduct the test
- Verify the results
- Communicate the results to stakeholders
- Create test reports
- Evaluate the test according to exit criteria

After the test phase, you need to evaluate the change to ensure it delivers value to the business. Change evaluation helps us determine whether the change meets the client's needs in terms of how the updated code is to be used and whether it delivers the expected level of service. Change evaluation ensures that you understand the intended and unintended effects of a change. Change evaluation monitors the predicted performance and manages risk.

Request fulfillment is part of operations and focuses on the process to complete routine requests. Request fulfillment streamlines the completion of routine requests to free resources to focus on more demanding and nonroutine requests.

11.13.2 Knowledge Management

The lifecycle processes covered under release control and validation provide the essential knowledge that is necessary to support reliable and effective services.

The knowledge management process captures a wide array of information that can help drive the entire process. The configuration management database and the configuration management system are part of the service knowledge management system.

The ITIL v3 framework is certainly a well-defined and widely accepted framework. Many organizations are also obliged to follow the guidance in the ISACA Cobit framework.

11.13.3 ISACA Cobit

The ISACA Cobit framework consists of high-level IT controls, including change and configuration management. The control objectives provide guidance on how to establish many of the same controls as described in the ITIL v3 framework and the IEEE and ISO standards. Cobit is most closely associated with compliance with Section 404 of the Sarbanes-Oxley act of 2002, although we have had healthcare companies tell us that the guidance is also well aligned with HIPAA and CFR 21.

We view these well-documented industry best practices as a key starting point for defining how your IT controls should be established to guide all aspects of your IT operations organization.

11.14 Business and Product Management

IT operations must keep a constant focus on the business and product management objectives, especially in terms of understanding risk management and the need for fast and reliable service. There are many times when a discussion with the business and product management professionals can provide a specific perspective that may alter the approach we take to provide IT operations services. The most common adjustment is that business would often prefer to take risks than slow down the rate of change. If the risks are well understood and communicated, we often find that our business and product colleagues are the first to encourage us to take calculated risks that can result in greater profitability.

> ### *Understanding the Risk of Not Making a Change*
>
> IT operations is always focused on ensuring that services are reliable and can operate without service interruptions. Discussions with business and product professionals often highlight the outside competitive pressures

that may justify taking a measured risk from time to time. The key to success is always to ensure that the risk is well understood and communicated to all stakeholders.

Business and product management professionals provide valuable insights. It is also essential for IT operations to have strong technical leaders to help interface across the organization.

11.15 Technical Management

Strong technical managers can provide the glue that helps the team focus and operate effectively. We view this role as being analogous to the conductor of an orchestra. Technical managers need to provide leadership and coordination and ensure tasks are completed successfully. Closely related to, and often combined with technical leadership, is IT operations management, which is focused on service delivery and ensuring effective communication across the entire IT operations organization.

11.16 IT Operations Management

The IT operations management function helps ensure that individual teams are successfully working together to guarantee effective service delivery and especially excellent communication across the organization. IT operations should also be interfacing with managers in other parts of the organization, including development, information security, business, QA, and testing. Although IT operations overseas effective day-to-day activities, we also need to establish the rules of the road, and that is where operations controls become an important consideration.

11.17 IT Operations Controls

Controls are general guidelines or rules that are established to avoid costly mistakes, often developed in compliance with audit and regulatory requirements. We will discuss establishing IT controls further in Chapter 16, but in this section, we discuss how controls affect IT operations.

IT operations controls need to be both well understood and reasonable, or else the entire organization will look for every opportunity to bypass them. IT controls should be the guardrails that everyone is glad to see put in place, but do not necessarily slow the efforts to be successful and compete with other companies in the same space. One example of an IT control is the *segregation of duties*, where the person who writes the code should never be the person who compiles, packages, and deploys the code. Implemented properly, this IT control is viewed as being reasonable and effective.

Teach Me Your Job

Segregation of duties requires that some knowledge be transferred from one person to another. We find that this is exactly where we identify steps that might have been missed in the documented procedures. We also find that many resist at first, but then are relieved when they can transfer support duties to the operation team, which is staffed to provide such services on a 24/7 basis.

Operations controls are essential, as is maintaining a secure and reliable physical environment.

11.17.1 Facilities Management

IT operations is also responsible for maintaining the physical environment. This consideration must include security and business continuity, among other factors.

Katrina in the Basement

We know of one international bank that had their offices near a major waterfront. When Hurricane Katrina occurred, it suddenly became apparent that the entire operations center could be completely underwater. The lack of awareness and disaster planning for flooding in a coastal region was astonishing.

The facilities must be maintained in a highly available and reliable way. The consideration must be in place for maintaining applications, including middleware and shared services.

11.18 Application Management

IT operations must usually organize support structures such that applications management is handled by a dedicated team, similar to (or perhaps the same as) the production support group discussed earlier in this chapter. Applications management within IT operations focuses on understanding how the application operates under full load in a production environment. We often see that the applications management team understands how the system operates in the real world in more depth than the developers who initially wrote the code.

11.18.1 Middleware Support

Understanding middleware typically requires specialized knowledge and is usually its own specialized function. Examples of middleware can include application queue management and web application servers such as Tomcat or WebSphere. We find that the complexity of these technologies requires that these support engineers have specialized skills, and the greatest challenge is often a lack of backups to the primary subject matter expert.

11.18.2 Shared Services

Shared services can include QA and testing services, which will be discussed in Chapter 20. Build and release engineering services are also typical shared services that should be provided consistently across the organization. Your organization can define other shared services that align with your business and technical requirements.

11.19 Security Operations

Security operations is a particularly important consideration from an IT operations perspective. We view security as being a full lifecycle endeavor. You cannot tack on security at the end of the application lifecycle, and we will discuss continuous security in Chapter 12. IT operations is responsible for access controls and ensuring that systems are configured to be secure and reliable. Just as we recommend standards and frameworks for establishing IT controls, so, too, do we recommend using well-respected security-related standards and frameworks.

11.19.1 Center for Internet Security

In previous engagements, we have used the consensus-based standards available from the Center for Internet Security (CIS) to guide the configuration of operating systems, including Linux. These standards provide short code examples that demonstrate exactly how to configure the operating system in a secure and reliable way. It turns out that it is very easy to use this code to create environment monitoring scripts to ensure that the configurations are maintained and are not changed, thereby compromising the security of the systems. Special considerations must be made when outsourcing IT operations.

11.19.2 Outsourcing

Outsourcing can create significant risks that need to be identified and addressed. Just because you are outsourcing work does not mean that you are no longer responsible for ensuring that proper security controls are maintained. We have been compelled to examine vendor controls, including site visits and audits. Reviewing vendor controls is also a consideration when using cloud-based resources.

11.20 Cloud-Based Operations

IT operations takes on some special considerations when working with cloud-based resources. We will discuss the agile ALM in the cloud in Chapter 17, but in this section we point out that the IT operations team must adjust its processes and functions for the special needs of the cloud. This includes understanding service-level agreements and exactly what tasks will be handled by the organization's IT operations versus those handled by the cloud-based provider. One key strategy that we will discuss in Chapter 17 is ensuring that you are never locked into one specific provider.

11.20.1 Interfacing with Vendor Operations

Interfacing with vendor operations can be a difficult task. Unless your organization has established a very strong relationship with a vendor, you may find that your operations team does not have sufficient transparency into vendor operations to ensure that your service will not be impacted. This is a common problem. Organizations typically choose vendors to save money, although you may find, in this case, that you get what you pay for.

11.21 Service Desk

The service desk is the customer-facing function that manages requests typically based upon a service catalog. In practice, we find many organizations struggle to maintain service desks that are able to meet their objectives without frustrating and alienating their end users. The dysfunctional relationship that we observe is sometimes due to the service desk having a different approach and terminology that does not match the business and development organizations, who are often working on an agile transformation. We view agile principles and practices to be a perfectly appropriate approach to guiding IT operations, including those using the guidance found in the ITIL v3 framework. Our recommended approach is to have the service catalog embrace agile terminology and service delivery managers in place to ensure that IT operations can align with the business and development requirements.

Aligning the service desk with the organizational culture is the first step required and begins with the centralized service desk function.

11.21.1 Centralized

The centralized service desk provides an essential interface to request services from the IT operations organization. We have seen many instances where users struggle to interface with the service desk, including developers trying to request resources they need in order to meet their goals and deliverables. Whereas developers, business users, QA, and testing are all focusing on agile principles and practices, IT operations needs to evolve to have terminology that is aligned with the rest of the organization.

> ### *Agile Principles in IT Operations*
>
> We have been working with IT operations organizations to provide a service catalog that is aligned with agile development. This can be a bit of a challenge for IT operations, but is a natural and absolutely necessary evolution.

Centralized service desks are often virtual organizations, a situation that does present some challenges.

11.21.2 Virtual

We see service desks taking a virtual approach instead of trying to collocate their teams. This does create some challenges similar to those we discussed earlier in the chapter with regard to help desks. Similarly, we find specialized service desks also have specific requirements.

11.21.3 Specialized

It is common for IT operations organizations to have specialized service desks, especially if the technology requires specific expertise and access. Specialized service desks are also closely related to requests for vendor services.

11.21.4 Vendor Escalation

Organizations that embrace Software as a Service (SaaS) and Platform as a Service (PaaS) often have to manage service requests through the vendor. Although users may initially reach out directly to the SaaS or PaaS provider, when things do not go well, IT operations typically needs to get directly involved by escalating requests to the vendor.

11.22 Staffing the Service Desk

Staffing the service desk requires that you find resources who have the requisite technical expertise and the demeanor to interface with end-user requests. One strategy is to make time on the service desk a tour of duty that leads to other opportunities, which has the advantage of ensuring that everyone on the team understands how requests come in and the need to satisfy one's customers, whether they be internal business colleagues or the developers trying to enhance and upgrade our systems.

> ### *Outsourcing the Service Desk*
>
> We have seen some organizations outsource the service desk function. In some cases, employees of the firm were transferred to the vendor taking

on the role of the service desk. In other cases, we have heard of significant resentment and a sense of helplessness on the part of the remaining staff. The service desk is a very important function, and having competent qualified resources is an important consideration.

IT operations also needs to manage incident and problem management.

11.23 Incidents and Problems

We discussed incident and problem management within the context of change management in Chapter 10. IT operations should have service delivery management resources to ensure that incident and problem management is handled successfully across the IT operations organization.

11.24 Knowledge Management

Capturing and managing knowledge is a key requirement in IT operations. There are many areas where specialized knowledge should be documented and reviewed with key stakeholders. Still, we find that many operations organizations struggle with capturing essential knowledge, a fact that contributes to development's view that IT operations staff are less technically skilled than other technology professionals in the organization. We consistently apply a DevOps approach to enhancing communication and collaboration, looking to consistently capture, review, and disseminate essential technical information.

11.25 Conclusion

IT operations performs a vital service ensuring secure and reliable systems. Although we fully support making use of industry standards and frameworks to establish and evolve IT operations processes and function, we also believe that agile and Lean principles should be embraced to align IT Ops with the culture of the rest of the organization.

Chapter 12

DevOps

DevOps is a set of principles and practices intended to help development and operations collaborate and communicate more effectively. DevOps is truly taking the industry by storm and, in some circles, reaching almost mythical proportions. I hear folks suggesting that DevOps can help solve almost any issue, which given the versatility of its cross-functional approach, is a view that has some merit, but some groups are losing sight of what this methodology is all about and how it can really help us implement the ALM. Unfortunately, some folks are also using DevOps to justify some very bad practices, such as allowing developers access to production machines, in some cases in violation of federal regulatory requirements for a segregation of duties. We absolutely believe that you can enjoy the great benefits of DevOps and still achieve your audit and regulatory requirements. In fact, we find that there are tangible benefits in adhering to regulatory and audit requirements if we approach them with a goal of creating right-sized processes and procedures that minimize risk and help ensure quality. DevOps should not be interpreted as all things to all people, but it does have a fairly broad focus and a great deal of potential to positively drive the entire application lifecycle. Make sure that you consider the maturity of your DevOps framework while also focusing on the primary goal of DevOps, which is to provide a fast and reliable deployment framework.

12.1 Goals of DevOps

The goal of DevOps is to ensure that we can reliably deploy code as often as evolving business needs require. DevOps has a strong focus on ensuring that there is a completely automated way to deploy changes, either in terms of systems configuration or application upgrades. DevOps also has a strong goal that development and operations work together collaboratively as a cross-functional and highly effective team. DevOps, by design, brings us both speed and reliability.

213

12.2 Why Is DevOps Important?

DevOps is important because it helps prevent mistakes leading to systems glitches and outages that have adversely affected many organizations, often in high-profile incidents that have tarnished the reputation and profitability of the firm. When DevOps is implemented successfully, organizations enjoy a significant competitive advantage, delivering business functionality and fixing defects in a rapid and secure way. DevOps enables agile development while improving both quality and productivity.

12.3 Where Do I Start?

We often find ourselves called in to help with implementing DevOps right after bad things have happened—usually, a failed release or serious cybersecurity incident that could and should have been prevented, or at least detected, by DevOps best practices. As always, we like to focus on assessing current practices, especially with regard to existing communication patterns, and incidents that can be attributed, in whole or in part, to less-than-effective communication and collaboration.

We always ask teams to explain exactly how they would verify that the correct code is running in production and to explain their procedures to detect unauthorized changes.

The call for DevOps sometimes comes after a serious application outage, often as a result of a failed systems upgrade or configuration change.

The CTO Looking for Answers

We often find ourselves in conversations with CTOs and other senior IT executives who are looking for a better overall approach, one that will address current challenges within their team. Such discussions usually consider how long systems should take to be updated and then evolve to addressing the intergroup dynamics that are impacting the performance of the technology teams.

After we discuss what DevOps is really all about, we are usually asked to describe what is involved with implementing improved application build, package, and deployment.

> ### *The Answer Within*
>
> The most fascinating aspect of our work is really just how often we find that the best solutions and suggestions come directly from people who are closest to the problem. Although we bring to the organization a comprehensive view of industry best practices, we find that very often we are simply providing a voice to technology professionals who are already in the organization and who have been trying to get their voices heard for a long time. It appears that we provide a filter to help senior management understand which views should be given consideration. Nonetheless, we have learned to listen carefully for good ideas from folks who have been trying to get their voices heard for a long time.

The assessment results in a document that explains the current practices ("as-is") and also specifies a target improved state ("to-be"), usually based upon industry standards (e.g., ISO, IEEE) and frameworks (e.g., ITIL, Cobit, CMMI). The best step is to implement the process improvements.

12.4 How Do I Implement DevOps?

Implementing DevOps must include both a strong focus on communication and a complete review of the systems and applications deployment technology, tools, and procedures. As always, we believe that you must first comprehensively assess your current practices and then compare them to industry best practices and afterwards create a reasonable plan to help your team move from where you are today to exactly where you need to be to meet your current and future business requirements. Implementing DevOps is both a culture and a technology shift. The new focus will be on automating everything that you do and ensuring that mistakes are minimized while speeding up the rate of change. DevOps moves from the team big-bang deployments to smaller, well-rehearsed rapid deployments that are repeatable and generally a lot faster.

> ### *The Results We Expect*
>
> We usually find that improving the application, build, package, and deployment can take a process from a two-week timeframe down to

> two hours with significant improvements in terms of reliability and quality. We also often hear that teams are confident that they could deploy every day without making mistakes.

To really understand DevOps, you need to appreciate the inherent conflict between developers and operations.

12.5 Developers and Operations Conflict

Developers and operations professionals have inherently different views and perspectives. Providing new features and innovations that meet the demands of the business is the goal of not only the application developers, but also just about everyone engaged in the software development process. The operations group has a very different view, which is focused on ensuring that systems are completely reliable and always available. Developers move us forward with rapid speed, often exhibiting what can seem like a reduced focus on caution with regard to avoiding costly defects and challenges. Developers see the system as working. Our operations colleagues are often in the role of telling us to slow down, pay attention to the road ahead, and above all avoid any possible risks that might cause a systems incident or outage. Ops is focused on reliability and security, whereas Dev wants to constantly update the application with new features and capabilities.

Although the perspectives of developers and operations often clash, both groups possess remarkable capabilities, and when they collaborate, organizations benefit greatly from the synergies of their talents and accomplishments.

12.6 Developers and Operations Collaboration

As DevOps evangelists, we help developers and operations professionals share their skills, expertise, and unique approaches, which yields amazing results. We find that developers are excellent at learning new technologies and building prototypes, but must rely upon their operations counterparts to ensure that there are repeatable processes and that the systems themselves will be supportable in production usage. Developers typically spend many months learning new technologies and then make critical decisions on their technical approach. They write the code and understand the intimate details of how the system was constructed. In contrast, operations understands how the application will behave in production under real work conditions. Our focus is on promoting collaboration, resulting in a more holistic understanding of the system, which ultimately benefits development, operations, and the business and end users.

The analogy of mountain climbing can be useful in understanding the DevOps perspective.

The Trip Up the Mountain

We frequently find ourselves describing DevOps in terms of mountain climbing. Developers excel at running up the mountain with amazing speed and agility. No mountain is too steep and no terrain is too challenging. The operations professional follows the developer up the mountain, noting the exact path and ensuring that others can easily run up the same mountain each and every time—without tripping.

Operations engineers are often excited to learn from developers, especially when it improves their technical skills. We sometimes see developers being surprised by how much their operations colleagues actually know and can contribute to the collaboration. Bob learned this lesson regarding wisdom from Ops while still in college at his part-time job doing research into blindness and disability.

First Lessons from an Operations Guy

Back when Bob was in college he worked as a research assistant at the American Foundation for the Blind (AFB). This nonprofit organization had a very high need for automation, but a very low budget for modern equipment, which gave Bob an opportunity to work with punch cards on a very old IBM mainframe. The computer operator would come over and look over Bob's shoulder while he was debugging his Fortran statistical programs. This gentleman knew how to rack tapes and handle punch cards, but had no real programming background. Still, the process of explaining the code always led Bob to find the bugs hiding in the program. Even when there is a huge disparity in the level of technical expertise, collaboration between operations and developers can be highly productive.

We have seen many other circumstances where development and operations were highly effective once they were brought to the table and agreed to collaborate.

> ### *Document Review*
>
> We had a deadline to take possession of documents that described the application deployment procedures. One part of this effort was the installation and configuration of some important systems software. The developers were supposed to write up comprehensive instructions, which were long overdue. Bob managed to get the developers to share a draft of their document on condition that he would help them edit and update the document. (Aware that Bob is an editor, they were appreciative of this assistance). Bob managed to convince them to allow him to schedule a review session to go over the "draft" document with the operations team. The operations team was glad to participate and helped out by completing the edits and even added some paragraphs from other similar documents. The development team moved from being afraid to show the incomplete draft to being thrilled that the operations team actually gave them significant help in getting the work completed!

Many organizations find themselves in a very demanding business environment with competitive pressures and other challenges.

12.7 Need for Rapid Change

DevOps is driven by an insatiable thirst for constant change. Years ago, businesses were often satisfied with changes to systems every few months, but expectations today are much higher. Organizations that cannot adapt to the need for rapid change are simply outgunned by other companies that have managed to become more agile, and consequently, more capable of promptly responding to and satisfying shifting business needs. Bigger companies are finding themselves having to make a choice between adapting to the new world and seeing their market share erode as more nimble competitors siphon off their customers. Some organizations find themselves having to restructure to become more competitive—effectively transforming themselves into many smaller autonomous units, with each acting as if they are a separate company. We have heard many people speak of sizing a team in terms of pizza delivery.

> ### The Two-Pizza Theory
>
> We often hear of teams that try to structure themselves into autonomous units, consisting of only eight to ten team members. The analogy goes that a team should stay under a size sufficient to be fed by two pizzas. Let's assume that they are big pizzas consisting of eight slices each. This means that the largest group should never exceed this eight- to ten-member limit.

Although the two-pizza theory sounds catchy, we believe that the underlying premise is the ability of the team to effectively communicate and collaborate. Some business problems cannot really be divided into such small chunks that they can be solved in a timely manner by such a small team—not to mention the inconvenient reality that coordinating across many small teams is not without its own problems of complexity. We saw one large organization enthusiastically take this approach, oblivious to the fact that their customers were unable to benefit from many small apps that were not well integrated. We conclude that the size of the team should have more to do with the complexity of the problem and its suitability to be deconstructed into smaller units versus how many pizzas you get delivered. Of much greater importance than team size is how you handle knowledge delivery.

12.8 Knowledge Management

The effective management and sharing of complex technical knowledge is a crucial aspect of DevOps. We find that the technology industry today is largely composed of specialists, who, although highly capable and accomplished, often have rather narrow areas of technical knowledge. DevOps can help discover, capture, and share all of the technical knowledge that exists throughout the organization. In our highly technical world, we find many areas of expertise are required to keep systems running smoothly; it takes considerable time to master languages, frameworks, and methodologies. Often, we find that silos develop across the organization to centralize specialized knowledge, but at the same time, it also leaves many technology professionals without the benefit of a wider "systems" view that is crucial for troubleshooting and understanding how the system behaves as a whole. Systems administrators often have their own view and even specialized lifecycles governing their work. Too often, DBAs and middleware administrators are equally as siloed, adversely affecting the creation of a comprehensive view of system architecture. DevOps seeks to enhance communication and collaboration across the organization to maximize sharing information, while still maintaining the existing organizational structures, which are often there for a good reason.

We would certainly be remiss if we did not acknowledge that some DevOps thought leaders actually want to eliminate organizational structures altogether, a practice that is more feasible when you are building your own Internet startup from your dorm room than dealing with today's large firms.

DevOps from the Dormitory

We hear many of our colleagues preaching the values of having teams handle all aspects of building, testing, deploying, and supporting their code throughout the lifecycle of the system. Having developers write and then deploy their own code to production may work fine when it is just three guys in a dorm room creating their first Internet startup. However, we view this approach as being impractical, if not downright impossible, for others, especially in large banks, healthcare firms, and other industries that have strict regulatory requirements. Our approach to DevOps seeks not to eliminate organizational structures, but rather to eliminate the negative impact of siloed behavior, while still allowing larger organizations to pass their audit and regulatory requirements.

The main building block for success is the cross-functional high-performance team.

12.9 The Cross-Functional Team

Cross functional teams are the very best aspect of taking a DevOps approach. With cross-functional teams, highly skilled professionals from different disciplines are temporarily assigned to work together as a team and collectively held responsible for the results. In practice, we find that these teams consist of developers, operations deployment engineers, testers, and usually a business subject matter expert. These folks still report into the organizations from which they come, but are temporarily assigned to the cross-functional team on either a full-time or part-time basis. The cross-functional team is able to avoid many dysfunctional behaviors that we often see when technology professionals from different parts of the organization interact.

Eliminating the Volleyball Game

Many groups operate in a fashion where they handle their own required tasks and then "throw it over the net" to the other team for the next step. This is often a very dysfunctional way of doing things and typically results in bickering over who is responsible for the next step. The groups act like they are in competition with each other. A cross-functional team model puts the responsibility for success on the entire team, thereby eradicating the competitive dysfunctional us-versus-them mind-set causing these "volleyball" behaviors.

To really understand and deal with disruptive organizational behaviors, we often find ourselves looking at how the managers of different groups interact.

Like Father, Like Son

Unsurprisingly, we often observe teams modeling poor behaviors that they see from their managers. Employees obviously are incented to act in a way that benefits their team and pleases their direct supervisor. Sometimes, we see managers who do not get along, and their teams mirror the same dysfunctional relationship. Sadly, this often goes on for a long time and can result in disruptive communication patterns and highly dysfunctional behaviors. There are rarely any easy answers in these situations when dysfunctional behavior is solidly entrenched in the organization. So any minimal progress should be noted and applauded.

DevOps is of great value to agile development, and, truthfully, the rapid nature of agile development makes DevOps an absolute necessity. However, this does not necessarily restrict DevOps to agile.

12.10 Is DevOps Agile?

The simple answer to the question of whether or not DevOps is strictly agile is no. We have employed DevOps successfully in many waterfall environments. Getting development and operations to collaborate and communicate effectively is imperative, regardless of whether the team is embracing agile, waterfall, or any other methodology. However, agile development, with its focus on rapid iterative development, cannot possibly survive without DevOps and its well-respected capabilities to streamline application build, package, and deployment.

DevOps does not depend upon agile, but agile depends heavily upon DevOps. The successful implementation of DevOps benefits greatly from taking an agile approach. When we implement DevOps, we do benefit greatly from agile principles, so, in that sense, it is true that the DevOps transformation is greatly enhanced by agile. But, rest assured that even if you are in a waterfall organization or have a project that must adhere to a waterfall methodology, DevOps will absolutely still provide great benefits. Also, please keep in mind that enlightened waterfall enthusiasts, echoing Winston Royce's original description, also consider their methodology to be iterative. Those who portray waterfall as not being iterative are almost always simply looking to discredit this approach.

> ### *Waterfall When Required*
>
> We conducted a CM assessment for a telecom engineering firm that created firmware and circuit chips for highly specialized communications applications. When asked why they were not using fixed timebox sprints, they explained that each circuit chip takes at least three months to manufacture. There was no way to test half a chip, so their lifecycle had to be three months, whether they liked it or not. Missing a key requirement meant that they had to start from the beginning. We worked on many process improvement efforts, but changing the duration of their lifecycle was just not an option.

12.11 The DevOps Ecosystem

Every organization exists within an ecosystem, and successfully implementing DevOps depends largely upon practices being aligned successfully within the existing structures. When we consider how best to implement DevOps, we spend considerable time understanding the existing organizational culture and history. We dig deeply into the communications patterns and existing means of operating. We also look outside the organization to the competitive pressures, economic environment, and the regulatory forces that may affect the business. DevOps will only succeed if you take this holistic "systems" view of the organization.

A fundamental aspect of this effort is to understand how each group operates and where in the software and systems lifecycle they are involved, as well as its interactions with other groups. We customarily try to help each group get involved earlier in the lifecycle, a practice referred to as *moving the process upstream*.

12.12 Moving the Process Upstream

Moving the process upstream means that the team gets involved earlier in the lifecycle. Traditional IT projects focused on determining requirements and deciding what should be built in the beginning of the software or systems lifecycle. Having only some stakeholders involved in the beginning means that some decisions will be made that impact others, who will only learn of these decisions later in the lifecycle when things are pretty much locked in. On the other hand, obviously, you cannot reasonably involve everyone up-front. Pragmatic choices have to be made, but increasingly we find that including certain key stakeholders up-front results in higher quality and increased productivity.

QA and testing definitely emerge as one of the disciplines that should be involved from the very beginning, especially since it has long been established that you cannot add quality in later.

> ### *Testing Moved Upstream*
>
> Obviously, you cannot do much about testing a system up-front until you have actually written the code. Test-driven development (TDD) focuses on writing test cases before the actual code, although this is often limited in scope. What we see that is far more dramatic is the value of designing the testing strategies and test cases up-front and giving these artifacts to the developers for their review. When we do this, we often find our development team saying, "Oh wow—is that what you wanted the system to do? Why didn't you say so?"

Moving upstream is sometimes called "left-shift."

12.12.1 Left-Shift

Left-shift refers to bringing in stakeholders earlier in the lifecycle. For example, we always try to bring operations into the deployment process from the very beginning because it is an extremely effective way to implement robust deployment pipelines. The alternative is to allow development to handle their own deploys in the beginning of the software development lifecycle, in what are usually called the *lower environments* (e.g., development test and integration).

Recently, we came across a scenario that we did not expect whereby operations developed an approach without bringing in development early enough in the process. We have decided to call the requirement for Ops to include development as *right-shift*.

12.12.2 Right-Shift

As a general rule, operations groups build their own tools and processes to manage the production environment. Recently, we came across a scenario where the operations group developed an essential infrastructure tool that affected the way in which software would be handed off from development to operations. This approach made quite a few assumptions about development, some of which were valid, and others that turned out to be less than accurate. The Ops team had kept quiet about what they were doing until the work was completed. From our conversations, we realized that the operations managers were not confident in how much they would be able to accomplish and therefore decided not to say anything until the work was done rather than be judged poorly for not delivering what they had said they would.

We now refer to "right-shift" as the need for operations to involve development in their efforts to build well-designed infrastructure to transition software and systems from development to production operations.

There are two key lessons here. The first is that technology professionals need to feel safe when doing their work. As Deming reminds us, we need to "drive out fear." The operations team kept their development counterparts in the dark because they were afraid of criticism if they didn't measure up to expectations. The second is that stakeholders need an opportunity to give their input when systems that will affect them are being designed.

DevOps should always involve both development and operations (and often other stakeholders such as QA, testing, and information security as well). In practice, we see much DevOps-related activity going on exclusively in development.

12.13 DevOps in Dev

DevOps in Dev refers to efforts by the development team to create automated application build, package, and deployment without any involvement from their operations colleagues. This is a common approach, and we would be remiss if we failed to discuss this reality.

When DevOps is exclusively in Dev, developers are focused entirely on build, package, and deployment to development test environments. This is usually accomplished through the use of a continuous integration server and often fails to adequately consider the requirements for deployment to the upper environments, including user acceptance testing (UAT), staging, and production. Some development teams are capable of building automation that can be seamlessly run by the operations team, but, by and large, we view DevOps as requiring collaboration between development and operations.

The real danger of DevOps in development is that the operations team will never reach a level where they can be effective at application deployment.

Outgunned and Error Prone

We worked with a bank in which the application deployment team was staffed by operations engineers who had very limited skills. No members of the Ops team could even write automated scripts, and the developers had long given up on these folks being able to really handle any complex technical tasks. The developers would come up with simple procedures and instructions as best they could, but sadly mistakes were common and often adversely impacted production systems.

Writing deployment automation is a key requirement for DevOps and should be treated as a full development effort.

12.14 DevOps as Development

Automating the deployment is often a full-scale development effort. Sometimes, teams consider this up-front and create applications that can be deployed effectively using automated procedures. But, more often than not, we find that we need to create automated procedures as part of a full development effort.

In these situations, we usually find it advisable to start by watching the developers doing the deployments to development test environments using manual procedures or perhaps automated scripts within the continuous integration servers. We almost always approach this effort as an agile iterative project whereby we start with the existing procedures, which may be less than ideal, and then iteratively work to improve the process by automating each successive step.

We call our approach the three-step process.

Three Steps to an Automated Build, Package, and Deploy

Getting to a "pushbutton" deploy often takes a little more effort than just writing a script or two. We find ourselves frequently handling this in three distinct steps. The first is to observe and document existing manual procedures. We then start scripting, with the goal of avoiding errors, even though manual intervention is typically required in terms of looking at a screen and hitting the Enter key. We call this interim step "attended automation." The third step is the fully automated approach, which includes steps to test the automation itself. Most of the value in terms of avoiding error and speeding up the process is realized during step 2 in terms of avoiding errors and speeding up the overall process.

Although we like to be pragmatic in our approach, the end goal is certainly the fully automated deployment pipeline.

12.14.1 Deployment Pipeline

The deployment pipeline, an automated encapsulation of the application build, package, and deployment, is the most common goal of any DevOps transformation. Creating the deployment pipeline sounds easy, but actually involves quite a bit of complexity.

Automating each step is often not an easy task at all, and some steps may be very difficult to automate without any user intervention. Although having a single pushbutton deploy is a nice goal, ensuring that you cannot make mistakes is a far greater priority.

Deployment pipelines should always be used consistently across all environments, from development test through production. They also should provide traceability, usually in the form of logging. Most importantly, we like to see at least half of the code focused on testing and verifying each step. The deployment pipeline should enable the team to handle many deployments without any chance of human error, and if something does go wrong, your deployment pipeline should "fail fast" so that the problem is immediately identified and may be addressed in a timely manner.

The DevOps approach facilitates the creation of the deployment pipeline by ensuring collaboration and communication across all stakeholders whose expertise is needed to successfully accomplish this goal.

Deploying application upgrades and fixes is essential, but equally important is understanding and managing application dependencies.

12.15 Dependency Control

Understanding and managing dependencies in any complex software architecture has always been a tough challenge. We believe this to be an area where DevOps can truly add value by ensuring that the various owners of software components are engaged in identifying and documenting dependencies.

All too often, this ship has sailed, in that the developers who wrote the code may have already moved on to the next project. When this happens, the best that you can hope to do is capture this information as part of the testing processes, as well as through incident management when things unfortunately go wrong.

Some companies have gotten very creative with discovering and understanding dependencies through a form of testing where they randomly cause components to stop processing correctly and then observe the impact. This approach has been coined by at least one company as a "chaos monkey."

> ### Those Pesky Simians
>
> Netflix has famously taken the approach of testing their infrastructure by randomly affecting their key service components. This has become fondly known as "chaos monkeys," meaning that little simians could be randomly impacting your services, and your infrastructure should be able to gracefully handle such interruptions with automated recovery procedures.

Another approach is to try to encapsulate all dependencies inside of a deployable structure. *Microservices* has emerged as an approach in which systems are divided into completely self-contained deployable structures. We are currently working on automating the deployment of microservices and see some value in this approach. However, where the business problem itself has many inherent dependencies and great complexity, microservices may be less than ideal because integration challenges will be numerous. Similarly, we are working with *container-based* deployments, which also hold much promise.

Containers are lightweight virtualization structures that allow for a complete structure capable of encapsulating dependencies and thereby reducing complexity during deployments to be created programmatically. The developer works within the container, which is created through code, and then deploys the code to each environment as a fully contained structure. Although we view containers as being an innovative approach, it will be some time before we fully understand its advantages and complexities. We remain convinced that you need to fully understand your architectural dependencies and design deployment approaches that can handle these essential considerations.

Understanding dependencies is essential for your success, and this is certainly no easy task. Just as important is an approach to handle the complexities of configuration changes.

12.16 Configuration Control

Configuration control is a key discipline for any deployment framework. Once again, understanding the configuration dependencies is the first step and benefits greatly from the DevOps approach to communicating and collaborating with key stakeholders. We see many organizations that struggle greatly with configuration control, often because key stakeholders may have moved on to other projects and their expertise may no longer be available. We view documenting the technical configuration as being a fundamental requirement. Verification of all configuration dependencies should be part of your overall environment management strategy.

You also need to verify that the correct code has been deployed—a procedure known as a *configuration audit*.

12.17 Configuration Audits

We generally start our DevOps assessments by asking if the organization can prove that the correct code has been deployed and that it has not been tampered with. The physical configuration audit, described in almost any industry standard or framework, verifies that the right code is running in production, usually by checking the version ID and often through the use of cryptographic keys such as MAC SHA1 or MD5. The deployment pipeline must conduct a physical configuration audit to verify that the correct code has been deployed.

We have given many examples of the physical configuration audit, and closely related is the use of cryptography to ensure that unauthorized changes can be detected in what we refer to as the *secure trusted application base*.

Similarly, the functional configuration audit verifies that the code is doing what it should be doing and is closely aligned with QA and testing.

12.18 QA and DevOps

We noted earlier in this chapter that agile depends upon DevOps because of the need to support rapid application deployments that are crucial to the success of the agile development effort. DevOps itself depends heavily upon QA and testing. It is common for the DevOps deployment automation to quickly outpace the QA and testing function's ability to certify that releases can be deployed to production. DevOps helps the QA effort by ensuring effective communication between development and the QA and testing function. There is much synergy in this approach because developers cannot usually test their own code effectively. However, the development organization does have a great deal of technical expertise that can help QA and testing better understand effective use of its limited resources. The QA and testing organization can have considerable synergies with the development organization in much the same way that operations also enjoys synergies with their development counterparts.

DevOps depends upon good testing and also helps facilitate excellent testing. We see a similar synergy between development and information security.

12.19 Information Security

Information security plays a key role in ensuring that the software and systems under development can withstand what has become a constant attempt to penetrate and adversely impact most production systems. We are confronted daily by stories of systems that have been harmed by hackers who often have malintent, including stealing personally identifiable information and using it for identify theft and other forms of fraud. Unfortunately, the information security group may be lagging behind in understanding the application and what must be done to safeguard corporate assets from those who would intend to steal them. Once again, we view a synergy between InfoSec and development in which development shares its technical expertise and benefits from learning security-related best practices.

One of the most important security competencies is the ability to build infrastructure as code.

12.20 Infrastructure as Code

Infrastructure as code means that you can programmatically build the systems environment from scratch using automated procedures. Most competent systems administrators automate every aspect of building and provisioning servers. DevOps itself was motivated by much of the thought leadership in the **agile systems administration** community. We have regularly worked to automate provisioning of operating systems to middleware and then, of course, the application deployments as well. Infrastructure as code has many advantages, including being able to quickly provision servers with identifiable and verifiable configurations on both bare-metal and cloud-based providers.

This is very important because when a security incident occurs, your best approach is to provision a completely new machine and quickly deploy your code. Infrastructure as code makes this possible. Without this core competency, you would be forced to try to identify the malware left on your machine and attempt to remove it without damaging the system. This is often impractical, so being able to completely reprovision your machines is a much better approach.

12.21 Taming Complexity

We have discussed many complicated topics in this chapter. DevOps places a strong value on taming complexity; it accomplished this by facilitating the cross-functional team to share knowledge and by providing a means to capture and store knowledge.

12.22 Automate Everything

Another key lesson of DevOps is how much power and control are gained by automating everything. Without automation, DevOps and the deployment pipeline would simply not be possible.

12.23 Disaster Recovery and Business Continuity

We view disaster recovery and business continuity as being key areas that also benefit greatly from the DevOps approach. The ability to rebuild servers using infrastructure as code, understand dependencies, and manage complex configuration changes are all essential aspects of managing significant interruptions in service that trigger disaster recovery and business continuity efforts.

12.24 Continuous Process Improvement

Implementing DevOps is no easy task. The most effective approach is to start small and continuously improve by approaching DevOps as an agile development effort. DevOps itself is an emerging industry capability, and thus it should come as no surprise that DevOps is also evolving and continuously improving itself.

12.25 Conclusion

The way that you approach DevOps in one particular organization may be quite different from how you implement it in another. The platforms and technologies may greatly affect your strategies. But the core DevOps principles do not change. We have discussed many of them throughout this chapter and the rest throughout this book. DevOps is a journey of discovery cooperation, which if embraced by stakeholders and implemented well, leads to enhanced communication and productivity throughout the organization.

Chapter 13

Retrospectives in the ALM

This chapter discusses the practical application of retrospectives to support application lifecycle management (ALM). The first section of this chapter will examine the main function of retrospectives, namely, to evaluate what went well and what needs to be improved. But that's just the beginning. Getting accurate information from all stakeholders in a retrospective can be very challenging. If you are successful, the retrospective can help drive the entire ALM process. There are many possible modes for conducting a discussion, from in-person group meetings to online virtual conferences. You should consider the many views represented by each of the stakeholders from developers to business end users. Ultimately, you need to have a cross-functional view, and the retrospective may take on a very different approach depending upon the culture of the organization and the stakeholders involved.

Retrospectives require leadership, and this chapter will provide guidance on how to succeed if you are responsible for implementing this function. This includes walking the fine line between gently questioning and stronger probing when necessary. Understanding retrospectives from a cultural perspective is also essential. Fundamentally, retrospectives are an important aspect of process improvement leadership. We will discuss how to employ retrospectives to support ITIL incidents and problem management, along with other industry standards and frameworks. Crisis and risk management are also key considerations along with IT governance and compliance. Retrospectives take on a different tone when used to manage vendor performance. We will complete this chapter by considering how much process is necessary, how to deal with politics (or, more accurately, *relationships*), and the use of effective metrics to drive the process improvement journey.

13.1 Goals of Retrospectives

The goal of a retrospective is to provide a mechanism to facilitate feedback from all stakeholders, which will be incorporated into plans for improving your processes. Very few organizations spend enough time discussing specifically how they can improve. Our experience is that everyone usually feels relieved and excited once we conduct an effective retrospective, usually wondering why we don't have this kind of feedback more often. The goal of retrospectives is to help you and your team improve your processes and procedures and ultimately achieve excellence in all you do.

(*Author's note:* There are a few places where we found it easier to write in singular first person. Wherever you see "I," you can assume that it is Bob speaking.)

13.2 Why Are Retrospectives Important?

Retrospectives are important because you don't want to make the same mistakes over and over again. Retrospectives provide a much-welcomed framework for assessing what is being done well and what could be improved. We often find that people are amazed at how much information is gathered at a retrospective, and usually we hear people ask "Why didn't we do this sooner?"

13.3 Where Do I Start?

Always begin by first asking participants to describe what went well. This discussion often elicits spontaneous remarks about what people feel could be improved. Ensure that everyone feels safe expressing their opinion and that even difficult topics can be comfortably discussed. You may need to structure your retrospectives based upon organizational dynamics and culture. For example, you might want to have a separate meeting among all of the DBAs (assuming they are a large group) and then have a DBA in the wider retrospective that includes representatives from development, operations, QA, and testing, as well as the business. Be careful with regard to stakeholders and their positional power. Many employees will not feel comfortable being open and candid in front of their direct manager. It is common to control participation to ensure that all those involved are able to speak freely and openly.

13.4 Retrospectives as Process Improvement

Retrospectives help drive the entire process improvement effort, especially in terms of defining application lifecycle management (ALM). This may not seem apparent at first, but your ALM must define the steps required to evaluate and solve problems. This is an ideal opportunity to identify processes and functions that should be added to your ALM. Retrospectives are effective at enabling the team to understand what went well and what needs active intervention to be improved. ALM should itself be defined in an agile iterative way, and that includes implementing retrospectives. Process improvement is hard. Identifying the processes supporting the application lifecycle is critical for your success. So, how exactly do you go about implementing these best practices?

The most basic retrospective involves an open and honest discussion on what went well and what needs to be improved.

13.4.1 Start with Assessing Success

Starting with the positive and upbeat discussion of what went well is often essential for a successful retrospective. Obviously, putting people on the defensive doesn't motivate anyone to be open and forthcoming about things that could be improved. We have found that asking people about what went well often helps them to feel comfortable talking about what needs to be improved. It is also important to identify what went well for a number of reasons. The first is that you do not want to fix something that is not broken

Assessment Tip: Don't Fix What Isn't Broken

We have seen team members who jumped on the process improvement bandwagon a little too quickly, sometimes identifying issues and problems that really weren't important to the current team or project. Sometimes, many have a tendency to focus on challenges and barriers that we experienced on the last project. Process improvement must be relevant, timely, and pragmatic.

Reinforcing what went well and what should be repeated is the first step. Next, the retrospective should dive deep into the issues and problems that occurred and what can be done to avoid repeating the same mistakes over and over again. Above all, it is essential that everyone participating in the retrospective feel safe expressing their views and observations in an open and honest way without fear of retaliation or punishment.

> ### Baseball Players and Mistakes
>
> Baseball players who can approach a batting average of .400 actually get a hit less than half of the time they come up, yet are amazing athletes and are often considered Hall of Fame material. We will discuss why we believe that mistakes are often helpful in terms of learning experiences. First, people are usually more alert after they realize that they have made a mistake. Second, some people will only learn and improve when they realize that their first attempt did not work. Mistakes are feedback loops that help us calibrate our approach. Baseball players are our favorite.

Understanding our mistakes is important for IT professionals—incidents and problems can point us in the right direction.

13.4.2 Incidents and Problems

Every development effort has its own share of challenges. Sometimes, these are minor issues that should be addressed (and hopefully are) in a timely manner. Sometimes, there are serious problems that require root-cause analysis. Taking a deep dive into analyzing why there was a problem and what we need to do in order to fix it will help avoid making the same mistakes time and time again.

Some people find it difficult to analyze these issues and problems and prefer to stay completely positive. These folks may appear to be uncomfortable having a candid, potentially contentious, conversation about what happened. This won't help the team grow and improve. We are not suggesting that you embrace being negative either, but the ability to honestly and accurate self-appraise is actually a strength. In fact, a healthy and balanced view that truly reflects performance allows for the most constructive retrospectives and opens the door for further progress

> ### The Football Analogy from Bob
>
> Many sports teams succeed or fail based upon the teamwork exhibited by each and every member. I like to remind my team that we need to always take an honest and open look at how we are doing. If we are on

a football team and I do a poor job of catching the ball, then you need to tell me honestly how I am doing. This is the only way that I can get much-needed feedback and improve my game, thus contributing more to the overall effort. Together, we can strive for that Super Bowl win. (*Editor's note:* No matter how much feedback you give him, Bob is terrible at sports.)

This discussion must be conducted in a way that ensures everyone involved knows it is safe to have an open and honest discussion about mistakes that were made, while also examining the issues and problems that occurred. Remember, too, that mistakes can be good if their dissection yields concrete knowledge of how the process needs to be improved.

13.4.3 Mistakes Are Good

Mistakes are not always bad, and it is very important that everyone knows that they can talk honestly about mistakes that were made. Mistakes can actually be good for identifying important issues that need to be addressed. These discussions are not always fun, and obviously many people find it difficult to have an honest and open discussion about mistakes for which they could be held responsible. Some people find it easy to be straight and objective, and others may try to avoid the tough discussions at any cost. Personality traits may have a lot to do with why some people find these discussions to be difficult.

13.4.4 Personality and Disposition

Some people are just dispositionally dismal and negative. Others are consistently upbeat and may have difficulty discussing problems and incidents that occurred. Be aware that people with low self-esteem are particularly sensitive to criticism and blame situations that trigger their feelings of inadequacy. Ideally, you need to foster a culture where everyone knows that not only are they safe to have an honest and open discussion, but they will be valued and respected for any insights and observations that shed light on the issue at hand. We discuss personality in more detail in Chapter 21, but in the context of retrospectives, keep in mind that personality factors may bias some people's participation. We see this behavior in people who just seem to always tell others what they believe that person wants to hear.

13.4.5 Don't Just Tell Me What I Want to Hear

I sometimes find myself reminding people that doctors often have to deliver news that is difficult to accept and digest. That doesn't mean that we don't want to know the information. You would never want a doctor to spare you from learning that you have cancer—especially if there was a chance that aggressive treatment could alter the outcome. We might not enjoy hearing that we are sick, but the only way to get better is to get the message and information in a clear and straight manner.

The mode of delivery of sensitive information is also important. When people deliver sad news, we usually prefer to have the person come in and sit down. The mode of delivering information can obviously affect how the message is received and understood.

13.5 Which Mode Should You Use?

We all have different preferred modes of receiving information. Choosing the right mode of transmitting information is essential for your success.

13.5.1 In Person Is Best

Agile certainly places a premium on having all of the resources in one location, with face-to-face communication being the optimal approach. But is this true for everyone?

> #### Blind and Agile (from Bob)
>
> I used to be blind, and direct face-to-face communication does not have the same appeal for me as it does for other people. I am just fine talking on the phone and can usually process audio information much better than visual stimuli. I recently taught a class to a lady who was deaf and found that in-person training was actually annoying and less than effective because we had to use a sign language interpreter. I was particularly annoyed with myself, because despite having an extensive amount of time with other people who had handicaps, I had never learned how to sign. It was much easier for me to give portions of the class via instant messenger, sharing a screen, because that put us on a level playing field.

So, blind and deaf people aside, is it always easier to communicate face to face? For the most part it is, although we can recall another instance where a colleague of ours had a great deal of difficulty with communicating in English because he did not speak English as a first language. When we communicated face to face, we were generally confused and he was, too. Interestingly enough, he did much better when we used e-mail to communicate with each other. More and more organizations are finding it helpful to use online and video conferencing to communicate between teams.

13.5.2 Online and Video Conferencing

Conducting a retrospective online or through video conferencing can be quite effective. With online and video conferencing, you can usually see and hear all participants. The technology for online and video conferencing is noticeably getting better day by day, although we have seen challenges with the video picture updating on a delay and even sometimes poor voice quality. The technical quality of the connection can affect the quality of the retrospective because of the difficulty understanding the communication. Sometimes, you may find that it is necessary to rely upon audio-only teleconferencing.

13.5.3 Teleconference

The standard teleconference is nothing new and may be perfectly adequate for getting everyone to express their views and give input. The challenge is that you cannot see all of the participants and may not even know if they have muted their line and decided to have a side conversation with someone who is at their desk. I usually find it best to poll all of the participants by name on the call to ensure that you get their input—and their undivided attention. In the past, using virtual worlds and a personal avatar has enabled me to participate in meetings that I would otherwise have had to forego.

13.5.4 Virtual Worlds

Some of the software standards working groups that I have been involved with have taken to using virtual worlds for their meeting place. This provides some interesting capabilities and challenges. The virtual world can provide some helpful backdrops, including conference rooms and side discussions. In one instance, I had to leave the meeting early. I left my avatar online and came back later to review the conversation that had been recorded for my review.

For all practical purposes, when I had to leave I had left a participant behind who carefully kept notes on the entire discussion. We have discussed some of the physical considerations inherent in conducting meetings, and most of us would prefer face-to-face meetings whenever possible. However, even when all parties are in the same room, you may find that there are a variety of different perspectives.

13.6 Perspective Is Essential

Each participant in the retrospective will likely have a unique perspective. That's not to say that there won't be a considerable number of shared views as well. Sometimes, the views are found to be distinguished by the function or role played by the participant. For example, developers often have a different view than customers.

13.6.1 Developers

In agile development, many developers play cross-functional roles that enable the technology professional to understand many different perspectives and views. That said, developers are still the folks charged with understanding the requirements and producing the system within a fixed time box (or sprint). Developers are often deep into the technology, confronting the many technical obstacles and forging solutions to deal with every possible challenge. Although the agile developer places a strong focus on the customer perspective, she or he still will likely have a different view than the end user.

13.6.2 Customers

The customer plays an essential role in agile development. Delivering the right features helps ensure that our company will be profitable and that we will all achieve success. The customer view should always be considered in the retrospective.

13.6.3 Tester

Testers also have a unique view, which focuses on ensuring that the system performs as specified and needed. We discuss QA and testing in Chapter 20, but in this chapter our focus is on using the retrospective to improve our processes, and the tester is a key resource in this effort.

13.6.4 Operations

Operations focuses on ensuring that systems are reliable and services are never interrupted. We discuss operations further in Chapter 11, but for this chapter you need to ensure that your operations team is well represented in all discussions on how to improve your processes.

Each of these perspectives is essential; the DevOps approach coaches us to include them all to yield a comprehensive and integrated cross-functional view.

13.7 DevOps: The Cross-Functional View

DevOps promotes the creation of a broad cross-functional view that allows us to understand each of the perspectives. This inclusive model is essential for conducting effective retrospectives with a holistic systems view.

13.8 Understanding the Use Case

Thoroughly understanding the use case points us to what we should test and how to actually perform the steps of the test.

13.8.1 Epics and Stories

Epics and stories describe the requirements of the system. This is also essential for us to discuss whether or not the system performed as expected and as needed.

13.9 Retrospectives as Leadership

Retrospectives provide a powerful opportunity to bring about positive change. Actualizing this potential often takes leadership and, especially, effective communication. Management needs to create an environment where each member of the team is comfortable expressing his or her own views without fear of retaliation. I have worked in a number of companies where many opportunities for improvement were missed because the team members did not feel comfortable expressing their views and opinions without fear of retaliation.

13.9.1 Removing Barriers

Retrospectives help us identify barriers that need to be addressed. In the scrum, the scrum master is responsible for ensuring that barriers are removed.

The retrospective also helps identify barriers that are discovered as part of the review process.

13.10 Running the Meeting

Running the meeting should involve creating an agenda and setting expectations and sometimes entry criteria for starting the retrospective. If the meeting is going to focus on a specific incident or problem, then obviously those involved should have reviewed the details before the meeting begins. Additionally, someone should be the scribe to capture notes and action items that are agreed upon during the discussion.

13.10.1 Probing and Questioning

We like to use very nondirective probing when comments are not forthcoming to avoid influencing people's responses. If this is not effective, then we may switch to being more direct with specific probes. Always remember that making everyone comfortable is of paramount importance if you are to get valid and useable data.

13.11 Retrospectives Supporting ITIL

Retrospectives should always be run in alignment with the culture of the organization. We find that many development teams are focused on agile development, whereas operations teams are often heavily focused on ITIL v3. It is always best if you can align the retrospective to match the terminology of your group. We sometimes find ourselves teaching agile principles to the operations team or explaining ITIL v3 terminology to developers, but aligning your approach to retrospectives will help your team achieve success.

13.11.1 Incidents

Retrospectives are often focused on understanding the circumstances in which an incident occurred. This approach can be effective at diving deep into how and why an incident occurred, as well as how it can be prevented in the future.

13.11.2 Problems

When the retrospective focuses on a problem, a wider group of stakeholders is usually involved and there is more of a focus on root-cause analysis. The ITIL v3 framework provides much-needed structure that can help ensure your retrospectives are effective and fruitful.

Retrospectives can also help triage defects.

13.12 Retrospectives and Defect Triage

When systems have challenges, we often find ourselves deluged with bug and defect reports. It can be challenging to prioritize and assign related work items to the limited stakeholders who have the knowledge of how best to address them. We have also seen many situations where even the subject matter experts (SMEs) were baffled. Holding a retrospective to triage bug and defect reports can be an excellent way to put some structure and priorities in place. Taking a DevOps cross-functional approach can also help by involving stakeholders from across the ALM in making the right decisions. The user or business expert can help set priorities where they may be difficult for developers to assess. The QA and testing group can create test cases to ensure that these defects do not come again in future releases, whereas the operations team may establish runbook procedures to work around systems issues in the future.

Understanding bugs and defects helps us address them, hopefully with bugfixes and features delivered quickly through our automated deployment pipeline. Having the entire team involved provides much-needed information and ensures that we are working toward ensuring the best possible service for our customers and other stakeholders.

13.13 Retrospectives as Crisis Management

We have seen some retrospectives that were held after a serious systems outage. In this case, we are not just trying to avoid the mistake again—we also might be discussing our response to the crisis itself. Life happens, and ensuring that your team always has an effective response ready and waiting is every bit as important as addressing the bugs and defects themselves. We have also seen situations where outages occurred due to circumstances completely beyond our control. Once again, the goal in this case is to ensure that our response itself is as effective as possible.

13.14 Supporting IT Governance

IT governance provides transparency to senior management, enabling them to make better decisions. We find that effective retrospectives can provide an excellent structure for gathering accurate information on what happened and what the team believes could help prevent issues from occurring again. It is common for the notes from a retrospective to be summarized and presented to senior management for their review.

13.15 Audit and Regulatory Compliance

Retrospectives often identify issues related to audit and regulatory compliance. Violating your own internal audit procedures can result in a serious impact, often involving senior management above you. When it involves regulatory compliance, sometimes federal laws may have been violated and the consequences can be even more severe. We have good news, though. It is almost always true that self-identifying the issue and coming up with a plan for addressing the incident can often help lessen the severity of any consequences. Although some regulatory violations have to be addressed by your legal and compliance department, in practice, identifying the issue and having a plan for avoiding the problem again in the future is most often an important step.

13.16 Retrospectives as Risk Management

Risk management is an important function in any organization, and retrospectives often provide important information to help ensure that risks are identified and an effective plan is created for addressing any possible contingencies.

13.17 Vendor Management

Vendors can be a source of serious challenges because they represent a factor that we cannot control. Having a retrospective when a vendor outage affects you can help identify strategies for addressing vendor-related risks and challenges. Sometimes, it also results in the decision to go and find another vendor, or at least avoid being locked into one who is not performing as needed.

13.18 Too Much Process

There is nothing worse than having too much process. When your team is mired in bureaucratic red tape, then everyone on the team will work hard to bypass your processes. When your retrospective identifies that you have too much process, it is clear that you should work with all of the relevant stakeholders to identify areas in which the process can be streamlined for increased efficiency and compliance.

13.19 Corporate Politics

Retrospectives sometimes become a discussion on corporate politics. Relationships are important, and understanding how things work in your company can certainly be a critical success factor, but try to prevent these discussions from just becoming a session to complain about things we cannot change. Although a little controlled venting can temporarily relieve frustration, coming up with a viable game plan that can really generate noticeable progress is a lot better.

13.20 Metrics and Measurement

It has been said that you can only improve what you can measure. Retrospectives are often a source of meaningful metrics that can help track gains as you improve your processes. Our advice here is to be careful that your metrics are valid and clear to all those involved. You want to avoid metrics that can be "gamed" by the stakeholders. For example, if my year-end bonus is based upon the number of bugs reported, then you might find my team fixing things without reporting them as bugs. Similarly, if my compensation is based upon the number of defects resolved, then you might find me reporting everything I can find just to show them as being resolved. Metrics need to be valid and reasonable.

13.21 Conclusion

Retrospectives can help you drive process improvement across the agile ALM. We view DevOps as being essential in implementing effective retrospectives because of its emphasis on the value of effective communication and collaboration across the enterprise. You need to implement effective retrospectives to successfully evolve your ALM over the course of your project.

PART IV

Scaling the Process

Chapter 14

Agile in a Non-Agile World

Being agile in a non-agile world can be difficult, and at times even seem impossible to accomplish. We have often found ourselves in organizations that insisted on a waterfall approach. What is most difficult is trying to predict things that are just not possible to ascertain up-front. Many are unaware that waterfall was originally envisioned as an iterative process because today it seems that some organizations expect their employees to be able to predict the future to a degree that is simply not reasonable. The real problem is that these are the same organizations that expect you to make the project actually conform to the plan once it has been developed and approved. Any deviations may be perceived as a lack of planning and proper management. Being agile in a non-agile world can be challenging and is fraught with its own set of risks and pitfalls. This approach is sometimes called *hybrid agile*.

14.1 Goals of Hybrid Agile

The goal of hybrid agile is to design a process that aligns with both agile and non-agile methodologies. This is no easy task, and many folks have criticized attempts to adopt hybrid agile approaches in software and systems development. We are not without our own concerns, but our report from the trenches is that hybrid agile is, in fact, the norm in many organizations. In every engagement, our goal is to come up with the best possible methodology, given the reality that we see on the ground in many organizations. In some cases, the goal of hybrid agile is to act as a bridge to adopting agile completely, whereas in other organizations, hybrid agile allows the organization to adopt agile principles and practices within the framework of the existing organizational structure and culture.

14.2 Why Is Hybrid Agile Important?

Hybrid agile is important because it provides a pragmatic approach to adopting agile principles and practices that can be implemented in situations that are less than ideal. We come across two common reasons why hybrid agile may be the only viable approach. The first is that you have a project that really must embrace a non-agile approach, as is the case in situations where requirements must be well defined and understood up-front. The second is a situation where agile would work just fine, but management will not agree to allow you to fully embrace agile development. This latter scenario is quite common in many of the organizations with which we consult. The degree to which your approach can adopt agile practices may vary. Hybrid agile may not seem ideal, but it is often the best approach for many real-world scenarios that you may find yourself having to manage (in a less-than-perfect situation).

> ### Hidden Agile
>
> We have implemented application build, package, and deployment automation in organizations where the official methodology was strictly waterfall. Senior management expected a full project plan up-front and well-defined requirements, albeit at a high level. Progress was tracked in terms of deliverables tied to phases. We found teams secretly adopting agile practices, including defining requirements as epics and stories, organizing in scrums with daily standups, and engaging in rapid iterative development, including continuous integration. To senior management, the team was working in a waterfall fashion. The day-to-day developer activities, however, took on an increasingly agile flavor. Although by no means a perfect situation, it is nevertheless one in which many teams find themselves.

In order to be successful, you need to understand where you are starting from.

14.3 Where Do I Start?

Always begin by understanding the situation and the culture in which you are trying to work. Is the business problem that you are trying to solve one in which agile is just not appropriate? Is your organization completely opposed to a non-agile methodology, making it unlikely you will be able to change senior management's view on how projects are managed? Alternatively, you may actually be working toward winning over your management by convincing them that agile is a viable approach and simply experiencing the stretching typical during any transitional period.

After assessing current hurdles, it is time to create a plan for adopting agile in a way that is aligned with your environment and organizational culture.

14.4 Pragmatic Choices

Making tough choices is part of everyday life. Many of our colleagues write books that focus on developing software that seems best suited for a perfect world that, more often than not, seems to us to exist only in their imaginations. We find that ivory tower–designed methodologies, while theoretically very interesting, are not always easy to implement in the real world—and the somewhat messy environments—the rest of us worker bees inhabit. However, most organizations, from banks to healthcare providers to defense contractors, do indeed exist within a less-than-perfect environment, and we suggest that good software methodology can play a huge role in helping manage those situations, benefiting the organization with great software that helps drive the business to success and profitability. We note that quite a few companies do represent themselves as having a great approach to delivering software. Some of these firms do not have the regulatory and compliance requirements that we see in large banks and other real-world firms. So although their approach might work for them, it is not always portable to other companies, and even if it was, their approach might not align successfully in a different corporate culture and ecosystem. The pragmatic approach is to understand your circumstances and design a methodology using all available industry best practices that have been shown to be successful in your situation.

Being pragmatic means that you understand fully what agile principles teach and what agile development brings to the table. Some folks take a seemingly hybrid agile approach because they are just ignorant of agile principles, and that is not what we are advocating at all. In fact, it could be argued that hybrid agile requires a stronger knowledge of agile because you must understand precisely what aspects can be tailored and adjusted to the circumstances within which you are operating. Done well, we have seen some advantages to a hybrid agile approach.

14.5 The Best of Both Worlds

Waterfall does have some distinct advantages. We have heard technology managers bemoan not having spent more time understanding complex requirements up-front and wishing that their project had not taken an iterative approach so early in the lifecycle. Agile, despite having some weaknesses and notable failures, also boasts several advantages that lead teams to a great deal of success in their development efforts. Our advice is to try to understand the choices that you have and to design a software methodology that matches the environment you are working in. This might mean that you spend a little more time up-front working on developing requirements, knowing full well that they may change. Designing a life support system or the software for a nuclear power plant requires a great deal of discipline initially to define requirements. We have had engineers from both of these disciplines in our public classes embracing agile practices, but from within their own development framework, with all of its regulatory and audit requirements. Sufficient understanding of both approaches will enable you to tailor an ALM that works within your world. We also think that your methodology may necessarily grow and adapt over time, and that might actually be the best choice for the world in which you are working.

14.6 Keeping It Agile

The transition to agile can be a long journey for many companies. Keeping your approach agile means that you apply many of the principles that you expect your team to adopt when they develop code to the way in which you adopt agility itself. Changing how your team works is not likely something that can be completely transitioned overnight. Certainly training, mentoring, and coaching are extremely valuable—and often essential for your success. But, even in the best of circumstances, you may find that your transition to agility cannot be described as flipping a light switch such that you turn agile "on" or "off," but rather a transformation that takes some time and quite a bit of effort, no doubt with a few mistakes and failures along the way.

How Agile Are You?

One of life's little mysteries is that many of the agile thought leaders certainly appear to be the least "agile" people around. We have colleagues who sound like they are advocating a rather orthodox approach to adopting agility, presenting it as an all-or-nothing choice. We suggest that sometimes there is no other choice than to actually employ the very same principles we learn from agility as part of the transition to agility itself.

The successful agile transformation often depends largely upon choosing the best pilot.

14.7 Establishing the Agile Pilot

Choosing the right pilot for your first agile project is an important step. Most often, we hear that it is really best to start with a new project that does not have any existing methodology "baggage" in place. We do not disagree with this choice, but note that we have come across highly motivated teams that did just fine transitioning their existing practices to agile methodology over time. You should always consider the experience and skill of team members when choosing an agile pilot. But frankly, you should especially focus on their culture in terms of collaboration and teamwork above all else. Be wary of teams where one or two members have strong dominant personalities and there is a lack of excellent teamwork, especially in terms of respect for each other.

14.8 Transitioning to Agile

We often see teams that are transitioning to agile, but since projects are already in play, they cannot easily just switch over. They may have deliverables that they have already committed to completing within a waterfall-based project. Transitioning to agile can be difficult and, in many ways, a balancing act. We have seen many situations where the senior managers insisted on deliverables that they were accustomed to receiving while the mid-level development managers were actively trying to help the teams transition to agile development. Missing a deadline will do little to increase confidence in your team and your approach, so we certainly believe that you should meet your deliverables as promised. But also start to look for opportunities to socialize and communicate your less visible transition to agile in terms of what you are doing to improve your own software development process.

For example, regularly scheduling demos of the systems that you are developing and reviewing the contents of your backlog may help enhance management's confidence that they will get a completed product on or before your deadline. Just as communication is important within your scrum, so, too, is managing the information being delivered to the senior managers who are responsible for approving your budget.

14.9 Having a Baby

Some endeavors take a specific amount of time and cannot be divided into sprints. Having a baby is one of them. Creating certain hardware and circuit chips is another. Many of these efforts require software or firmware to be developed in parallel.

> ### *Bob Waking Up Attendees*
>
> Bob enjoys teaching public classes at conferences and usually gets really great reviews from the attendees. But one challenge is waking the attendees up after the lunch break. To regain everyone's full attention, Bob usually gets up and asks for help in finding nine women who would be willing to help make a baby in one month. This silly example highlights the inescapable fact that some deliverables must be handled in a waterfall fashion.

Acknowledging that some tasks just take a fixed amount of time is important. Equally important is realizing that many of us find ourselves working in environments that are not optimal. We acknowledge that we are perhaps called in more often when these challenges exist, but the elephant in the room is that most organizations have environments that are less than perfect.

14.10 The Elephant in the Room

Although many of my colleagues will not admit this, the proverbial "elephant in the room" is that many, or perhaps most, organizations are working with agile in atypical situations. We have discussed hybrid agile and that senior management may indeed place demands upon any project, which means that we will have to meet their requirements. Living in an imperfect situation is the norm, and that is exactly the world within which we must produce results.

We are often compelled to define requirements in a waterfall manner. We also may have to employ a project management strategy that has much more ceremony than one would expect from an agile process. One important governance issue is management wanting to know exactly when the project will be completed.

14.11 Are We There Yet?

Knowing when a project will be completed is a common requirement. We see many project budgets in the millions of dollars, and frankly no one is going to give you that much money without adequate governance over the project in terms of how the money will be spent, including a clear schedule on when the work will be completed.

Family Vacation

Most parents know the joy of taking children on a summer vacation trip. Driving for hours in the car with several children can certainly be quite the challenge. Those of us who have done this are quite familiar with the experience of starting off on an hours-long drive and hearing the littlest child asking "Are we there yet" after the first block. Our experience is that some very senior managers can be just as impatient when it comes to taking long trips. Be prepared to give an accounting of when you are going to reach your destination, or project completion, as the case may be.

Many development managers may feel that senior management's requirements for accountability are unreasonable, but the truth is that many agile projects have failed. You need to take a pragmatic approach as to how and why agile projects can fail in order to avoid the most common causes.

14.12 Agile Disasters

The most common problem we have seen is code from a release iteration that was not at a point where it was really ready to be seen being delivered to a customer prematurely. Far more serious, however, is releasing code that has just not reached a state where it meets quality standards.

Larger projects may be at greater risk for disaster. There have been a number of very large-scale projects that did not meet their goals, even after spending their budget and burning through their development schedule.

Although there may be significant challenges, many developers successfully manage to operate in these situations.

14.13 Developer View

Developers are a resilient bunch, and we often see agile development being successfully conducted under even the most difficult circumstances. Agile in the trenches, even under these circumstances, often involves agile practices such as scrums, requirements tracked in user stories, and information radiators. Developers often do a great job of making their development environments agile even under the most difficult circumstances.

We also have run into circumstances where corporate rules directly impacted the agile practices that could be adopted by the team.

14.14 No Information Radiators Allowed

We worked in a bank where there were many rules and regulations. The corporate security department did not allow any work products to be left out on the desk after hours, much less any diagrams or posters related to systems architecture or other technical requirements. Agile developers often make *information radiators* that display important information about the project, its status, and its deliverables. In this company, we were not permitted to have any information radiators on display after hours for fear of corporate espionage. The rule was so strict that we could not leave business cards on our desk, even if we gave them to other colleagues all the time. Sometimes corporate rules can get in the way of the most basic things.

14.15 Waterfall Is Iterative, Too

We like to remind folks that waterfall as it was envisioned by Winston Royce was iterative by design. This means that the original view was that analysts tracked requirements, designed the system, coded, tested, and started from the beginning to iteratively develop a system that met the users' requirements.

That is not to say that waterfall is not without its challenges by any means. We have seen folks have to pretend that they understand requirements before it was conceptually possible and to make estimates about new technology that were completely impossible to guess at up-front. However, the waterfall methodology itself should not be blamed for this dysfunctional behavior; rather, the way in which it has been implemented in many organizations is the real root of many problems. There are many circumstances in which defining requirements as thoroughly as possible is an absolute must-have.

14.16 Document Requirements as Much as Possible

The best approach for many projects is to define as many of the requirements as possible while simultaneously identifying risks and other open issues that just cannot be understood and specified up-front. In this regard, having more requirements defined is better, but one should never be forced to lie about what is known. This tends to be one of the biggest problems with the waterfall approach. The folks who have made Lean methodology so popular in software development have come up with a clever solution to address this dichotomy.

14.17 Last Responsible Moment

Many of our colleagues in Lean development have used the phrase "last responsible moment" to describe the practice of waiting to make decisions until all, or at least most of, the essential information is available. Waterfall often results in analysts trying to define requirements about things that they do not completely understand. Putting off the final decision until more information is available results in better decisions and better designs. Even if you are using a hybrid approach, *never* define requirements until you have the information that you need to specify them correctly. Taking an iterative approach and seeing prototypes of the system being constructed often enable you to make better information decisions. It also helps you identify and mitigate technology risk.

14.18 Technology Risk

Technology risk is inherent in any development effort, especially when the team is using newer technologies that have not previously been implemented by this team. The hybrid agile approach can facilitate iterative development and allow the developers to acquire some valuable experience by building prototypes. Even if the team is not embracing fixed timebox sprints, technology risk should be identified and a strategy specified for mitigating this risk. In practice, we always like to learn a new technology by iteratively developing components of the system in as simple a way as possible.

14.19 Understanding the Ecosystem

Development processes must align with the culture of the organization and the environment within which the company must compete. Understanding the ecosystem can help you identify the most appropriate approach to enhancing productivity and quality.

14.20 Mature Agile

As we discussed in Chapter 4, mature agile processes should consider the whole lifecycle and all of its requirements. Although we certainly value working software over comprehensive documentation, hybrid agile is often focused on the so-called items on the right, including comprehensive documents, processes and tools, contracts where needed, and, of course, having a pragmatic approach to planning.

14.21 Meeting IT Governance Requirements

IT governance focuses on ensuring that senior managers receive the information they need in order to make good decisions. The information could be project status, sales and profitability, or even identified risks that should be raised up the chain of command. Many companies will not adopt agile, specifically because they have an IT governance framework in place that is well established throughout the enterprise and management decides to compel each group to continue to provide information in this standard way.

> ### Does Your Manager Make Good Decisions?
>
> Many employees believe that senior management is too detached to have the accurate information required to make good decisions. Even though some managers work their way up the organization, it is still the view of many employees that those in the trenches have the most accurate view and should be involved with decision making. IT governance is the team's opportunity to manage valid and useful information up the ladder to those in senior positions who are responsible for making the key decisions.

14.22 Conclusion

Many technology professionals who would like to embrace agility must function within an organization that has considerable non-agile structures in place. This situation is actually more common than you might think. Sometimes non-agile processes exist in organizations that are just beginning their agile transformation. Other times, non-agile processes are part of the established fabric of the organization and are unlikely to go away anytime soon. Implementing agile practices in a non-agile environment may not seem ideal, but nonetheless, it is the world that many of us actually live in.

Chapter 15

IT Governance

IT governance provides transparency to senior management so that they can make the best decisions based upon the most accurate and up-to-date information. The ALM provides unique capabilities for ensuring that managers have the essential information necessary for evaluating their options. From the CEO to the board of directors, information must often be compartmentalized due to the practical constraints of just how much information can be consumed at any point in time. Achieving this balance empowers your leadership to make informed decisions that help steer your organization to success.

15.1 Goals of IT Governance

The goal of IT governance is to ensure success of your project by providing valid and up-to-date information to those who are empowered to make decisions. IT governance is usually focused on informing senior management, who in turn must answer to the board of directors, shareholders, or other executives who are responsible for the overall well-being of the company. Your goal in IT governance is to provide the information that is needed for executives to do their job effectively, which obviously affects the entire organization.

IT governance places a strong focus on transparency, so that all concerned are assured that projects are going as planned and are informed when there are deviations from the plan or other challenges.

For the agile ALM, IT governance takes on a very special role communicating project status and barriers to success and also raising awareness of identified risks. In our view, DevOps plays a key role in ensuring that decision makers are receiving communication that helps them govern projects and take the steps necessary to ensure success and to address issues when they occur.

Unfortunately, we find that many mid-level managers to do not understand the importance of IT governance, often because the structures in place do not facilitate focusing on the most important issues.

15.2 Why Is IT Governance Important?

IT governance is important to ensure project success and corporate profitability by establishing the oversight needed to successfully direct and guide projects within the ALM. IT governance is also essential for driving out siloed behavior by "being the adult in the room" when individual teams cannot manage to get on the same page.

Integration between development and operations is the starting point for most DevOps initiatives. But Dev and Ops are not the only corporate structures that need to be aligned effectively. What most folks fail to understand is that senior management needs to be integrated with the rest of the organization as well. When your management structure seems to be out of touch with the "worker on the street," then there is an overall lack of cohesion in the corporate culture. IT governance is important because it provides a means for senior management to stay aligned and be supportive of the efforts within the corporation.

15.3 Where Do I Start?

Our experience is that most organizations have an existing IT governance structure in place, and any efforts at process improvement must be implemented within this framework. It is best to start by asking about the information that is communicated to senior management and what additional information might help the senior management team make better choices. It is important to start by considering how information is collected so that the support for IT governance does not take too many resources away from the mid-level management team, those responsible for day-to-day operations. Our concern here is that we have seen teams stretched very thin, trying to meet their deliverables, resulting in them having to cut corners when putting together the data requested by their senior management team. What is needed is a plan and operational processes to regularly gather the information necessary to support both day-to-day operations and the IT governance function.

In Chapter 7, we discussed the need for excellent tooling to support the ALM. It is very much our intent that these efforts should include an automated mechanism to gather and disseminate the information needed for IT governance. Some strategies for accomplishing this are suggested in this chapter.

15.4 Senior Management Makes Decisions

Senior management can sometimes make very poor decisions that greatly impact the future success of the company. Occasionally, this is because executives are motivated more by short-term results and do not sufficiently consider the long-term success of the firm. Sometimes, though, bad decisions are directly the result of incomplete or inaccurate information being delivered to the folks empowered to make these decisions. We view IT governance as an opportunity to provide valid data to help guide the decision-making process.

> ### The Frustrated CTO
>
> We recall a conversation with a frustrated CTO who hired us to conduct a configuration management (CM) assessment. This executive listened attentively to our findings and seemed genuinely delighted to be getting important information from his team. At the same, the CTO was also a little frustrated that his own employees had not come to him sooner to express their concerns, and he further indicated that he had actually suspected that these problems existed. We were essentially the catalyst for getting information that helped raise his awareness of issues that were blocking progress and also communicating risks identified by his team. Although it is true that we helped filter out some noise and especially helped him see this data compared with other organizations, we were largely giving him advice and suggestions that had come from his own team. The good news is that we learned that this effort empowered the team, and they became much more proactive in ensuring that important information reached his desk in the future.

The best way to view this effort is that you are effectively managing "up" the ladder by providing the best information possible to influence your boss's boss and to effectively promote your suggested approach.

15.5 Communicating Up

The key to success with IT governance is understanding that you are actually managing information up the chain of command. Viewed in this way, IT governance can help technology professionals influence the decision making at the top of the organization. But we can tell you from our hands-on experience that it is no easy matter to figure what information should be communicated and the best format for presenting the data. We are sometimes baffled by how often senior executives seem to be addicted to pretty pictures and charts, which convey a message, but seem to take much more work to create than they probably should. The challenge is really to understand what information needs to be presented and the best format for the presentation.

> ### What If You Are the Senior Manager?
>
> It is always best to put yourself in the shoes of the executives who run your company. If you were the boss, what information would you need to have in order to make wise decisions? If you are the manager at the top, keep in mind that you have a lot of information coming in from many different sources. Your board of directors has probably placed demands upon you to ensure growth and profitability. You may have regulatory requirements that are putting pressure on your company to establish IT controls, which may be expensive to implement. Of course, pressure from competition may also be adding complexity to your efforts to steer the ship. With all of this incoming information, you would really appreciate your own staff helping you make the right choices based upon a clear and compelling presentation. Do you understand now what your executives are up against?

Communicating up also means that you get a chance to show the good work that you and your team are doing. Marketing your accomplishments to the folks who make decisions about your compensation and future promotions is obviously a great idea, but communicating up positive information is not your only concern.

Sometimes, you also want to ensure that you are communicating challenges that you are facing so that perhaps you can get some support in removing barriers that are affecting your ability to do your job. Most importantly, you always want to go on record when there are risks and other threats to the organization.

This effectively shifts the responsibility from your shoulders to those above you who are in a position to act. This is not just playing the "blame game," but effectively freeing you up to focus on getting the work done by getting others involved. Deming said to "drive out fear." In this case, we might be driving it up the chain of command to others who are better positioned to address challenges that are above your pay grade.

> ### *Police Chiefs and Patrol*
>
> Bob spent many years as a volunteer leading a cross-functional multi-cultural team patrolling the streets of a major city. Sometimes, police–community issues could become challenging due to incidents reported in the press or other social issues. As a volunteer cop, Bob had the ability to walk into the police commander's office to discuss challenges and strategies. This police chief also had Bob's cell phone and never hesitated to request help when he needed an experienced community liaison. The police–community partnership is a great example of where managing communication can help avoid serious issues that can have far-reaching impact.

Having far too much work to complete within the time allotted and resources allocated is the norm for any complex technology project. Getting more budget allocated and perhaps adjusting deadlines to be more realistic are essential to ensuring that teams can deliver quality code without working unreasonable hours, which ultimately leads to burnout and skilled technology professionals looking for more reasonable opportunities elsewhere. The key to handling this strategy is ensuring that your executives understand just how much work is really getting accomplished.

15.6 How Much Work Is Going On?

Technology professionals are constantly operating in an environment where they are simply overloaded with work that needs to be completed and no shortage of discretionary tasks that they would love to complete as well. We are all as busy as could be and all too often feeling overwhelmed with just how much work we need to complete within the timeframe that we have been allotted. Communicating the work that is being done is important, not only in terms of senior management and decision makers, but also in terms of providing transparency across the organization. We find that well-designed governance can often be the catalyst for teams with similar challenges becoming connected and empowered to combine their efforts to address challenges.

Governance and Tools Selection

In one organization, we found teams looking at one tool and then immediately putting in a purchase request without any evaluation or even a proof-of-concept. We requested, and senior management approved, that the purchasing department reject requests without due diligence. Pretty soon, teams wanting to look at similar tools came to us directly, and we connected different teams, who then worked together to perform joint tool evaluations. With the increased transparency, management was much more confident in approving the purchase. In this case, IT governance removed barriers to choosing and getting the money for tools.

Communicating your existing workload and deadlines for deliverables can also give you some much-needed support when you cannot possibly complete all of your deliverables within the time allotted. Similarly, you may find yourself empowered to hire more staff or give more budget to help you accomplish your goals. Communicating how much work you have and your risks of missing your deadlines does not always result in other managers coming to the rescue, but it is also true that bad news does not get better with age, and the sooner that you communicate the status, the more likely that you will get the support you need in order to be successful. Often, the most critical aspect of IT governance is identifying and communicating risks.

15.7 Identify and Manage Risk

When risks are identified, key information should be communicated to those in a position to make decisions about the best course of action. Naturally, this effort should include the recommendations of those closest to the action, and one certainly hopes that senior management is wise enough to make the right choices. We find that many managers are afraid to deliver tough messages, but as we have said before, "bad news does not get better with age." Communicating risks and other challenges often does have the effect of transferring responsibility from the mid-level manager to the executive team.

> ### *Don't Say That I Didn't Tell You*
>
> We have seen situations where managers identified serious problems that could potentially lead to disasters. Keeping that information to yourself effectively puts the responsibility on your shoulders. Reporting the risk up the chain of command often transfers the responsibility to the most senior manager advised of the situation. Bob worked early in his career for a major radio network in New York City. One of their systems efforts was poorly designed and almost certainly going to fail. Bob wrote a letter documenting the issues and sent it up the chain of command. When things went south, the most senior manager was held accountable and terminated.

One of the biggest risks, one with far-reaching implications, is a lack of sufficient time and resources to meet the required deliverables.

15.8 Time and Resources

Estimating the amount of time and resources required to complete a project deliverable on time can be a difficult challenge. IT governance should include the current state of a project and whether or not the development efforts are likely to result in the deliverables being completed on time and within the allotted budget. When that is not possible, decisions must be made to either scale back on the goals of the project or to provide more resources to ensure that the work can be completed as planned.

We have seen situations where the team was running at full speed and on a trajectory to meet the target deliverables, but the executive staff expressed concern as to whether or not the team efforts could really be sustained over the entire course of the project. They were doing fine working long hours for the first few months, but more experienced heads realized that even the most dedicated IT professionals can burn out if they are expected to exhibit such a huge effort for a long period.

Communicating time and resources expended can help the decision makers determine if adjustments need to be made to ensure that the team can complete the project without everyone reaching burnout as we reached the finish line.

> ### Trading Firms and Hedge Funds
>
> We have seen quite a few trading firms and hedge funds that maintained a long-term culture of teams working very long hours for extended periods. In some cases, the development organization was compensated substantially for their over-the-top efforts, which motivated many to work long hours and weekends. Interestingly, however, we did not observe senior management being advised of progress, deliverables, and challenges. Instead, we found that the culture was simply focused on getting it done, regardless of the sacrifice. We don't advocate for or against such cultures, but just note that they exist. These organizations are highly competitive and often very successful, although the stress and fatigue can certainly be seen over time. We also note that many of these same firms were responsible for some of the catastrophic outages that have impacted our industry.

When existing time and resources are insufficient, decisions should be made as to whether or not more resources might be obtainable and whether or not they could help with essentials such as scalability.

15.9 Scalability with More Resources

The agile ALM can help identify when resources are insufficient to support the level of scalability that might be a necessity. In large-scale systems development, it is not unusual for project scope to expand to meet emerging business requirements. The well-designed ALM can help identify when scalability is essential, and IT governance should be the vehicle to communicate this information to senior management.

If your request for more resources to meet demand is not approved, you may have to deal with delays and other challenges.

15.10 Delays Happen

When delays occur, you need to ascertain whether additional resources are necessary. Otherwise, a change in scope of deliverables or schedule is required. As any experienced IT project manager will tell you, it is common for projects to experience delays for any number of reasons. The agile ALM should provide sufficient information that can be disseminated to those at the top to communicate delays that are unavoidable.

Effective communication always helps to reduce anxiety and facilitates the decision-making process. Keeping everyone on the team advised of the project status is absolutely essential and avoids anxious managers from becoming helicopter moms.

15.11 The Helicopter Mom

When anxiety is high, senior managers can sometimes provide a little too much supervision. This most often happens when these executives get surprised by a report that a project, thought to be on track, is discovered to be behind schedule. The sponsor of the project or other executives responsible for the success of the effort can feel compelled to suddenly get directly involved. Our view is that effective IT governance can help avoid these situations, which often have an unintended and less-than-helpful impact. You want to funnel information up to those in charge so they don't feel the need to stand over your shoulder to get their information.

Another dysfunctional situation is when managers seem to have forgotten what you have already communicated.

15.12 I Told You That Already

We have seen many managers find themselves being grilled by those above them, only to feel like the information was already communicated. This can happen because the data that was delivered up the chain of command was not entirely clear to those managers who are directly involved with the action and aware of the nuances that others take for granted. In these situations, we see managers who react negatively because they feel that they had already communicated these issues. This happens when IT governance is not implemented effectively, and although lots of data may be getting sent to the senior management team, effective communication is just not happening.

Make sure that status reports and information dashboards are designed to provide effective communication. This documentation can help avoid the accusation that senior management has not been sufficiently informed.

Another important requirement for IT governance is ensuring that we always communicate and learn from our mistakes.

15.13 Learning from Mistakes

The most effective organizations make it a practice to learn from mistakes. When mistakes happen, effective managers take responsibility, learn from what happened, and then move on. You should be able to have this discussion and utilize even the most serious incidents as a learning experience.

> ### The Best Managers
>
> The best managers empower their employees to own their mistakes. When serious incidents occur, prompt managing of that information up the chain of command is essential. Our view of IT governance is that you always want to proactively provide the information required to decision makers.

15.14 Governance Ecosystem

IT governance exists within a larger ecosystem with many stakeholders who should be kept informed. When viewed as a holistic system, it becomes readily apparent that there is a tremendous amount of information to be managed and interpreted. When there are too many surprises, it becomes likely that either the wrong information is being delivered or the information has not been successfully presented. Regulatory compliance and outside forces such as competition are both important aspects of the governance ecosystem.

15.15 Continuous Process Improvement

IT governance requires ongoing efforts to improve on a continuous basis. You need to start by understanding where you are today and what you need to do in order to improve. The best approach is usually to measure where you are today in order to track and communicate your improvements. One important aspect of process improvement is ensuring that IT governance is aligned with your compliance requirements.

15.16 Governance and Compliance

IT governance is commonly associated with compliance. We will discuss audit and regulatory compliance in Chapter 16, but what you need to know is that IT governance helps manage and guide the compliance effort. When auditors or outside regulatory authorities become aware of issues, it is the executive team who is most often required to respond to the findings and communicate the firm's intention to address any shortcomings.

Once again, you want to be proactive in how you communicate this information and ensure that your senior management team has the information they need in order to address any compliance issues.

15.17 Conclusion

IT governance is an importance mechanism for you to communicate the information that will help your executive team make intelligent decisions. You want to proactively drive this effort and not force your senior management team to come asking for information. This is your chance to influence the decision-making process, and doing this well can make your job much easier.

Chapter 16

Audit and Regulatory Compliance

Audit and regulatory compliance require that you establish IT controls to guide the way in which the team works. Your auditors may be internal employees or external consultants engaged by your firm. The internal audit team usually focuses on internal policy, whereas external auditors are often engaged to ensure compliance with federal regulatory guidelines. Whereas many technology professionals look at audit and regulatory compliance as just something that you have to do, others view it as an obligatory yet unfortunate waste of time and effort. Our focus is on establishing effective IT controls that help avoid both defects and risk. This chapter will help you understand how to use audit and regulatory compliance to ensure that you prevent the sorts of major systems glitches and outages that we read about all too often.

16.1 Goals of Audit and Regulatory Compliance

The goals of audit and regulatory compliance are to identify and then mitigate risks. As we have said before, risk is not always bad, especially when it is clearly identified and a plan for mitigating the risk established. But audit violations and failure to comply with regulatory standards are always bad. We have seen organizations that had serious violations with regulatory authorities actually issuing one or more warning letters outlining the violations and criteria for corrective action. If corrective actions are not forthcoming, the warning letter(s) could potentially be followed by a "cease and desist" letter, which could effectively force the company to leave a particular business area as a consequence of the noncompliance or, even worse, as a consequence of a serious incident. The goal of audit and regulatory compliance is to ensure that you do not run afoul

273

of the rules that your company is required to follow. You should have a goal of using this guidance to improve your productivity and quality.

16.2 Why Are Audit and Regulatory Compliance Important?

Audit and regulatory compliance are essential to the success of your organization. Without meeting these criteria, your company could literally be forced out of areas that are the bread and butter of your business, fined, or sanctioned in other ways. News of violations can also tarnish your corporate reputation and result in your customers choosing the services of your competitors instead of you. We often hear managers disparage audit and compliance as a waste of time. Our view is these resources can be enlisted and directed to focus on valid risks, helping the firm address challenges and avoid costly incidents.

Security is also a key concern. Understanding and successfully implementing industry guidelines help avoid incidents, including those related to security.

We strongly believe that audit and regulatory compliance should really be focused on avoiding errors and reducing operational risk, as well as keeping you out of the news as the latest major incident. The controls that you establish will help your team to achieve excellence and your company to be successful.

16.3 Where Do I Start?

The first step is to understand the industry that you are in and your audit and regulatory compliance requirements. You start by adhering to the rules that you are compelled to follow, but next you need to understand your firm's unique risk profile.

What are the things that could potentially go wrong with your systems? Could you accidently make a million-dollar trade, resulting in significant losses for your firm and your shareholders or expose confidential employee information? Could you accidently expose confidential patient information in violation of Health Insurance Portability and Accountability Act (HIPAA) regulations? Obviously, the risk of causing a problem in a life support system is more critical than exposing your favorite social networking password. But these days, there are many risks and consequences. You need to start by considering your organization's profiles and priorities. Then focus on making your journey to implement IT controls and compliance an effort that focuses on improving quality and productivity.

You also need to consider the cost of compliance. Establishing IT controls takes time and resources. Of course, the cost of noncompliance could potentially be more—indeed much more. Our message is to move beyond just going through the motions and actually focus on assessing and improving your operational processes.

16.4 Compliance with What?

Establishing controls to meet audit and regulatory requirements really requires that you understand the guidance you are trying to follow. Your internal audit team likely has their own policies and will also review and follow the guidelines of other groups, such as information security in the organization. We will discuss compliance with laws such as the Health Insurance Portability and Accountability Act of 1996 (HIPAA) and Section 404 of the Sarbanes-Oxley Act of 2002. These practices are typically guided by industry frameworks and standards. Common frameworks include ISACA Cobit 4.1, itSMF ITIL v3, and the Software Engineering Institute's Capability Maturity Model Integrated (CMMI). Standards are typically based upon the consensus of working groups from the International Organization for Standardization (ISO) or the Institute of Electrical and Electronics Engineers (IEEE), among other standards organizations.

Companies may choose to comply with ISO 9001, which establishes a quality management system (QMS). Many firms focus on security-related guidelines such as National Institute of Standards and Technology (NIST) or ISO 27001.

Whatever your specific industry focus, you need to determine which standards and frameworks make the most sense for your company to use as a guideline for establishing your own IT controls.

16.5 Establishing IT Controls

IT controls are the guidelines that help you meet audit and regulatory compliance. IT controls are essential for a number of reasons. The most obvious is that many organizations have to comply with federal laws. We believe that good corporate citizenship should be an even more compelling reason to make sure you are in compliance. The rules that we will discuss just make sense, and organizations should comply regardless of whether or not their lawyers have found some way to avoid it. One serious area of concern is that many hedge funds do not have to comply with establishing IT controls and compliance. Sometimes this results in organizations where production passwords are openly shared and there is no separation of duties. We view this as a huge mistake and feel strongly that all compliance laws should apply equally to all financial services firms, not just banks. There is also a need for these types of controls for firms in other industries, such as pharmaceutical, medical, and military contractors, which, by and large, take these practices very seriously. Implementing these controls just makes sense, and their successful implementation is essential for any organization.

16.6 Internal Audit

The internal audit team is usually completely outgunned, and sometimes regarded by developers and other stakeholders as just a waste of time and energy. Our experience is that they are actually a source of untapped talent who, with some training, can fill a valuable role as the "beat cop" on the street. Too often the internal audit team is intentionally kept in the dark, relegated to writing up a few issues here and there. We have provided training to internal auditors so that they actually know what to look for and then sent them out to visit each development team. The key to success was to focus only on valid and useful IT controls that everyone agreed were the most essential best practices.

The Auditors Are Here

We put together a slide deck and went through some technical training with the internal IT audit team of a large bank. The auditors would then visit each development team and ask them specific questions on how the team was baselining their code and to describe their procedures for managing bugfixes on branches. The focus of the audit was simply on the basic skills for supporting baselined releases, including variants. This was a huge help to us because the development teams were motivated to come to us for help using the version control and build automation tools in an effective way. The groups who came to us for training were pretty well guaranteed that they would pass their audit. These audits became a valued change agent, and some of the developers were openly surprised that the IT audit team actually knew what to ask for!

There was another positive effect from working proactively with the internal IT audit team, and that was receiving their support with senior management. We had accomplished two very important things with this effort. The first was that we trained and utilized the internal IT audit team to help us spread best practices throughout the firm. The second was unintended, but more important. With the training, the internal audit group no longer was writing up irrelevant stuff that wasted everyone's time. The message here is that the DevOps approach should be utilized to facilitate communication and collaboration between the internal IT audit team and the other stakeholders who can help identify and reduce risk. Although the internal IT auditors are really part of the team and should be included in your DevOps implementation across the ALM, external audits can be a little more unpredictable.

16.7 External Audit

External auditors usually come in with a predetermined focus. Although many managers insist that you should never volunteer any information at all to an auditor, our approach is to accurately describe the IT controls that we have in place. Because we know that these best practices are aligned with federal regulatory requirements, along with industry standards and frameworks, we have always been confident interfacing with the external auditors.

> ### Audit and Accountability
>
> With so many major incidents affecting international banks and trading firms, it is actually remarkable that external IT auditors are not doing more to lead the adoption of effective IT controls. Many of the external IT auditors who we have met certainly seemed to lack the technical knowledge and experience to be effective at identifying technical risk. We believe that this is an essential area for stricter controls in the future. In fact, the firms who do this work should be leading the way to establish effective IT controls that prevent human errors, improving system reliability, as well as security and quality.

One of the most important considerations from an audit perspective is ensuring compliance with federally mandated guidelines.

16.8 Federally Mandated Guidelines

There are many federally mandated guidelines, but we will start with those commonly known as SOX.

16.8.1 Section 404 of the Sarbanes-Oxley Act of 2002

The Sarbanes-Oxley Act of 2002 (SOX) was originally written by Senator Paul Sarbanes and Representative Michael Oxley as a response to several high-profile corporate scandals, including the much-publicized debacle at Enron Corporation. In this incident, there was a complete breakdown in corporate governance leading to huge losses for shareholders, many of whom were employed by the company. The purpose of the SOX legislation was to hold senior management responsible for seeing that financial reports were accurate and that there was full financial disclosure and transparency in corporate governance. In short, SOX requires that companies have accurate financial reports and that they establish proper IT controls. Section 404 of the Sarbanes-Oxley act specifies the requirements for management assessment of internal controls.

Section 404 requires that "[w]ith respect to the internal control assessment required by subsection (a), each registered public accounting firm that prepares or issues the audit report for the issuer shall attest to, and report on, the assessment made by the management of the issuer." In practice, this meant that the public accounting firm established a tool for the organization's subject matter experts (SMEs) to attest to compliance with each of the 34 required Cobit 4.1 controls. This was supposed to involve assessing current practices and then attesting to compliance. Where noncompliance existed, we proactively worked with the development teams to improve their configuration management (CM) practices so that they could pass their next audit. Even if the teams failed the first time, the important issue was that we had a short-term plan to help them quickly come into compliance. In most cases, this took less than a month. Unfortunately, we have also seen organizations where this effort was little more than a rubber stamp. In fact, we recall one incident where a senior manager in charge of compliance expected that the attestation would happen before the groups were reviewed and assessed! This organization obviously did not take SOX compliance seriously, and that was truly a lost opportunity, as these best practices can improve both productivity and quality.

Management Assessment of Internal Controls

As specified in the text of the act, Section 404 requires internal controls and accurate reporting:

(a) RULES REQUIRED.—The Commission shall prescribe rules requiring each annual report required by section 13(a) or 15(d) of the Securities Exchange Act of 1934 (15 U.S.C. 78m or 78o(d)) to contain an internal control report, which shall—

(1) state the responsibility of management for establishing and maintaining an adequate internal control structure and procedures for financial reporting; and

(2) contain an assessment, as of the end of the most recent fiscal year of the issuer, of the effectiveness of the internal control structure and procedures of the issuer for financial reporting.

(b) INTERNAL CONTROL EVALUATION AND REPORTING.— With respect to the internal control assessment required by subsection (a), each registered public accounting firm that prepares or issues the audit report for the issuer shall attest to, and report on, the assessment made by the management of the issuer. An attestation made under this subsection shall be made in accordance with standards for attestation engagements issued or adopted by the Board. Any such attestation shall not be the subject of a separate engagement.

After the Sarbanes-Oxley act was passed, a number of organizations began working on establishing an effective control framework so that corporations would have adequate guidance and could comply with the requirements set forth under law. One of the first organizations to work on this effort is known as COSO.

Committee of Sponsoring Organizations (COSO)

The Committee of Sponsoring Organizations of the Treadway Commission (COSO) is a voluntary private-sector organization composed of five sponsoring professional associations. COSO is dedicated to guiding executive management and governance entities toward the establishment of more effective, efficient, and ethical business operations on a global basis. It sponsors and disseminates frameworks and guidance based on in-depth research, analysis, and best practices. In 1992, the Committee of Sponsoring Organizations outlined five essential components of any internal control system:

- Control environment
- Assessment of risk
- Control activities
- Accounting, information, and communication systems
- Self-assessment or monitoring

Cobit as a Framework for IT Controls

Although COSO is generally considered a proper starting point for establishing financial controls, Cobit is commonly used to assess IT controls. In the Cobit 4.1 framework, there are 34 high-level IT processes and 34 control objectives. These control objectives include guidance on establishing change and configuration management.

Cobit is a common framework, but it is not the only source of information on IT governance.

16.8.2 Financial Industry Regulatory Authority

Financial Industry Regulatory Authority, Inc. (FINRA) is a self-regulatory organization (SRO). Overseen by the Securities and Exchange Commission, FINRA provides a variety of services focused on regulatory oversight of securities firms. FINRA was formed by a consolidation of the member regulation, enforcement, and arbitration operations of the New York Stock Exchange, NYSE Regulation, Inc., and National Association of Securities Dealers (NASD). We have seen guidance from FINRA help public securities firms, including banks, benefit from FINRA's well-defined cybersecurity governance structures and policies, along with training and awareness of potential risk vulnerabilities, including

- Data security standards
- Vendor management
- Incident response planning
- Independent cybersecurity penetration testing
- Cybersecurity planning and intelligence
- Safeguarding of personally identifiable information (PII)

From our experience, one of the most valuable services provided by FINRA is the self-administered risk assessment surveys, which help identify potential risks that need to be understood and mitigated. Although FINRA focuses on financial services firms, some of its guidance is of value to other industries as well. Many pharmaceutical and medical firms need to comply with HIPAA regulations, including safeguarding personally identifiable information, from Social Security numbers to confidential medical records.

16.8.3 Health Insurance Portability and Accountability Act of 1996

The HIPAA Privacy Rule protects the privacy of individually identifiable health information. The Patient Safety Rule also has confidentiality provisions, which protect identifiable information from being used to analyze patient safety events and improve patient safety. I have had technology professionals from pharmaceutical companies contact me to implement IT controls that were similar to those required by SOX and Cobit. In both cases, the organization has to comply with regulations that are described in a specific framework. I have been told that pharmaceutical companies may have their IT controls subject to review by agencies such as the Food and Drug Administration (FDA).

16.8.4 ISACA Cobit

ISACA Cobit is a framework commonly used to achieve compliance with Section 404 of the Sarbanes-Oxley act of 2002, which we discussed in Section 16.8. Our experience with the Cobit framework has been mostly focused on the 4.1 version, which consists of 34 high-level processes. We have found that the control objectives in this framework, including those focused on change and configuration control, are helpful in establishing effective IT controls. These same controls are described in other standards, including the IEEE 828-2012—Standard for Configuration Management in Systems and Software Engineering and the itSMF ITIL v3 framework.

16.8.5 Government Accountability Office

The Government Accountability Office (GAO) reviews government agencies and the subcontractors who work for them, making recommendations on areas where processes and procedures should be improved. The GAO describes the results of their reviews on their public website. For example, the GAO reviewed and commented on the configuration management practices used by the Federal Deposit Insurance Corporation (FDIC). The GAO cited several areas where the FDIC configuration management controls needed to be improved. For example, in May 2008 the GAO issued a report that said there were weaknesses in configuration management controls in two key FDIC financial systems. The GAO report stated that the FDIC did not adequately (1) maintain a full and complete baseline for system requirements; (2) assign unique identifiers to configuration items; (3) authorize, document, and report all configuration changes; and (4) perform configuration audits. This was not the first time that the FDIC had come under scrutiny for inadequate configuration management controls. In 2005, the FDIC Office of Inspector General (OIG) retained IBM Business Consulting Services to audit and report on the effectiveness of the FDIC's configuration management controls over operating system software.

The report also noted that CM is a critical control for ensuring the integrity, security, and reliability of the information systems. Absent a disciplined process for managing software changes, management cannot be assured that systems will operate as intended, that software defects will be minimized, and that configuration changes will be made in an efficient and timely manner. The objective of the audit was to determine whether the FDIC had established and implemented configuration management controls over its operating system software that were consistent with federal standards and guidelines and industry-accepted practices.

16.8.6 Office of the Comptroller of the Currency (OCC)

The Office of the Comptroller of the Currency was created by Congress to charter national banks; to oversee a nationwide system of banking institutions; and to assure that national banks are safe and sound, competitive and profitable, and capable of serving the banking needs of their customers in the best possible manner. The OCC issued guidelines on internal controls.

The OCC also has identified cases in which internal control weaknesses included improper and untimely reconcilements of major asset or liability accounts resulting in bank losses. In others, the bank did not institute or follow normal separation of duties between the physical control of assets and liabilities and the record-keeping functions involving those assets and liabilities.[1]

In practice, banks need configuration management best practices to maintain a separation of duties between the software developers who write the code and the operations teams that maintain the production systems. The calls that we have received were in regard to getting build engineers in place to compile, package, and deploy the code in a repeatable and traceable way. We have worked in organizations where the developers would do their own build and deployment, which was very bad for many reasons. In most cases, the procedure was not repeatable, and the developers relied upon being able to access production to fix last-minute problems that had been overlooked. This meant that when their build and deployment process was broken, the operations team could not roll back to a previous release, and there was little or no traceability into changes that were made to production systems. Developers, focused on writing great code, are not to blame. Another team was needed to provide traceability and repeatable deployment processes.

---

1. Internal Controls—A Guide for Directors, Office of the Comptroller of the Currency, Washington DC, September 2000.

16.9 Essential Compliance Requirements

Understanding what is essential for meeting compliance requirements is very important. The fact is that companies that must comply with federal regulatory regulations usually have legal experts on staff (or on contract) who help interpret these regulations and guide the firm in understanding what they really need to do. You certainly need to be guided by your own legal advisors, as they will be with you, defending you, should any violations be identified. That said, we find that most of the controls focus on establishing an appropriate segregation of duties to avoid collusion. Our experience is that these controls also avoid human error, as we have described throughout this book, including in Chapter 6. Traceability is another key consideration in that, even if mistakes are made, being able to show exactly what changes were made to production is an essential practice required by every set of regulatory guidelines that we know of.

Too many folks focus on just meeting the letter of the law, often wasting time on silly, ineffective controls that allow the company to claim that they met the regulatory requirement, but all too often are simply busywork. We strongly prefer to establish effective IT controls that not only allow you to meet the letter of the law, but actually improve your quality and productivity as well.

16.10 Improving Quality and Productivity through Compliance

If you take the time to really understand audit and regulatory requirements, then you will see that their main intent is to avoid human error and reduce risk to the firm. Throughout this book, we have described how to implement IT controls that improve quality and productivity. In this chapter, we have explained the requirements for audit and regulatory requirements and gave several practical examples. But your focus should be to go even further and create an agile ALM that meets these requirements, thus helping your organization achieve success.

16.11 Conducting an Assessment

Assessing your existing practices and comparing them to the relevant industry standards and frameworks helps identify the important IT controls that you really need to establish. We are often involved with these efforts and have found that teams usually have some effective strategies in place, yet there are often many areas where improvement really needs to occur. Your task is to find the right balance and avoid just meeting the letter of the law, but rather bring about real change that helps your team achieve success.

16.12 Conclusion

Meeting audit and regulatory compliance is a critical objective. To be successful, you need to understand what you are required to establish and the practices that will help your team avoid errors and reduce risk. We view these practices as being essential for your success and the success of your organization.

Chapter 17

Agile ALM in the Cloud

Cloud-based computing promises, and often delivers, capabilities such as scalable, virtualized enterprise solutions, elastic infrastructures, robust services, and mature platforms. Cloud-based architecture presents the potential of limitless scalability, but it also presents many challenges and risks. The scope of cloud-based computing ranges from development tools to elastic infrastructures that make it possible for developers to use full-size test environments that are both inexpensive and easy to construct and tear down, as required. The first step to harnessing its potential is to understand how application lifecycle management (ALM) functions within the cloud.

Technology professionals often use cloud-based tools at each stage of the development lifecycle to manage the workflow and all of its required tasks. Cloud-based ALM tools commonly include source code management, workflow automation (including defect and task tracking), knowledge management, and community-based forums. Many organizations make good use of the technology by maintaining their own private cloud. Virtualized environments enable continuous delivery and robust testing environments. The main advantage of cloud-based computing is its ability to deliver enterprise architectures at low cost and then scale the architecture as demand increases. Companies that use cloud-based technologies can focus on operating expenditures (OPEX) instead of capital expenditures (CAPEX). Therefore, businesses can keep initial costs low and pay only for actual resources utilized, adjusted as system needs vary. Making the right choices requires that you understand the goals of the ALM in the cloud.

17.1 Goals of ALM in the Cloud

The goal of ALM in the cloud is to establish a comprehensive suite of automated tools to support your entire development effort at very little cost. We discussed automating the ALM using tools in Chapter 7, but this chapter makes the assumption that you have a limited budget, although you may need to scale up in the future. The agile ALM, and especially DevOps, relies heavily upon a robust tools infrastructure to support the entire software and systems lifecycle. We make the assumption that your environment will likely need to scale because it has become standard practice to begin with a small pilot project or proof-of-concept (POC) and add more resources once the project has been approved and funded.

We also have another related goal, which is using our ALM implementation in the cloud to help us learn more about cloud-based development, because we may be supporting the development of software and systems that themselves may very well be in the cloud. If the application being built will eventually run in the cloud, then it is a very good idea to manage its ALM in the cloud using the same service provider and the same infrastructure.

17.2 Why Is ALM in the Cloud Important?

ALM in the cloud is important because it is common to have a limited budget in the beginning of a project. This is especially important for startups, which may have very limited budgets or perhaps are even self-funded. We see many teams adopting low-end tools with limited functionality that cannot scale to meet the full long-term needs of the agile ALM. Starting in the cloud allows you to establish the right tools at a fraction of the cost and then scale up as the project demands. It is important to plan to use the best tools, ones that have the security and features you need to support agility at scale.

There is another reason why using the cloud is very important; it gives the team some practical experience working in the cloud, often with the same tools that they have to deploy when the code is ready for production. The cloud provides a flexible sandbox for development and operations to make the journey together as the agile ALM evolves to the meet the needs of the software and systems development lifecycle.

17.3 Where Do I Start?

It is common for development teams to begin with inexpensive or even completely free tools just to get started. Low-cost (or no-cost) tools are often sufficient in the beginning, and perhaps even complete the POC, thereby securing management approval for the pilot or POC and also your funding. Some teams choose to use cloud-based service providers who offer robust ALM tools as Software as a Service (SaaS) or Platform as a service (PaaS). The SaaS approach means that the service provider handles the software installation, configuration, and maintenance. You generally use the SaaS-based product via a Web browser, perhaps with the use of a browser plugin. The PaaS approach typically involves more of the configuration and administration. There are many agile ALM cloud-based solutions, from version control to project and workflow automation tools. If these solutions do not work for you, you may decide to use Infrastructure as a Service (IaaS), where your cloud-based provider simply provides virtual servers and you handle the software installation, configuration, and administration. Your total cost to get started will likely still be much lower compared with buying machines and having to provide space in a physical datacenter, a practice that is commonly referred to as "on premises" (on-prem).

Many commercial tools vendors offer no-cost "community editions"—robust products that may have some limitations compared with the commercial version yet can still be used by a small team, often up to ten users. This means that your scrum team can get started using products that can scale to thousands of users. We have worked with several teams where we implemented the most robust ALM tool suites using community editions and then efficiently converted up to the commercial versions once the funding and approvals for purchase and implementation had been attained.

We coach teams to avoid starting with tools that cannot scale to full production usage and instead start with the best tools, even if they are only community editions, implemented on cloud-based infrastructures. This approach allows you to start small and then grow to full production usage.

Most teams start by choosing an approach to version control and then a service provider for the infrastructure. Many teams begin with a tool to provide and configure infrastructure, followed by application build, package, and deployment.

17.4 Understanding the Cloud

Cloud-based providers are evolving their services into remarkably powerful (and complex) tools and solutions. Understanding cloud capabilities and then implementing these solutions can be a daunting task, requiring engineers with considerable training, skills, and experience. In many organizations, the DevOps engineer is routinely assumed to be an expert in managing complex cloud-based resources. Actually, although the cloud has enormous potential, DevOps is just as essential on physical servers (or, as many like to say, "bare metal").

It is common for cloud systems engineers to spend considerable time learning how to work with the complex offerings from cloud vendors, who themselves are getting very good at turning almost anything into a scalable SaaS or PaaS offerings.

We have seen numerous instances where getting into a particular vendor's offering was initially easy, but then sometimes the service became less than acceptable. It is often difficult to then move to another service provider when poor service actually affects your business. Using DevOps best practices, you should be able to structure your implementation steps so that you can switch providers as necessary. This may require a little extra work up-front to abstract the implementation details, but is well worth the effort to ensure that you can always choose the best cloud service provider or bring your operations back in-house on physical servers should you so choose. In fact, architecting your ALM so that you can pull back out at will is a must, as there are often times when cost, security, or concerns warrant such a move.

17.5 Developing in the Cloud

Software and systems development in the cloud can feel like being a kid in a candy store. There are so many powerful resources from which to choose, and the potential seems to be without limits. Many groups are discovering the value of developing in the cloud, using evolving technologies such as virtualization and container-based deployments. The DevOps approach of requiring that developers work in production-like environments is remarkably feasible when cloud-based resources are available, and the agile ALM is greatly enhanced by this limitless potential. We also feel that DevOps can help ensure you are not locked into the cloud, but retain the ability to bring your environments in-house when necessary, including deployment to physical servers. There is some concern regarding security and reliability in using powerful source code management and workflow automation solutions in the cloud.

17.5.1 Source Code Management in the Cloud

Many popular source code management cloud-based solutions also offer a framework for workflow automation and release coordination. Some of these providers allow you to use their resources and restrict access to only your own internal employees. We have been using a number of these services for quite some time and are impressed with their capabilities, delivered at a low cost. However, we are not without our concerns in terms of reliability and security. If your source code information contains valuable intellectual property (IP), then you need to make an informed decision as to whether or not you feel comfortable trusting a service provider to maintain security, or if you view this responsibility as something that you need to bring in-house. We are not saying that cloud-based providers are more or less secure per se, as some of them have a great deal of experience managing security and a large, experienced staff on-hand dealing with this responsibility on a daily basis. But if you are a contractor working on a healthcare system, you must be aware that outsourcing the management of your ALM in no way outsources your regulatory responsibilities, such as adhering to HIPAA regulations as well as other requirements.

17.5.2 Build Automation in the Cloud

We find that cloud-based build automation is more commonly performed on servers provisioned on elastic infrastructure providers. DevOps absolutely requires fast builds, so virtualization of build machines is an absolute must-have. That said, we currently see most folks managing the complexities of their application build, package, and deployment directly, so although cloud resources may be part of this effort, it is generally handled as infrastructure. We know that cloud-based providers are working on improving SaaS and PaaS build, package, and deployment solutions, and these may very well become more popular in the future.

17.5.3 Release Engineering in the Cloud

Release engineers are benefitting greatly from all that the cloud has to offer. Being able to harness unlimited resources and production-like environments makes our job much easier to accomplish. But there is also some danger out there, and release engineering needs to focus more on creating release packages, whether they be web packages (e.g., JARs, WARs, EARs)[1] or simply GNU tar[2] or zip[3] files, that are cryptographically signed and contain a manifest with a full list of configuration items along with their own MAC-SHA1 or MD5 signatures. Cloud-based development values the procedures inherent in release engineering, but also requires the more advanced security-related techniques that some folks foolishly skip. Your release containers should always be tamper-proof (using

---

1. Java Archive (JAR), Web Archive (WAR), and Enterprise Archive (EAR) are packages used to simplify the deployment process.
2. GNU tarball.
3. ZIP file.

cryptography) and be verifiable as coming from the trusted source, in a manner that is called nonrepudiation. *Nonrepudiation* means that you have signed the tamper-proof container with your private key, which is verifiable with your public key.

17.5.4 Deployment in the Cloud

Deployment in the cloud is getting interesting. Virtualization and container-based deployments have led many of us to reconsider how we approach the deployment of complex systems. Being able to rapidly build and provision a virtual machine and then deploy applications through a fully automated deployment pipeline have quickly become expected capabilities. The potential of applications running on multiple servers (via a load balancer or proxy) and updated during the working day without any impact to end users is even more exciting. This practical approach to *continuous delivery* is accomplished by upgrading a few machines and then proceeding on to the rest, if there are no problems, within a specified timeframe. If the upgrade appears to have some technical issue, then the modified servers are taken offline and reverted back to their original state. The idea is that having a couple of servers die is an acceptable price to pay to avoid impact to the larger system, and more importantly, to the customer.

> ### Canaries and Deployments
>
> Years ago, coal miners would work in very dangerous conditions where carbon monoxide and other dangerous gases could, and in some cases did, cause the death of one or more of the mining workers. One strategy that was used was to bring small birds, such as canaries, into the mine. The thought was that the bird was likely to get sick before the miners, providing a crude "early warning system" when the environment had turned toxic. We are pleased to report that no animals have been harmed in cloud-based "canary deployments."

17.6 Change Management in the Cloud

Cloud-based change management solutions help manage the automated workflow required for processing and tracking change requests (CRs). These solutions are often part of a comprehensive IT process automation solution. The change management approach should include support for the change control board (CCB), which manages the review and approval of CRs. The CCB maintains a change calendar to avoid scheduling conflicts, which could result in serious incidents. The change management process should also review and evaluate technical risk. Every change request incurs a risk of the change being made and also a risk of the change *not* being made. The change management process should review the technical risk of each change and its potential downstream impact. To accomplish this task, the CCB must rely upon subject matter experts (SMEs) who possess deep and thorough knowledge of what might happen if each change is approved. We recommend determining the assets affected by each change request and enlisting the help of the experts who understand the potential impact of each change on the asset itself. It is a best practice to appoint these SMEs to a change advisory board (CAB) to assist the CCB with reviewing and approving change requests.

Terminology Confusion

Unfortunately, some organizations have chosen to rename their change control board (CCB) to change advisory board (CAB). This is unfortunate and confusing. The CCB is a process control function that is very important. The CAB consists of the technical experts who can advise the CCB on what might happen if a particular change is made (or perhaps not made). We view these two functions as being quite different, and they should not be combined. Some folks are very good at establishing and following process. Others have excellent technical knowledge. In practice, we see a different group of people serving in the CCB than those who should be assigned to the CAB. You need both entities working together in order to help the organization manage technical risk, significantly improving your system's reliability and security.

One key concern is to understand the management of changes made by the service provider. In fact, it is essential to include service provider notifications in your change management function.

17.6.1 Service Provider Notification

Many cloud-based providers do a great job of ensuring reliable service. But sometimes outages cannot be avoided. Third-party notifications must be part of the change management process.

> ### Upselling and Other Bad Services
>
> We have seen some service providers that forced upgrades in their SaaS and PaaS offerings, but actually handled dependency management very poorly. One particular ISP developed a reputation for causing outages, which their support staff insisted could be best handled by purchasing more services from them. Each time they caused us an outage, their response was to attempt to charge us more money. In response, we automated our deployment process, allowing us to take our business elsewhere, thus preventing future mishaps and saving money in the process.

When you decide to use the cloud to manage your ALM, you should ensure that you take a wide and comprehensive view of managing the entire lifecycle.

17.7 Managing the Lifecycle with ALM

Managing the lifecycle with robust ALM tools must take a very broad view. We have discussed many examples of using the cloud to manage the ALM. You may find other aspects of the ALM that need to be handled as well. You should also consider whether or not management of the ALM will eventually be brought in-house and "on-prem," as is often the case when the ALM has to scale to the enterprise. We will discuss this further in Chapter 19.

17.8 Cloud-based ALM Tools

Cloud-based ALM tools usually include workflow automation; support for agile development; and specialized tools to support application build, package, and deployment. In some cases, you may be able to implement large, comprehensive ALM solutions, such as those that exist for customer relationship management (CRM). In others, you may have to create toolchains to integrate one or more vertical solutions.

17.9 Achieving Seamless Integrations

Using vertical solutions involves tools that perform a specific task well, but that may need to be integrated with other tools. There is often a tradeoff between a comprehensive ALM solution and integrating vertical solutions. We discuss managing tools integration in Chapter 7, but the cloud does bring some unique challenges. For example, trying to integrate different cloud-based solutions may present specific challenges. Cloud-based ALM solutions are especially helpful with iterative development.

17.10 Iterative Development in the Cloud

Iterative development is well suited to the cloud. Supporting the ALM lifecycle may involve a fair amount of effort. Sometimes, the frameworks offered by cloud-based providers are sufficient and can therefore save time and work. But you may find that, over time, you need more robust tools support. Once again, this is exactly where cloud-based development benefits greatly from the elasticity and flexibility of the cloud.

17.10.1 Development Models in SaaS

We have seen some SaaS-based solutions that had established ALM lifecycle processes that were not only available, but actually required. In some ways, these solutions are mature and well supported. However, we have also seen that they are sometimes limited and fall far short of solutions we have implemented. In one instance, we were forced to use the provider's user acceptance testing (UAT) environment, which did not fully match the production environment, which increased the risk of defects occurring in production that were not successfully identified in UAT. Development models in the SaaS can be quite mature, but you may still find yourself less than satisfied if you have become accustomed to robust ALM lifecycle solutions.

17.11 Interfacing with Your Customers

Keep in mind that your customers will hold you responsible for the success or failure of your application lifecycle methodology. Selecting a cloud-based provider may save you some time, but outsourcing this work does not outsource your responsibility. If your service provider fails to maintain acceptable security standards, you run the risk of failing to adhere to required regulatory compliance requirements. In other words, if you are supposed to adhere to HIPAA and your service provider has an incident that discloses personal identifiable information (PII), then you will still be left holding the bag for the breach caused by the service provider's failure to secure the environment.

17.11.1 Fronting Service Providers

Many cloud-based providers allow you to brand their solutions with your own skin. Providing a seamless interface is important for many businesses and something that you may be able to implement.

17.12 Managing with SLAs

Service providers do typically offer a service-level agreement (SLA) with their customers, which specifies target uptimes and agreed-upon procedures for resolving issues. It is important to understand the SLA and evaluate whether or not it is acceptable for your business. There is usually a cost for a "premium" SLA, providing better service and response, but, of course, there is usually a cost to systems being down as well. Either way, you are always dependent upon your cloud-based provider, as it is the factor over which you have the least control.

17.12.1 Reliance upon Service Providers

You must rely upon your service provider to maintain an acceptable level of support. This is another reason why some projects start by using cloud-based providers in the beginning, but then choose to bring the ALM tools support in-house using on-premises machines.

17.13 Managing Cloud Risk

The cloud, despite all of its advantages and potential, also has a great deal of risk. As we have said previously, risk is not always bad. You need to understand the risks inherent in cloud-based computing and come up with a plan for communicating and mitigating them. In some cases, these risks are acceptable, or perhaps unavoidable, in the beginning of a project. You may be required to implement your ALM in the cloud with a long-term plan of bringing your ALM back in-house and on-premises as the project approaches completion. One area where the cloud clearly excels is its limitless capacity for robust development and test environments.

17.14 Development and Test Environments for All

Developers benefit greatly from access to robust development and test environments. Unfortunately, it is all too common for developers to be limited to their own laptop and the number of virtual machines (VMs) that they can squeeze onto their own machine. The cloud excels at providing low-cost development and test environments that can significantly improve programmer productivity and especially the quality of the code. With the cloud, developers can test on production-like environments as early and as often as they wish. This approach also implicitly promotes managing infrastructure as code, a key DevOps objective.

We also find that it is a very sound practice to start small and then grow as needed.

17.14.1 Starting Small

The cloud enables one to create environments both large and small. However, we have observed that it is often a wise choice to start with a small footprint and then grow. This approach keeps the work required to stand up the environment to a minimum.

17.15 Environment Management

Environment management is often overlooked, but is actually especially important in the cloud. You should not just rely upon your cloud provider, as they may not have the same sense of urgency for your business operations as you do. We find that most outages are actually related to a lack of good environment management. You should always understand and monitor your runtime dependencies. When you do this well, you will often get notifications in advance of actual outages and, more importantly, you will likely be able to take corrective action before customer impact occurs. One important consideration is ensuring that you have gold copies of all production baselines.

17.15.1 Gold Copies

Your ALM not only should, but in our opinion must, safeguard baselined production releases of your system created through the ALM. You need to have a storage facility, often called the definitive media library (DML), for these production baselines. Any and all changes to the production baselines need to be tracked and verified. This is best accomplished with the support of a CMDB.

17.15.2 CMDB in the Cloud

The configuration management database (CMDB) contains records that describe both the expected and current states of all configuration items (CIs). This information is maintained in a configuration management system (CMS), which is usually a relational database that provides supporting information for the CMDB. You should have automated procedures in place to verify that all configuration items are recorded and any discrepancies identified. Many CMDBs fail because the information cannot be updated in a timely manner using fully automated procedures.

17.16 DevOps in the Cloud

DevOps in the cloud has its own special set of challenges, often due to the dynamic nature of the cloud and the iterative development that accompanies agile development. You can manage these requirements by having a fully automated set of procedures to build your infrastructure and seamlessly deploy your applications. This approach is especially valuable in responding to a cyberattack or other unauthorized changes, which may threaten the reliability of your systems.

17.17 Controlling Costs and Planning

Controlling costs and planning can be especially challenging in cloud-based development. We find that some cloud providers are less than completely clear about what things cost, and their PaaS and SaaS solutions often have hidden costs that may be difficult to predict. We recommend that you invest the time to understand the vendor's cost model and also set up a credit card that notifies you immediately when charges are incurred. We had one experience where we set up a small environment for testing and then deleted all of the servers and resources, but we kept getting charged small amounts. We contacted the support line, who were also unable to help us figure out what was still causing us to incur charges. Finally, we deleted the account.

17.18 Conclusion

Managing your ALM in the cloud has significant advantages, although not without some challenges, and certainly not without effort. If the application that you are building will eventually run in the cloud, using the same cloud provider to manage your ALM is usually a very wise choice. In some cases, using the cloud is only a temporary solution. In all cases, DevOps can help you manage the ALM for success.

Chapter 18

Agile ALM on the Mainframe

The mainframe is alive and well. Many corporations have been planning the deprecation of their mainframe infrastructure for years, but yet the mainframe continues to be in use. Application lifecycle management (ALM) on the mainframe typically enjoys a specific workflow. Despite a culture that lends itself well to step-by-step defined procedures, ALM on the mainframe often falls short of its potential. Sure, we can specify steps of a process, and everyone accepts that process tollgates are necessary on the mainframe. But that does not mean that our mainframe processes help improve productivity and quality. It is essential that ALM on the mainframe be agile and help the team reach their goals and the business achieve success.

18.1 Goals of Agile ALM on the Mainframe

The goal of agile ALM on the mainframe is to define processes that help you deliver updates and bugfixes while achieving the highest levels of quality and productivity. On the mainframe you will likely focus on iteratively improving your existing processes rather than adopting a whole new approach. It is likely that you also have the goal of aligning your mainframe processes with ALM processes for distributed systems. We discuss aligning the ALM across the enterprise in Chapter 19. But this chapter focuses on being agile on your mainframe.

18.2 Why Is Agile ALM on the Mainframe Important?

The mainframe is still the trusty workhorse in many organizations, and many technology professionals work on projects that must include, in whole or in part, mainframe systems. Coming up with an effective strategy on your mainframe is very important, or else you will find that your ALM is constantly held up waiting for those Cobol copybooks to be updated.

> ### Mainframe Culture
>
> The most interesting aspect of working with the mainframe is its well-established culture and operating procedures. We find that many technology professionals are totally fine with adhering to mainframe procedures that they would immediately reject if they were on Linux or Windows machines. We know of no actual technical rationale for this phenomenon, but have seen this dynamic play out in many organizations. IT controls are just part of the culture of mainframes. That is not to say that some folks find clever ways to bypass these controls, as we discuss in this chapter.

Getting started with ALM on a mainframe will likely have you first reviewing many well-established processes and procedures. Mainframe technology professionals often have large binders of technical and process-related information, which are often out of date and seldom maintained. Instead we find that "tribal" knowledge exists both in terms of process and technical procedures. Approaching process improvement in a mainframe environment should always begin with a careful assessment of the current state.

18.3 Where Do I Start?

Mainframe developers and systems administration have long had well-established procedures. The issue that we hear frequently is that the mainframe deployment procedures are reliable and traceable, but far from agile. We usually start by examining the existing procedures, looking for ways to help the team accelerate their delivery without compromising quality.

> ### Defining the Mainframe ALM
>
> Mainframe processes are often well established, although often based on "tribal knowledge," without updated written documentation or instructions. The initial rationale for checkpoints and other IT controls are often long forgotten, with available documentation often being out of date

by ten or more years. When we probe deep enough, we often find that the existing rigid controls are not always necessary—and often cleverly bypassed. Challenging the way that things have always been done on the mainframe is not easy, and many people will warn you not to try to change what has worked for so long. Nonetheless, it is our approach to challenge each step by finding out exactly why the existing controls are in place. To make this happen, we have found ourselves reviewing ancient CLIST, EXEC2, and REXX scripts. Make sure that you get help with this effort, because the technical details are often nontrivial and *always* essential.

With the support and help of skilled programmers and systems administrators, mainframe systems are often extremely efficient, crunching through vast amounts of data at a remarkably fast and efficient rate. We don't doubt that distributed systems can also efficiently handle big data, especially when you have the luxury of limitless cloud-based resources. But existing infrastructures (and investments) on the mainframe in many cases would take years (and a large budget) to replace without any real return on investment. Mainframes are good at what they do, and it is often pragmatic to improve mainframe processes without trying to replace these complex and reliable systems.

We do find that mainframe technology experts often have great ideas on what can be improved; therefore, reviewing and adjusting mainframe processes is often an excellent approach. Even the smallest mainframe incurred a huge investment of time, money, and effort to set up, so there is a great deal of value in focusing on process improvement and achieving better quality.

Bypassing Change Control

We have seen organizations with well-established bureaucratic quality assurance (QA) and change control processes. Unfortunately, these guidelines are not always respected and followed. In one organization, we learned that the QA group took so long to test and approve mainframe changes that developers had learned to adapt by waiting for an emergency change to be approved and then slipping in an extra hundred lines or so of changes that had not been fully reviewed or tested. The verbose QA processes had motivated these folks to find a way to circumvent the mainframe IT controls. Obviously, this was a huge risk to the firm, as we learned during our configuration management (CM) assessment.

Many organizations do not think of including the mainframe in their efforts to implement an agile ALM. We view this as a lost opportunity, and our goal is always to approach process improvement on the mainframe in a way that aligns with its culture and technology, while also harmonizing with processes in the distributed world.

18.4 DevOps on the Mainframe

We have had several engagements where we worked to implement DevOps on the mainframe. The procedures were usually well defined, and changing them was most certainly no small matter. We made some tangible improvements by reviewing and improving on the CLIST and REXX scripts, although this project felt more like a corporate anthropology study than a code review. Sometimes, we were able to make modest improvements in the deployment processes by working with stakeholders and soliciting their suggestions and relying largely upon their technical expertise and knowledge of history within the organization. Many of the suggestions were considered to be significant changes in the mainframe world, but normal and accepted controls in any Linux/Unix environment. We managed to improve communication and collaboration between developers and operators on the mainframe, although again these roles were well entrenched, and protocols for interactions had generally been in place for many years. Process improvement on the mainframe must focus on taking baby steps with robust communication and collaboration.

Getting Root Access on a Mainframe

Implementing DevOps often involves taking root access away from developers who have formed the bad habit of deploying their own code into production. Although we don't generally find the same issue on mainframes, a similar risk occurs when developers who have been around for a while have RACF security privileges that allow them to bypass controls and even run JCL without going through the normal change control process. Always make sure that you understand risks from the viewpoint of the technology in which you are working.

18.5 Conclusion

In many organizations, the mainframe is alive and kicking. You should always include the mainframe in your process improvement initiative, including designing and implementing the agile ALM. Remember to understand the mainframe from within its own culture and technology, while also working to align its processes with the rest of the organization, as we will discuss further in Chapter 19, "Integration across the Enterprise."

Chapter 19

Integration across the Enterprise

Understanding the ALM across the entire organization requires an understanding of the organization at a very broad level. It also requires that you understand how each structure within the company interfaces with the others. In DevOps, we call this *systems thinking* when we are examining an application from its inception to implementation, operation, and even its deprecation. DevOps principles and practices are essential in integrating the ALM across the organization.

19.1 Goals of Integration across the Enterprise

The goal of integration across the enterprise is to help the team understand how the systems and software development effort affects the entire organization. We live in a time when technical knowledge is highly specialized. Unfortunately, this often means that technology professionals have only a very narrow understanding of the organization along with its systems and processes. Using a DevOps approach, you can drive your ALM to be effective across the enterprise and align with both business and technical processes. We find that the key to success is creating cross-functional teams, whether they are engaged for months on a specific project or just for the hour in which we are all joined on a call, sharing a screen to solve a problem or just accomplish a task. This approach significantly improves communication and collaboration across the enterprise.

19.2 Why Is Integration across the Enterprise Important?

Integration across the enterprise is important because you want to align your technology efforts with your business objectives. In fact, stakeholders throughout

305

the enterprise should all have well-defined roles in your agile ALM. We find that, too often, software and systems lifecycles cover the concerns of those writing and configuring the code, but fail to consider other key stakeholders. The itSMF ITIL v3 framework has provided much-needed governance in terms of running IT operations, including transitioning the system from development to operations, but other stakeholders, including IT audit, information security, and business and procurement, should be involved and informed who are often not fully engaged.

Procurement and Standards

Your procurement team is essential for implementing an agile ALM, and many folks do not realize just how helpful they can be. In many organizations, the procurement team processes purchase orders and approves expenditures related to software and systems purchases. We usually ask the procurement team to insist that purchase requests for ALM-related software, such as version control systems, workflow automation, and deployment frameworks, include documentation of a well-structured product evaluation, proof-of-concept, and even a bake-off when feasible. Our secret goal is to ensure that we do not have each team purchasing a different set of tools. By getting the evaluations out into the "light of day," we are able to help guide each team in adopting uniform corporate standards and avoid the "urban sprawl" of different toolsets being implemented for each team. This obviously affects our ability to ensure effective integration across the enterprise.

Taking a wide view of the agile ALM is essential and should even extend to procurement and similar functions. To be successful, you need to make knowledgeable decisions regarding where to begin.

19.3 Where Do I Start?

Getting started with integrating your ALM across the enterprise should always begin with the core software development processes. We find that nothing gets done without both a version control system (VCS) and workflow automation. As we discussed in Chapter 7, the VCS and the workflow automation tools should be integrated. From there, we like to see a consistent method for capturing the requirements for the software being built, whether using agile stories or a classic requirements-gathering approach such as the Open Unified Process (OpenUp). Ultimately, you need to make sound decisions on the functions that you wish to add to your agile ALM. You cannot include everything all at once, so taking an agile iterative approach to designing and implementing your agile ALM works really well. Start at the beginning and keep iterating until you have a well-defined and comprehensive agile ALM. DevOps principles and practices are extremely effective at helping you drive the development of your agile ALM across the enterprise.

19.4 Multiplatform

Integrating the ALM across the enterprise usually involves working across the range of platforms that are in use. There can be challenges integrating the procedures used by Windows C#/.Net developers with those favored by full-stack Linux experts. You need to take into consideration not only the technical aspects of the platform, but the culture of each development organization as well. We briefly discuss the agile ALM on the mainframe in Chapter 18, and most of the book takes a broad view of distributed development. You need to be able to consider your own multiplatform environment when designing and implementing your agile ALM. One key consideration is coordinating across your various systems.

19.5 Coordinating across Systems

Coordinating across systems always involves understanding the essential dependencies between the systems impacted. It also involves the groups or teams involved, along with their cultures and operating procedures. Coordinating across systems can be complicated and challenging. Ensuring that development, operation, QA, testing, information security, and other groups work as a cross-functional team can be challenging to accomplish. This is precisely the situation where taking a DevOps approach can be effective. Make sure that you pay close attention to the interfaces.

19.6 Understanding the Interfaces

Understanding the interfaces between systems can be difficult given that we are often working across systems and technologies involving different subject matter experts, procedures, and team cultures. In practice, we find that the best chance for success is to have the IT leaders agree to having the required resources work together as a cross-functional team, which may last for months or just for an hour, sharing a screen to accomplish a specific task or solve a problem. To really get the team working together in a collaborative way, you need to understand the enterprise ecosystem.

19.7 The Enterprise Ecosystem

The enterprise ecosystem includes many groups and technologies and likely different vendors and service providers. Integration across the enterprise requires that you thoroughly understand the environment in which the technology professionals and their teams operate. This can be a challenging task and an excellent opportunity to utilize a DevOps approach. We are often coordinating across technology professionals from different teams and platforms. In addition to understanding your ecosystem, having an effective release coordination function is important.

19.8 Release Coordination

Release coordination is a very important project management function that seeks to track required tasks from each of the stakeholders. We like to describe release coordination as the person with the clipboard ensuring that all tasks are completed in the proper order and that everyone is kept aware of the status of any remaining tasks to be completed. Too often, release coordination only focuses on scheduling on a calendar, when what is really needed is facilitating communication and collaboration across organizational structures.

19.9 Conclusion

Integration across the enterprise is a challenging function that must align with the business goals and take a comprehensive view of each group or function within the organization. Understanding the ecosystem and the interfaces is key to your success at ensuring your agile ALM effort can align with your organization and your business.

Chapter 20

QA and Testing in the ALM

Quality assurance (QA) and testing are essential to any software or systems life-cycle. Most technology professionals view the QA and testing process as simply executing test cases to verify and validate that requirements have been met and that the system functions as expected. But there is a lot more to QA and testing, and this chapter will help you understand how to establish effective processes to help ensure that your system functions as needed. DevOps helps us build, package, and deploy software much more quickly. Too often, the QA and testing process cannot keep up with the accelerated deployment pipeline. DevOps cannot succeed without excellent QA and testing.

20.1 Goals of QA and Testing

The goal of QA and testing is to support the iterative nature of agile ALM by ensuring that there is an automated testing process that can keep pace with the DevOps approach to application deployment. After so many process improvement successes, many organizations find that their QA and testing functions are actually left in the dust. Your goal should be to have a comprehensive approach to testing that can help your DevOps and agile ALM reach its full potential.

20.2 Why Are QA and Testing Important?

QA and testing are important because your customers want you to deliver defect-free code that accomplishes its objectives. It is absolutely vital that your testing process be both comprehensive and yet able to keep up with the rapid rate of change inherent in agile development and DevOps in particular. Without excellent testing, your developers will be mired in supporting system issues and fixing bugs. Testing must be started from the very beginning of the process, including unit testing through functional and regression testing and more. QA and testing is the lifeguard in the pool.

The First Rule of Being a Lifeguard

Both Bob and Leslie have served as certified lifeguards and emergency medical technicians. When Bob first took the lifeguard class, he was surprised to hear the instructor explain that the first rule of being a lifeguard is "don't get wet." But this is actually a very accurate view of QA and testing. We want to deliver defect-free code without having to jump in and pull anyone out of the water. The focus should always be on prevention. Code reviews are among the many methods that help developers deliver clean code. That said, don't go into a deep pool without a lifeguard present, and always make sure that your testing procedures are comprehensive and able to keep up with the rapid rate of change inherent in agile development and especially DevOps.

20.3 Where Do I Start?

Getting started with QA and testing involves understanding your existing processes along with the demands of your emerging DevOps practices. We find that teams may have adequate manual testing, but these measures won't meet the needs of rapid application delivery when organizations adopt a DevOps approach. You must assess your ability to automate your testing throughout the software and systems lifecycle. Although unit and functional testing are a must-have, effective testing needs to include a much deeper approach, such as testing directly at the application programming interface (API) level. With this foundation, you can successfully move on to creating message proxies and implementing emerging techniques such as service virtualization testing, which we will discuss in the next section.

The nature of the agile iterative development process and the high rate of deployment enabled by DevOps are often limited by the lack of robust automated testing. Many teams are finding that even if they can deploy faster, QA and testing approvals often lag behind.

The Slowest Function

With many efforts to improve the development effort and our ability to rapidly build, package, and deploy, we have seen some teams finding that their QA and testing functions lagged behind. Unfortunately, in some instances, we uncovered developers looking for clever ways to bypass QA and testing, defending their shortcuts with the rationale that they needed to get bugfixes into production immediately. These same folks would also frequently sneak a few new features into production without having gone through the formal QA and testing process either. We have even been told by a few developers that agile allows them to deploy buggy code, which can be fixed in the release. We are grateful that these folks were not working on life support or missile defense systems.

To ensure effective and timely QA and testing, you need to have a comprehensive test plan that is simultaneously pragmatic and comprehensive.

20.4 Planning the Testing Process

The people responsible for planning the testing process need to take a comprehensive view encompassing the entire agile ALM. We like the term *continuous testing* because it denotes the need for an approach that encompasses the entire software and systems lifecycle.

Developers benefit greatly from starting with unit testing and especially test-driven development (TDD). Functional and regression testing are also fundamental and, for many projects, another basic starting point. But there needs to be a much deeper approach to testing that provides more comprehensive test coverage. When applications have an exposed API available for use, then automated testing can utilize the published API for robust automated testing. Many testing tools make use of messaging protocols, which provide an effective and comprehensive approach to automated testing.

We have seen robust testing tools, which included proxies to capture messaging protocols, effectively creating a "record and playback" script. These tools usually allow you to make copies of the message package and modify them, effectively making test cases that follow logical paths that may not even be accessible from the user interface. A number of excellent testing frameworks allow you to effectively create virtualized test assets that function in a way similar to mocks. This approach has become known as *service virtualization testing* and should be on your list of must-have testing approaches. Make sure that you don't forget to embrace performance testing and nonfunctional testing as well.

Since your testing process needs to take a comprehensive approach, we strongly recommend that you at least evaluate and consider some of the excellent testing frameworks available today

Creating Your Own Framework

Your testing framework can start with unit, functional, regression, and performance testing. But to really meet the demands of testing in a DevOps context, you need to also have comprehensive API testing and service virtualization testing. Although agile depends upon DevOps, a comprehensive approach to testing will help you keep up with the demands of the DevOps transformation.

Some of these popular techniques are pretty complicated, and we have seen considerable success with taking a DevOps approach in which the developer works closely with a test engineer who is familiar with these tools, much like XP-paired programming. With this approach, you get the value of a technical resource who knows the application, combined with the expertise of an engineer who understands the test tools.

Embedding Testers

It has become a popular view that testing is everyone's job and that a truly agile team has testing embedded throughout the development lifecycle. We do not dispute this principle or its merit. However, we have seen organizations that disbanded their QA and testing function and moved the headcount into the development teams. The vision was that each team would have a dedicated testing resource embedded within the scrum. What actually happened, though, is that the development teams used the headcount to hire more development resources and the test function essentially disappeared. We prefer having testers sit next to developers and functionally embed them into the scrum. We believe that testers should always report to the head of QA and maintain the positional power to do their job effectively, even if that means deciding that the release cannot be certified for promotion to production.

Similarly, you should take a DevOps approach to writing comprehensive test cases.

20.5 Creating the Test Cases

Test cases should explain what you are going to test and what you expect the results to be. Test cases can help supplement requirements documents or agile stories by explaining how the application is expected to work. We view the test script as providing the step-by-step instructions on how to execute the test, and this information is essential. Requirements documents are often incomplete due to real-life constraints, but your test cases and scripts must be comprehensive and up to date in order to ensure that you maintain quality.

20.6 Ensuring Quality

There are many ways to ensure quality. From defining requirements to test cases and test scripts, eliminating defects is a key goal of the agile ALM. Taking a DevOps approach to quality will help you achieve success. For example, cross-functional team code reviews are known to be extremely effective. Yet, ensuring high overall quality demands a much wider approach.

Effective version control procedures, including the best use of branching and merging, build engineering (described in Chapter 6), and continuous integration (described in Chapter 8) are a critical component. Throughout this book, we have been describing many strategies that help ensure quality. You need to ensure that you are taking a holistic and comprehensive approach. QA and testing are absolutely required, but the fact is that your entire ALM helps provide quality. Make sure that you always build in quality from the beginning of the agile ALM.

20.7 Ensuring Quality from the Beginning

The best way to approach quality is to focus on it from the very beginning. We like to invoke the term "left-shift" to denote the involvement of operations engineers early in the lifecycle. Getting the QA and testing function involved from the beginning of the software and systems delivery process is crucial. Professional test engineers know how to structure the testing process to be comprehensive and efficient. Taking a DevOps approach of pairing developers with test engineers is the best approach. Have them start with unit testing and work their way all the way through the software delivery process to production and ongoing systems support. We find that some test scripts actually form the basis of environment monitoring, discussed in Chapter 11, which is a key consideration in ensuring that systems are reliable and secure.

20.8 Conclusion

It is always best to take a comprehensive approach to QA and testing. Although certainly a necessary and good first step, unit testing is usually limited in scope. Functional and regression testing are also typically limited to the user interface and consequently also limited in scope. For optimal quality, you need to adopt automated continuous testing from the very beginning of the software and systems delivery lifecycle. We advocate embracing evolving API and service virtualization testing to create a holistic approach to automated testing that can truly enable the DevOps capabilities to deploy as often as desired.

Chapter 21

Personality and Agile ALM

Top technology professionals often have remarkable analytical and technical skills. However, even the most skilled professionals often have great difficulty dealing with some of the interesting behaviors and personalities of their colleagues. Implementing an agile ALM requires you to be able to work with all of the stakeholders and navigate the frequently thorny people issues inherent in dealing with diverse groups of very intelligent, albeit somewhat idiosyncratic, and often equally opinionated, people.

21.1 Goals of Personality and the Agile ALM

The goal of understanding personality as it affects the agile ALM is to help identify strategies for dealing with the many people issues that often come up when implementing application lifecycle management. DevOps places a very high value on communication and collaboration processes, which, in turn, put a very strong focus on the skills necessary for effective human interactions. In this chapter, we will examine some of the personality-related challenges we have encountered in implementing DevOps and the ALM and identify specific and proven strategies that can help the team achieve success.

21.2 Why Are Personality and Agile ALM Important?

The value of understanding personality and behavior cannot be overstated; you can have the most well-designed processes in the world and still find that your team gets derailed due to dysfunctional human interactions. This chapter will examine some of the common personality-related challenges that can impair team morale and productivity. As part of this discussion, we will introduce you to some very effective and proactive techniques emphasized in an emerging discipline known as *Positive Psychology*.

21.3 Where Do I Start?

Understanding personality dynamics usually begins by taking an honest and objective assessment of the quality of communications and behavior between members of the team. Sometimes we observe dysfunctional behaviors and exchanges between workers that are so blatant and prevalent that our starting point is obvious.

When Managers Collide

We have consulted with several organizations where teams just did not work effectively together. After several discussions with team members, we learned that the root cause was that their managers simply did not get along and made no secret of their decision to not work together. In this case, the team was simply following exactly what they saw their leaders doing.

In order to be effective, you need to understand the corporate culture.

21.3.1 Understanding the Culture

The DevOps transformation compels us to revisit the way we manage communication and culture. When guiding a team to embrace new ways of collaborating, the DevOps coach often comes right up against the characteristic communication style and organizational culture that, for many corporations, has evolved over many years or even decades. Many organizational silos have developed defense mechanisms that shut down communication while strengthening existing policies and entrenched rules of engagement. These practices block attempts at organizational change.

We often assess existing practices and make recommendations for process improvement based on industry standards and frameworks. While implementing our recommendations, many organizations ask us to mediate discussions between teams mired in very counterproductive behaviors. One pattern we often see is the very bright technical guru who has quietly become an expert in a particular niche and carefully maneuvered himself into a position where he is the only trusted resource in this area—essentially, a "keyman risk." The resulting problems become apparent when the teams get ready to deploy their code.

In most large organizations, there are federal regulatory requirements for maintaining a well-delineated separation of duties. These rules make sense because having the developer turn over his code and build procedures helps to ensure that corporate assets, along with the procedures to build, package, and deploy the code, are safeguarded. In our practice, we often hold working sessions where we have the developer and operations personnel on the same call to iron out the procedures being established to automate the application deployment. This is an essential step in implementing continuous delivery and continuous deployment successfully. Very frequently, however, we feel like we are playing referee in a full-contact rugby game as we make the different teams aware of one another's perspectives. The biggest issues are often related to communication styles, with culture coming in a close second.

Communication styles vary significantly from one person to another. Some technology professionals find it particularly difficult to communicate with each other. Too often, we see people getting defensive and attempting to shut down the conversation. DevOps strives to increase communication and collaboration so that people who are by nature uncomfortable communicating may begin to contribute more, rather than following their usual pattern of retreating and withdrawing. We also find that cultural norms can impact explanatory and response styles.

International corporations, by definition, include many people from different countries, who each bring along a set of expectations that affect their behaviors and communication styles. Although no one wants to stereotype a cherished colleague, most people realize that one's culture impacts how they interact with the world. Some cultures can be characterized as relatively passive and conflict-avoidant. We see colleagues who struggle, or just simply refuse, to deliver bad news and say "yes" too much—possibly because they just were not socialized to be assertive and thus lack the ability to turn down a request directly. Others seem to be easily intimidated by managers with significant positional power. Highly effective organizations have cultures that empower all members of the team to speak freely, especially when the news may be bad. Although loyalty is certainly important, failing to share important information out of a misguided reluctance to appear negative may lead to serious problems within the team.

Organizational structures are essential for any large corporation. These entities require management guidelines to operate and function effectively. Good managers instill loyalty in their staff, but there is also a dark side: organizational silos can act as if they are in competition with each other. Interdepartmental rivalry results in behaviors that often resemble a volleyball game, with each side throwing responsibility over the net to the other group. In DevOps, we remind each member of the team that the enemy is not on the same payroll. Teams should be incentivized to work together for the common good. The only way you can make this happen is if you understand the personalities and behaviors of the people on your team.

Savvy managers listen carefully to the way their team members communicate and interact with each other. True leaders exhibit behaviors that encourage positive interactions, including excellent communication and collaboration. The accomplished manager will also understand the cultural norms of the technology experts who are on their teams. The rapid rise in globalization of commerce and social networking means that most employees now find themselves working in a culturally diverse international community. It behooves today's professional to understand how we can utilize our strengths and abilities to work together in the most effective way possible.

One construct that we find very useful to understand organizational culture is called the *collective unconscious*.

21.3.2 Probing Deeper into the Organization's Psyche

Process improvement requires that we understand and influence human behavior by helping people improve the way in which they perform their work. Sometimes this involves identifying sources of error, and other times we are simply helping team members strive for the next level and continuously improve.

Later in this chapter, we will discuss how positive psychology can help us understand effective behaviors, including leadership, which are essential for successful organizations. But positive psychology is primarily focused on the individual, and we have learned that understanding the ecosystem of the organization, along with its culture, is also essential for our success.

In our practice, we usually focus on helping teams improve their configuration management best practices, with particular attention to communication-related factors. Often, we are asked to assess existing practices and then form a plan for a long-term process improvement initiative. These initiatives will only succeed if they are aligned with the organizational culture and the overall environment within which the team must operate. This means our approach for a defense contractor may be very different from that of an Internet startup or a large international bank. To succeed, we first must understand the basics and then adapt our approach to the organization's unique identity.

To the outsider, many organizations may appear to be mired in bureaucracy, impeding any attempt to make things better. It can sometimes seem impossible to overcome resistance to change and get the team moving forward. When things get really bad, catastrophic mistakes occur, and this is frequently when the senior managers of these organizations call for help. You may find yourself in just such a situation, especially when starting a new job—if you are very lucky, this might be exactly the reason that you were hired in the first place. To be successful, you need to understand not just the technical processes and structures within the company, but the organizational culture as well. We encourage you to embrace the opportunity, but to go in fully aware that you need to size up the situation pretty quickly in order to be effective.

We have found from experience that psychotherapist Carl Jung's construct of a *collective unconscious* can be very helpful in getting a basic understanding of how and why folks behave the way they do in a particular organizational environment. Dr. Jung believed that we are all products of patterns of behaviors that he called *archetypes*. Archetypes provide the structure of a collective body of knowledge that defines basic human behavior and situations. Dr. Jung's view considered many factors, including images, symbols, and public knowledge that everyone in the culture "just seemed to know."

Our approach is to listen to the "rhythm" of communication within the organization. In one company, we noted that several engineers in different groups all seemed to be afraid to offer their opinions regarding anything outside their direct responsibilities. With a little probing, we found that these colleagues were each intelligent and knowledgeable, just very cautious to speak out of turn.

In other conversations, we found team members who acted as if they were in competition with each other, and they were not motivated to really help each other out. We later learned that promotions were indeed competitive and these employees were actively fighting against one another to attain the next pay grade. Another team in the division had been acquired as part of an organizational merger. Many of their colleagues had been let go during the transition, and they were the "survivors," left to cope with a distracting mix of feelings, including worry, fear, and guilt.

You may not be able to modify every cultural challenge in the organization. But understanding what you are up against may help you form a strategy that can encourage and promote initiative in even the most stifling organizations. At the very least, you can acknowledge the stress and frustration that team members express.

We believe that most organizations operate based on a type of collective unconscious. If you listen carefully to the "rhythm" of their communications, you may find that you are much more capable of designing effective process improvement strategies, from change control to release management, that are aligned with the corporate culture and thus considerably more likely to be accepted and implemented.

21.4 Group Dynamics

Understanding group dynamics can be challenging. Organizations are typically structured in a way that requires navigating across different groups, each with a defined role or area of responsibility. Although specialization can have a positive impact when it is focused on developing expertise, sometimes these structures can be highly dysfunctional. For example, some teams operate as if their primary focus is the health and well-being of the silo and not the organization itself.

21.4.1 Using DevOps to Drive Out Silos

DevOps and the ALM rely upon effective communication for all of its interactions, whether technology related or not. Many organizations consist of separate departments that operate as isolated silos, with little or no effective communication between teams. The DevOps movement has been focusing on a set of principles designed to facilitate better collaboration between developers and IT operations professionals by emphasizing effective communication. DevOps also helps the QA and information security organizations operate more effectively within the development and operations structures.

Many professionals, although experts in their technical niche, are sometimes less than perfect at communicating effectively with colleagues from other departments. The end result can be departments that fail to work effectively together, thus resembling silos more than a collaborative and cohesive organization.

Teams sometimes behave in a dysfunctional and self-sabotaging manner. They may compartmentalize information and refuse to collaborate with other members of the organization even when there is a clear need to know. Other members of the organization frequently attribute such behavior to fear and distrust. There have been many studies [1] of what sociologists and psychologists describe as in-group and out-group behavior, where team members typically act more favorably toward members of their own team and may deliberately not cooperate with those outside the group. This tendency to "protect one's turf" may be especially problematic when trying to implement a complex system requiring cooperation from stakeholders throughout the organization. Covering up mistakes or working to maintain complete control over a function that should be shared between stakeholders is another commonly recurring dysfunctional behavior. It can be helpful to understand some of the personality traits that can be seen in members of the team who act in a way that hampers the success of the team and to understand what traits help facilitate great teamwork and success for the entire organization.

The organization needs to ensure that all of the stakeholders understand the need for transparency, even when there is a requirement for a separation of duties (as is often the case with development and operations). Much has been written about the natural tension between development and operations. Developers are required to produce successive releases of the system with improved functionality and new features on a regular basis. In fact, without new features the organization may not be able to keep up with the competition and could actually cease to exist as a corporate entity. Meanwhile, operations staff members are generally focused on maintaining continuous and uninterrupted services. It is no surprise that some people are drawn to one area of focus or another, and that is also true for those who become quality assurance analysts or information-security specialists. There are also times when groups that must interact are indeed not even part of the same organization; this is especially true with cloud-based development.

Development in the cloud inevitably places a dependency upon support organizations that may be external to the business function. Cloud-based development has many advantages, but one clear disadvantage is sometimes seen when the cloud supplier support organization does not believe that it needs to be transparent with the client-support organization. Service-level agreements (SLAs) can only go so far when communication is hampered by the supplier-client relationship. This is also true when organizations depend for support upon vendors who may not have the same sense of urgency as the business entity that will be directly negatively affected by a service outage.

21.4.2 Managing Power and Influence in DevOps

DevOps helps improve communication and collaboration between development and operations, leading to smoother and more reliable deployments without the drama often associated with large-scale system outages. The DevOps transformation often uncovers a level of imbalance that exists between organizational structures—sometimes creating a little disruption along the way to process improvement.

We often see organizational dynamics that adversely impact the team's ability to achieve success. This dysfunctional behavior may be observed as a mismatch in organizational power between existing organizational silos. There is a natural tension between development and operations. When this relationship is in balance, each side helps the other. But when there is imbalance, bad things can happen.

Some operations groups have very strong positional power and can actually shut down new approaches, essentially stifling organizational agility. When this happens, operations becomes a bottleneck in the development process, resulting in a loss of productivity and quality. Some operations groups hide behind their existing rules and insist that any deviation will result in significant risk to the firm. By shunning innovation, operations is sometimes responsible for slowing down the deployment process, which itself can result in significant risk to the firm. However, operations is not the only potential bad player.

Development can also yield an excessive amount of power within an organization, often because they are in the best position to know the latest tools and technologies. Unfortunately, they sometimes keep operations in the dark until the very last moment. I have seen development teams use their superior technical knowledge to run rings around the operations team and exhibit significant power to bypass existing IT controls, often with the excuse that operations lacks the technical expertise to support the application themselves. DevOps is supposed to help address these issues, but some developers basically use DevOps as a rationale to usurp the role of operations by deploying their own code direct to production. When this happens, some developers are actually motivated to keep operations in the dark even more so that they can maintain free rein in production.

Personality plays a key role in these situations because individuals tend to fall back on the behaviors they find most comfortable and familiar. Some technology professionals have a strong need to maintain absolute control and will orchestrate the balance of power to ensure that they can maintain their own positional influence. We have observed developers who actually try to bypass their operations colleagues in order to maintain their position of being the only smart person in the room. Likewise, there are operations folks who know that they could be a little more flexible, but they distrust the developers, so they stick with adhering to the letter of the law.

Technology practitioners who engage in turf wars and power grabs are obviously not going to fit well into a high-performance cross-functional DevOps team. Distrust and fear—which are often significant motivators driving individuals to try to maintain their positional power—can sabotage the goals of the team.

Positive psychology teaches us that the best way to combat these dysfunctional behaviors is to model and empower strong leadership and good teamwork. When we see these problems in a group, we help the leadership understand their role in creating a collaborative and positive environment. With top-down support, we can then assist the professionals engaged in the day-to-day work.

DevOps enables groups to find the right level of balance by promoting the creation of cross-functional teams, an organizational structure in which everyone has a shared goal as well as common responsibilities. The DevOps team focuses on sharing knowledge and building trust through a mutual experience.

Unfortunately, some team members prefer to remain on their own and actually may not be able to adjust to the demands of a cross-functional team. Although these individual contributors still may be able to provide value to the organization, it is important to ensure that their roles are clear and they do not adversely impact the DevOps transformation.

The balance of power between highly skilled development and operational professionals provides a valuable set of checks and balances that helps the team achieve agility, along with exceptional productivity and quality. Strong leaders ensure that their teams maintain this equilibrium along with the teamwork needed to reach excellence. If you can maintain an appropriate balance, then your organization has a much greater chance of achieving success, while also meeting and exceeding your customers' expectations.

21.5 Intergroup Conflict

Dealing with conflict between groups is unavoidable. Sometimes this is related to competition, and frequently it is because teams are afraid of being blamed and held responsible for situations over which they have little control. The key to understanding intergroup conflict is to recognize its presence and come up with effective strategies to deal with its potential impact. One common problem that we see is individual employees who are afraid to express their views and decide to just agree with whatever the person in charge appears to be saying. Although these folks may appear at first to be very agreeable, big problems can occur if their acquiescence goes unchallenged.

21.5.1 Overly Agreeable People and Other Challenges

Technology professionals often need to get along with some interesting personalities. Dealing with overly agreeable people can be fraught with obstacles quite different from those usually associated with the stereotypical stubborn geek who seems unable, or consciously unwilling, to bend or compromise.

Psychologists have spent decades researching personality [2] and developed many different models to explain the behaviors that we observe in the people with whom we interact on a daily basis. One of the most well-respected models, based upon many studies, is known as the five-factor model. The five factors—openness, conscientiousness, extraversion, agreeableness, and neuroticism (OCEAN)—describe essential dimensions of personality. We all express some degree of each of these five factors in our own personality, although the specific range of each factor can certainly vary considerably from one individual to another.

Successful sales professionals are typically high in extraversion, whereas police and law enforcement personnel are often focused on conscientiousness. Folks who have personalities more geared toward being agreeable typically exhibit highly social behaviors and enjoy the company of others, often demonstrating more kindness, empathy, and affection for others than the average person. Sometimes these people come across as "pack animals" that seem to be most comfortable operating within the context of a group. By definition, folks who are agreeable prefer to get along and are more comfortable concurring with others, and that is exactly why problems may arise.

The dysfunctional side of agreeableness manifests itself in extreme conflict avoidance. These are the people who just cannot take a stand and always seem to forgo their own will for the sake of "getting along" with others. In our book on configuration management best practices, we discussed the middle child who is often the peacemaker in the family [3]. This behavior is not always a problem and can come in handy in helping others understand others' differing views.

Unfortunately, being agreeable becomes dysfunctional when the person just cannot take a stand or will not engage in uncomfortable conversations, including what most of us would regard as necessary negotiation. The overly agreeable person will often avoid letting you know where he or she really stands on the issues and will typically do almost anything to avoid conflict. Agreeableness is nice, to a degree, but someone who habitually goes along with the crowd may reach a breaking point in which he or she just cannot take the disparity between what he or she says and what he or she feels. Sometimes, if tension has been building for a long time, the resulting response may appear unduly extreme, and a usually pleasant and mild-mannered colleague will have a sudden and loud outburst over some seemingly minor difference.

Technology professionals often need to analyze tough problems and collaborate to arrive at a consensus on how best to address and resolve problems. It's no surprise that smart people don't always agree on how to fix complex technology problems. When dealing with a systems outage, the situation may be very stressful, and effective technology professionals must be able to calmly express their views and listen to the opinions of others too. In a crisis, tact and diplomacy may be in short supply, and people with a thin skin may find it hard to cope with the stress of feeling that they are under attack.

Some people back off and actually become passive-aggressive, allowing those with either positional power or perhaps just a loud voice to drive the decision making, which may or may not be the optimal choice. Effective leaders create environments where everyone can feel safe expressing their professional views and experience-based opinions.

Dealing with a smart analytical person who tries to steer clear of conflict may require some very strong people skills, and this is exactly where you can emerge as a leader within your group. Creating an environment where everyone's opinion is expressed and the team collaborates to reach consensus is by far the best problem-solving strategy. The most effective teams frequently consist of diverse personality types and actively promote a common value of respect and consideration for each person.

Most people enjoy the validation of hearing opinions in alignment with their own views. But it is also true that successful technology teams encourage the selection of correct decisions based upon facts, whether they come from the most popular member of the team or the quiet nonconfrontational guy in the corner who just happens to really know how to configure the software to get your system up and running!

21.5.2 Learned Helplessness

There have been many high-profile system glitches leading to an increased focus on the role of IT operations and other key personnel in maintaining a stable and reliable system environment. The technologies involved are obviously complex with many moving parts, any of which could be responsible for a system crash, potentially affecting thousands of users and, ultimately, the company itself. Some organizations foster a highly effective environment where employees feel empowered to always do the right thing. Unfortunately, some organizations have a highly dysfunctional culture that results in employees who do not believe that they can be effective and, worse, are not motivated to take appropriate action when serious incidents occur. Instead, they focus on protecting themselves and ensuring plausible deniability.

Dysfunctional operations teams are often a consequence of a dysfunctional organizational culture that breeds distrust and results in employees who just sit back and allow disasters to occur. What kind of organization do you want to work in and, if you are in a leadership position, what type of environment do you want to foster?

The majority of high-profile systems incidents—from the reliability-challenged www.healthcare.gov to outages affecting numerous trading firms and trading exchanges—have almost all had one thing in common: published reports indicating that technology professionals had warned of issues and problems that could, and did, eventually result in risks and potential systems outages. These warnings were largely ignored, or even overruled, by senior officials who had the positional power to make decisions that ultimately led to disasters. No doubt many of the technology professionals who spoke up and tried to warn of impending danger were frustrated and discouraged seeing that their alarms went unheeded as they watched helplessly while serious incidents threatened their jobs and the very existence of their firm. It is certainly difficult to be optimistic in these circumstances.

Martin Seligman is credited with developing a new branch of psychology that focuses on promoting the type of positive behavior that helps create effective teams and successful results. However, decades prior to his work on positive psychology, Seligman was already quite well known and highly regarded for his work on a phenomenon he termed *learned helplessness*. In order to really appreciate the importance of positive psychology, we need to first understand learned helplessness.

In early studies on learned helplessness, researchers discovered that dogs subjected to repeated situations in which their actions had no discernible direct effect on whether or not they were shocked soon stopped responding at all. Related studies involving other animals, as well as college student volunteers, yielded similar results, thus providing more support for the assertion that some people (and animals) just stop trying to overcome problems when repeated experience indicates that there is no point in attempting to prevent such incidents from occurring. Related dysfunctional behavior included cognitive learning deficits and depression. To summarize, the results suggest that subjects who have been conditioned to consider themselves helpless essentially give up trying to have any impact, have difficulty learning, and are depressed about their inability to affect their situation.

So how do these frustrating situations manifest in IT and how can we help our teams overcome learned helplessness? Operations teams may find that they do not have the required training, procedures, and knowledge available to be effective at identifying and addressing issues when they occur. Development teams may find that they have to write complex software without well-defined requirements, and testers may feel that they just don't get enough time in order to really ensure that the software is free from defects.

Published reports indicate that all three of these issues occurred with regard to the much publicized release of the fault-riddled www.healthcare.gov website. Technology professionals involved with this effort have indicated that requirements shifted late in the process, warnings about system reliability went unheeded, and essential security testing was not completed due to insufficient time. When key warnings such as these are ignored, it is no wonder that some professionals become discouraged and resigned to the fact that the system just won't work as required.

A related problem is management's frequent dysfunctional reaction to inevitable mistakes. Many organizations severely punish employees for serious mistakes, creating a culture in which employees are afraid to step forward and admit when an error that could potentially impact the systems and the organization has occurred. Successful organizations understand that mistakes can be acceptable (and even beneficial) if people learn from them. Quality guru Joseph Juran referred to mistakes as "gold in the mine" [4], a reference to the value that comes from a lesson learned. You need to create an environment in which employees are willing to step forward and acknowledge when they have made a mistake, confident that the entire team will refrain from finger-pointing and help address the problem.

Successful organizations ensure that their employees believe they can be successful and feel empowered to identify and report risks. Senior management should demonstrate they value their technology professionals' input and respond to the advice of those who are most knowledgeable and capable of assessing potential issues. If you want your organization to be successful, you need to drive out any aspect of learned helplessness and embrace a positive culture that conveys a can-do attitude!

21.5.3 Introspection and the Postmortem

Technology professionals know all too well that, despite everyone's best efforts, sometimes things still go wrong. When software glitches occur and disruptions to mission-critical systems affect users, there are often substantial consequences. Most companies will conduct meetings to understand the sequence of events that led to a serious systems outage. Sometimes these fact-finding meetings are called a postmortem, which derives from the medical term for the examination of a body to determine the precise cause of death.

How you handle an IT postmortem depends on your leadership approach, the culture of your organization, and, of course, your own personal strengths.

We all know that mistakes happen. The important thing is that we learn from our mistakes and try to avoid making the same mistakes again. Unfortunately, technology teams often engage in dysfunctional finger-pointing that results in some team members blaming each other instead of taking an open and honest approach to understanding exactly what went wrong and how similar problems can be prevented in the future.

Why do some people get defensive and others stand up and courageously admit their mistakes? Psychologists note that some people have personalities that predispose them to act in a defensive way, whereas others have the self-esteem to act with confidence and integrity. People who are defensive often find it difficult to have an honest discussion regarding mistakes that occurred and therefore have difficulty improving their own performance. Sometimes people will tell you they had previously tried to do the right thing, only to be punished by the organization. Consequently, they focus on self-preservation, even if it means providing incomplete or misleading information to protect their image and professional reputation.

This dysfunctional behavior can adversely impact the behavior and performance of everyone around them. Successful managers engage in strategies that address these problems, including exhibiting more helpful traits and behaviors themselves. So, what exactly are these desired personality traits that result in the best behaviors, even under stress?

Positive psychology teaches that traits such as humility and modesty, along with self-control, lead to effective behaviors. Employees who do not feel threatened obviously find it much easier to act with humility, modesty, and self-control. Similarly, folks who value fairness and equity along with a strong sense of justice may find it easier to discuss mistakes and how they can be prevented. The priority should always be to figure out what mistakes occurred and how they can be prevented in the future. The truth is that it takes courage to be completely honest when under stress. Where does this courage come from, and how does one ensure that the members of their organization feel comfortable doing the right thing all the time?

Organizational culture often sets the stage for whether employees feel they are safe admitting their own mistakes. W. Edwards Deming focused on this when he advised managers to "drive out fear." Personality factors, including strong self-esteem, certainly predispose people to exhibit courage and integrity. But, at a practical level, employees who feel safe are more likely to tell the truth about what occurred and to admit their own mistakes. Obviously, those who fear losing their jobs are more likely to engage in dysfunctional behaviors, such as finger-pointing and generally blaming others. Those who genuinely fear losing their jobs may indeed feel justified in lying and deceiving others to protect themselves from what they view as unfair consequences for their mistakes.

Positive psychology teaches us effective tactics for avoiding these problems and turning mistakes into lessons learned. Start by using a more positive approach to incident debriefing, such as an agile retrospective, which focuses more on what went well and what can be improved. Agile retrospectives help teams adapt and improve their efforts with a strong focus on open and effective communication.

If your organization insists on sticking with the postmortem, then at least help the team keep a positive attitude—and, above all, eliminate finger-pointing and the blame game. The best approach is to encourage honesty and integrity in a culture that tolerates human error-based mistakes as long as they are a catalyst for process improvement. If your team can learn from their mistakes, then they will constantly improve and achieve success.

21.6 Managing Stress and Dysfunctional Behavior

Managing stress and the dysfunctional behavior that usually comes with it can be challenging. Your first step is to try to understand the personalities who are involved and the behaviors that you are observing. Psychologists discuss a behavioral pattern, called *learned complacency*, in which environmental factors essentially "teach" the person to not attempt to resist what they perceive as being inevitable. We view this type of acceptance of the status quo as an institutional variant of the learned helplessness that Seligman observed in individuals.

21.6.1 The Danger of Learned Complacency

The software configuration problem that shut down the Chicago Board Options Exchange (CBOE) trading system in April 2013 was yet another high-profile financial system failure reportedly caused by the complexity and challenges inherent in upgrading complex mission-critical financial trading systems. Given that similar crippling service disruptions had occurred at several other major stock exchanges and trading firms, one might be tempted to think that this outage was unremarkable, possibly even inevitable. What is striking, though, is that there was a published report regarding this incident that described how employees had warned that the system was not working correctly, and yet the CBOE nonetheless chose to not revert to its backup system.

We often come across technology professionals who try to warn their management about risks and the possibility of systems outages that could affect essential services. When conducting configuration management (CM) assessments, we often find ourselves being the voice for validating and communicating these concerns to those who are in a position to take appropriate action. What is troubling, however, is that we have seen many companies in which employees have essentially learned to no longer raise their concerns because no one is willing to listen. Even worse, they may have suffered consequences in the past for being the bearer of bad tidings. We refer to this phenomenon as *learned complacency*.

Additionally, some people are more passive than others. This may come from a personality trait in which a person feels that getting along with others is more important than blazing a new trail and standing up for one's convictions. Many people strongly desire to just go along with the crowd. As previously explained, psychologists often refer to this personality trait as *agreeableness*, one of the primary personality traits in the well-known big five. Usually considered a positive attribute, this personality trait can be problematic in certain situations.

Some people who like to avoid conflict at all costs display a dysfunctional behavior known as *passive-aggressiveness*. A passive-aggressive person typically refuses to engage in conflict, choosing instead to outwardly go along with the group while inwardly deeply resenting the direction that he feels is being forced upon him. A person with a passive-aggressive personality trait may outwardly appear to be agreeable, but deep down he is usually frustrated and dissatisfied. In fact, he may engage in behaviors that appear to demonstrate acquiescence, yet he actually does nothing or even obstructs progress, albeit in a subtle manner. Some IT professionals who have a passive (or passive-aggressive) personality trait may be less than willing to warn their managers of systems problems that may cause a serious outage.

We have seen folks who simply felt that, although they were close enough to the technology to identify problems, they could not escalate a serious issue to management because it simply was not their job. In some cases, we have come across employees who tried to warn of pending problems, but were counseled by their managers to not be so outspoken. For example, one manager we knew frequently used the phrase "smile and wave" to encourage his staff to tone down their warnings, which no one really wanted to hear anyway. Not surprisingly, that firm has experienced several serious systems outages that affected thousands of customers.

However, not everyone is afraid to stand and be heard; some employees have personality traits that are naturally associated with being a strong leader.

Technology leaders know how to maintain a positive demeanor and focus on teamwork while still having the courage to communicate risks that could potentially impact the firm. The recent rash of serious systems outages certainly demonstrates the need for corporations to heed Deming's clarion call regarding the need to eliminate fear and instead reward and empower their technical leaders to communicate problems without concern about retribution. There is certainly no greater situation where we need leaders to be fearless than when warning of a potential problem that could have a significant impact upon large-scale production IT systems.

Although some individuals may be predisposed to avoid conflict, it's an even greater problem when a corporation develops a culture in which all employees become conditioned to maintain silence even when they are aware of potential problems. The IT industry needs leaders who are accountable, knowledgeable, and empowered to create working environments where those who protect the long-term best interests of the firm are rewarded and those who take short-sighted risks are placed in positions where they cannot adversely affect the well-being of the firm. We will see fewer systems outages when each member of the team understands their own role in the organization and feels completely safe and empowered to speak truthfully about risks and potential problems that may impact their firm's critical systems infrastructure.

There are times when risk taking is appropriate and may result in significant rewards. However, firms that take unnecessary risks endanger not only their own corporation, but they may affect thousands of other people as well. Those firms with thoughtful IT leadership and a strong, truthful and open culture will achieve success while still managing and addressing risk in an appropriate and effective way.

21.6.2 Dealing with Aggressive Team Members

Technology teams often attract some "interesting" personalities. Some of these folks may simply exhibit odd, perhaps eccentric, behaviors unrelated to their work responsibilities, and others may engage in behaviors that undermine the effectiveness of the team or, perhaps conversely, actually stimulate teamwork and contribute to success. The personalities of the folks on your team certainly affect not only how happy you are to show up for work, but also the overall success (or failure) of the organization. So, what happens when members of your team exhibit overly aggressive or downright combative behaviors, such as insisting that the team adopt their approach or showing a lack of teamwork and collaborative behavior? Since you're unlikely to change your colleagues' modus operandi, it is wise to consider instead how your DevOps effort can benefit from taking into account some typical behaviors of people with type A or type B personalities.

First, a quick overview of the history of personality types is in order. Dr. Meyer Friedman, a cardiologist trained at John Hopkins University, developed a theory that certain behaviors increased the risk of heart attacks [5]. Together with another cardiologist by the name of Dr. Ray Rosenman, he suggested that people who exhibited type A behaviors—including being overly competitive, hard driving, and achievement oriented—were at higher risk for developing coronary artery disease. Fascinating, and not without some controversy in the medical establishment, this research makes one ponder how other members of the team might react to interacting regularly with a type A personality on the team.

Software development is largely a type A endeavor. In fact, many highly effective teams have several members who are very aggressive, intense, and highly competitive. One important mitigating factor is that technology professionals also need to be right. You can exhibit whatever personality traits you want, but the software just won't work if you didn't get it right. Additionally, current technology is so complex that few people in today's global organizations, if any, are able to work entirely on their own, so these type As must interact frequently.

High-performing teams often have specialists who depend upon each other and must collaborate. Even though some degree of competition may be common, continuous collaboration is a daily necessity—it is just not optional. If you have ever been in a meeting with someone who just stuck to their point despite objections from other team members (and seemingly oblivious to any sense of logic), then you probably have experienced this type of obstinate behavior firsthand. Many technology teams often struggle to overcome a fair amount of conflict and drama.

In the midst of a highly confrontational meeting, it might be tempting to consider how much less contentious the workplace would be with the more easy going type B personalities. Harvey Robbins and Michael Finley point out that some teams actually don't work well when their leaders are unwilling to fight for the team [6]. So, how exactly can one determine what is the right amount of type A versus type B behavior in a DevOps team?

There is a natural tension between the aggressive behavior of highly motivated software developers and the operations professionals who are charged with ensuring that we maintain consistent and continuously available services. Operations often focuses on maintaining the status quo, whereas development presses hard for introducing new features based upon customer demand. It shouldn't surprise you that both types of behavior are essential for a successful DevOps organization. You need to have aggressive personalities with a strong achievement-focused drive to create new features and improved systems. But you also need to temper this aggressiveness with the more balanced type B behaviors that encourage review and careful analysis. Encouraging and optimizing this balance is exactly what the burgeoning DevOps movement brings to the table.

DevOps brings together the views of those engaged in QA activities, software development, operations, and information security and improves communications between and within teams, requiring the participation of stakeholders with different viewpoints and often very different personalities. Keep in mind that many people are attracted to each of these essential disciplines, in part, due to their personalities, as well as by how these roles fit into the goals and objectives of their respective teams.

Successful cross-functional teams harness this diversity to help ensure that the sum is more robust and efficient than its component parts working independently. The most effective managers understand the basic personalities and communication styles that are often found in cross-functional teams and become adept at developing strategies that utilize these differences productively. With encouragement, competitive type As and more laid-back type Bs can learn to "play nice" so that each of their strengths are incorporated and contribute to overall team success!

21.6.3 Extremism in the Workplace

One of the most difficult personality types to deal with is the person who always seems distrustful of others. Sometimes, this lack of trust is well justified, but it can also be a manifestation of some dysfunctional personality issue. Hopefully, you won't encounter cases in your workplace where the person is actually so paranoid that he or she is dissociated from reality. Psychologists diagnose this mental illness as paranoid schizophrenia, which may require medications and intensive therapy to manage. What is far more common, however, is the person with a borderline personality who manages to operate within a normal workplace environment, but always seems to be a little "off." Eccentric behavior is not, in and of itself, a reason to suspect that someone suffers from mental illness. However, sometimes the behavior and personality of a coworker may be so extreme and off-putting that it affects other people's ability to work.

Harry Stack Sullivan, an American psychiatrist, noted that paranoia may be associated with suspicion, a tendency to blame others, and a sense that one is being persecuted [7]. Some folks just have a disposition such that they are always expecting the worst from others. Quite often, this tendency may actually result in a self-fulfilling prophecy in which a person's quirky behavior elicits negative responses from others that actually reinforces this person's view that everyone is always out to "get" them.

As Dr. Sullivan noted, it is common for the person to then resort to blaming others in an attempt to protect himself or herself in what may seem like a silly turf war. Unfortunately, many of these folks take these incidents seriously and may truly feel that they are being persecuted. These defense mechanisms may be quite destructive to not only the person, but also to everyone with whom he or she interacts.

People who have trust issues often find it difficult to collaborate and cooperate with others. This can make it very tough in a technology organization in which everyone has to rely upon each other for specialized expertise. Sometimes, people with difficult personalities actually focus on being experts in a specific technology area that enables them to feel safe because they have complete control and power due to their specialized—and often extensive—knowledge of institutional history. But consider for a moment that sometimes a little suspiciousness can actually be justifiable and perhaps partially a consequence of a particular situation.

In fact, some organizations just do not foster trust and collaboration. Employees who work in dysfunctional organizations may understandably exhibit counterproductive behavior. If you are the new guy on the block, you may not know all of the organizational history and, consequently, may not fully understand why some employees seem unusually distrustful or have developed other defense mechanisms to defend their turf.

One example is the organization that attempts to "motivate" its employees through a constant threat of layoffs or other forms of termination. Creating a state of fear does not result in productive, effective, and loyal employees. Some managers use their positional power to try to control and motivate others through fear and intimidation. Although respect for authority is important, there are much more effective ways to motivate employees than instilling fear, particularly the fear of losing one's job and livelihood.

If you find yourself dealing with a person who seems unreasonably distrustful, listen carefully to his or her view and then try to be clear about your position. Conflicts in the workplace are often the result of a misunderstanding or even some institutional history that occurred long before you even joined the organization. You should also consider who else might be able to help you navigate these choppy waters.

Your own manager may be able to fill you in on what factors have led to this state of affairs. Sometimes dysfunctional behaviors are a consequence of corporate politics, but also consider that there may be some other much more benign factors in place. We all go through life stresses. You may be catching someone as they are trying to handle their "day" job while also dealing with a demanding family situation that would make anyone stressed. Another possibility is that the person is taking medication for some medical condition that results in behavioral side effects. Employees obviously have a right to privacy, but sometimes managers are made aware of these issues by HR so that the company can be as supportive as possible.

The best organizations consider the needs of their employees and try to provide a workplace that is conducive to success and productivity. However, even in the best organizations, you may still encounter difficult personalities. Hopefully, you won't have to deal with too many people who are truly paranoid, but you will probably encounter at least a few colleagues during your career who seem remarkably distrustful, blame others, and seem to believe that they are being persecuted. These situations are never easy, and your best approach is to try to communicate effectively; if possible, you should strive to understand the other individual's position while explaining your case. When possible, reach out to your own resources such as your manager, and, in extreme cases, to HR.

The workplace must be free of hostile and disruptive behavior from both a legal and business perspective. The best work environments are both productive and respectful of their employees, and, with good communication, you should be able to navigate successfully even when confronted with some difficult personalities.

21.7 Taking a Positive Approach

Positive psychology, which focuses on proactive positive behaviors that parallel the medical establishment's current emphasis on wellness, continues to gain in popularity. Much of our consulting involves applying positive psychology principles in the workplace.

21.7.1 How Positive Psychology Can Help Your Organization

Difficult behaviors, such as paranoia or the learned helplessness that we see in many IT operations shops, are common distractions in many workplaces. Psychology has long focused on pathologies in a valiant effort to identify and cure mental illness. However, one limitation with this approach is that focusing on the negative issues can sometimes become a self-fulfilling prophecy. Additionally, viewing one's situation as a problem often creates a debilitating sense of immobility and powerlessness that adds to the existing stress.

For instance, first-year medical students are notorious for thinking that they have almost every illness that they learn about in medical school. If you want an effective and healthy organization, then it seems obvious that it is essential to focus on promoting healthy organizational behavior. Psychologists Martin Seligman and Mihaly Csikszentmihalyi have pioneered a new and exciting focus on a positive view of psychology, which suggests very promising techniques.

Technology leaders from CTOs to scrum masters work every day to foster the optimal behaviors that lead to improved productivity and quality. That said, we all know that dealing with difficult people and dysfunctional behaviors can be challenging and sometimes disheartening. Seligman and Csikszentmihalyi wrote that "psychology has become a science largely about healing. Therefore, its concentration on healing largely neglects the fulfilled individual and thriving community" [8]. Instead of concentrating so much energy on remediation, it would be better to empower technology leaders to focus on and encourage positive and effective behaviors in the workplace. Martin Seligman and Mihaly Csikszentmihalyi note that "the aim of positive psychology is to begin to catalyze a change in the focus of psychology from preoccupation only with repairing the worst things in life to also building positive qualities [8]."

Seligman delineates 24 strengths, ranging from curiosity and interest in the world to zest, passion, and enthusiasm, which he suggests are the fundamental traits of a positive and effective individual [9]. Notably, playfulness and humor, along with valor, bravery, and a sense of justice, are also listed among these traits that Seligman describes. So, how do we apply this knowledge to the workplace, and how can we use this information to be more effective managers? The fact is that we all know people whom we admire, and we have all had more than a few employers who seemed less than completely effective.

Effective leaders do indeed exhibit valor, bravery, and a sense of justice in identifying barriers to organizational success. The best leaders are not afraid to deliver a tough message and use their positional power to help teams achieve success. Technology leaders are often particularly motivated by curiosity, interested in the world, and most certainly exhibit enthusiasm and passion for their work.

Other traits observed in strong leaders include kindness and generosity, along with integrity and honesty. Successful leaders also exhibit perseverance and diligence, as well as a love of learning. It hardly comes as a surprise that the positive psychology movement specifies so many of these strengths as beneficial traits. In fact, many of these attributes had been discussed earlier by both Abraham Maslow and Carl Rogers in their respective classic texts on humanistic psychology, a discipline that focuses on helping people achieve success and realize their full potential.

Positive psychology is providing a useful framework for understanding the traits that lead to success, both at an organizational level and for each of us individually. Positive psychology can create an environment where each stakeholder feels empowered to do the right thing and speak up when there are problems or barriers to success, thus aligning well with the agile mind-set and methodologies that many organizations are finding to be so beneficial.

Long ago, quality management guru W. Edwards Deming noted the importance of healthy behaviors, such as driving out fear, in order to ensure that your employees are willing to speak up and warn of potential issues. Clearly, positive behaviors lead to highly effective teams and successful organizations.

Positive psychology cannot solve every problem, and there is no doubt that many organizations have cultures and environments that just do not foster success. However, if you are a technical leader (or wish to emerge as a technical leader), then understanding the significance and impact potential of encouraging positive traits is essential for your success. Helping your organization embrace and cultivate positive and effective behaviors will increase the productivity and success of every endeavor.

21.7.2 Three Pillars of Positive Psychology

The focus of positive psychology is on encouraging positive and effective behaviors [8] that help bring out desired behaviors and applies well to many business and technical situations. Dr. Seligman noted in his writings that there are essentially three pillars that make up the scientific endeavor of positive psychology. The first two relate to individual behavior, and the third is the study of positive institutions, which Seligman suggested was "beyond the guild of psychology" [9]. This section will focus on that third pillar, which is within the realm of organizational psychology and of great interest to anyone who wants to be part of an effective organization. The first two pillars of positive psychology focus on positive emotion and positive character, each of which contribute to the development of a sense of self-efficacy and personal effectiveness; these are both important to individual success. Organizations, not unlike the people who comprise them, often have unique and complex personalities as well. For example, individuals who join the army or the police force certainly experience the culture of the organization in a very real way.

When people fail in their jobs, it is sometimes due to factors beyond their direct control; perhaps they could not fit into the culture, and the expectations of the organization itself or the organization's culture made success difficult to attain. What traits might we want to highlight when looking at an organization from a positive psychology perspective?

Organizations that encourage curiosity, interest in the world, and a general love of learning provide an environment that is consistent with what Dr. Seligman had in mind with his first cluster, which he termed wisdom. Technology professionals could understand these traits in terms of organizations that encourage learning new technologies and frameworks and provide opportunities for professionals to constantly improve their skills. Judiciousness, critical thinking, and open-mindedness, along with ingenuity, originality, and practical street smarts, are also attributes found among employees in effective organizations. Social, personal, and emotional intelligence describes organizations that encourage their members to respectfully understand both individual and group differences, including cultural diversity.

Organizations that encourage employees to feel safe when speaking up or taking the initiative can be understood to exhibit valor and bravery, qualities that fall within the cluster that Seligman termed courage. Integrity and honesty, along with perseverance and diligence, are also grouped with these particular positive traits. The degree to which these characteristics and their active expression are valued in an organization will significantly affect that firm's functioning and results.

Positive organizations encourage their employees to take initiative and ensure that employees feel safe, even when reporting a potential problem or issue. Dysfunctional organizations punish the whistle-blower, whereas effective organizations not only recognize the importance of being able to evaluate the risks or problems that have been brought to their attention, they proactively solicit such self-monitoring efforts.

The cluster of humanity and love consists of kindness, generosity, and a strong commitment to social interactions and developing solid relationships. An intrinsic sense of justice broadens the perspective to include how one relates to larger groups such as one's community and nation. This cluster includes many virtues such as duty, teamwork, loyalty, and fairness. Organizations that encourage a genuine sense of delivering value to customers and the idea of giving back to their community model these behaviors and are more likely to see employees living these values on a daily basis. Of paramount importance are good citizenship and teamwork, as well as a strong culture of leadership. Although many organizations may have individuals who exhibit these strengths, highly effective organizations make these values a cultural norm, which, in turn, becomes the personality of the organization itself.

The cluster of temperance includes self-control, humility, and modesty, all of which can be understood in terms of delivering quality to all stakeholders, including ensuring real value to stockholders rather than "fluffy" advertising and marketing hype. Gratitude is a fundamental trait of many successful organizations; this involves modeling positive behaviors and actively participating in helping the communities that support them. These are often the same organizations that have a strong sense of hope and optimism and are mindful of the future; again all traits found in Seligman's view of positive psychology. Some organizations have a culture that exhibits spirituality, faith, and even religiousness, which aligns with their personality. Most importantly, playfulness and humor, along with passion and enthusiasm, all make for a corporate environment that fosters successful and loyal employees.

Over the years, many organizations have unfortunately become associated with greed and dysfunctional behavior. However, the study of positive psychology provides an effective, comprehensive, and attainable model to understand those companies that exhibit cultures that encourage and nurture the positive behaviors that research indicates lead to success and profitability.

21.7.3 Using Positive Psychology to Motivate Your Team

Motivating a team can be a difficult task. Managers often need to spend a considerable amount of time ensuring that their team members are motivated to do the best work possible. Although pay, benefits, and a flexible work environment are often put forth as a key reason to apply for a job, truly motivated employees maintain a high level of discretionary effort on an ongoing basis.

So, how do you effectively motivate employees to be the best and do the most even under difficult circumstances? Effective leaders motivate others through their own behaviors and create an environment where each team member has multiple opportunities and reasons to be successful.

Psychologist Abraham Maslow proposed a theory of motivation that is based upon a hierarchy of needs and drives. It begins with physiological needs, including basic necessities such as food and water, progresses to less concrete requirements such as safety, and then reaches for more conceptual ideals such as a sense of love and belonging. Self-esteem and self-actualization sit at the highest levels of Maslow's hierarchy, which remains one of the most widely respected models in use.

Maslow's work is easy to operationalize and very compelling due to the simple fact that most people intuitively "get" the progression. The bottom line is that the majority of employees are indeed motivated by the need for pay and benefits such as medical insurance and paid time off. Once these basic needs are satisfied, many then seek a comfortable work-life balance, which is aided by a flexible work environment. Many technology professionals also value technical training and projects that allow them to learn new technologies and feel that they are continuously growing and improving.

Autonomy is one of the most cherished factors in job satisfaction, and many employees are highly motivated to demonstrate their abilities in exchange for flexible work arrangements that carry with them significant autonomy. Many successful companies are learning that providing flexible environments that accommodate working moms or dads who are highly skilled but desire a personalized work-life balance helps the organization attract and retain valuable employees. Positive psychology is taking motivation much further by focusing on providing opportunities to bring out positive behaviors through various reward and recognition programs.

Some technology firms go as far as providing time off for employees to work on side projects. For example, hackathons (also known as codefests) provide opportunities for employees to work on special projects in a highly competitive environment. These approaches combine technology innovation with a sense of friendly competition and the promise of recognition by peers, which can also be motivating.

Successful managers look for opportunities to elicit and motivate positive behaviors. One example of this phenomenon is the open-source industry, in which many accomplished technology professionals work long hours to produce high-quality software and then give it away for free. Maslow would point out that many software engineers who help with open-source projects have a day job that satisfies their basic physiological and maintenance needs. Participation in volunteer activities provides a sense of belonging, self-esteem, and, ultimately, self-actualization as their peers recognize them as industry leaders.

Positive psychology focuses on the factors that lead technology experts to exhibit positive behaviors. Moving beyond the individual, it is essential for organizational culture to support positive behaviors. Successful managers create environments where employees feel empowered to exhibit positive behaviors. This should include setting clear, achievable goals that can be measured and understood by key stakeholders. Some organizations add a sense of competition to the ecosystem by identifying outside competitive forces that threaten the success of the firm. Employees who perceive these outside forces to be legitimate may indeed be highly motivated. Although managers who try to motivate solely via fear may find themselves losing their best talent, challenges that are perceived to be legitimate may be quite motivating for some individuals.

Teams can also be highly motivated by positive environments that are fun and rewarding. Organizations that value learning and creativity and understand the importance of work-life balance and autonomy encourage the type of culture the positive psychology movement has proven will usually bring out the best in employees.

21.7.4 Learning from Mistakes

Mistakes happen. But too often, team members engage in highly dysfunctional behavior after they have made mistakes. Even though mistakes are often the best learning experiences, many organizations suffer serious consequences, not just because a mistake was made, but also often as a direct result of the attempt to save face and cover up after an employee has made a mistake. W. Edwards Deming's research indicates that addressing mistakes in an open and honest manner is essential for any organization in today's competitive business environment. Here's what we learn from positive psychology about creating an environment where employees can be empowered to address their mistakes in a straightforward way.

Positive psychology teaches us that most people want to cultivate what is best within themselves and to enhance their experiences of love, work, and play. The trick is to guide your employees into exhibiting appropriate behaviors to accomplish these goals. Otherwise, you may find very dysfunctional behaviors, such as hiding mistakes, denial, and even blaming others, which obviously disrupt the workforce and can adversely affect the business in many ways. Many organizations have silo infrastructures and cultures that further detract from the organization's goal of addressing mistakes and resolving problems in the most efficient way possible. DevOps principles and practices can help by encouraging teams to work in a collaborative, cross-functional way, which is essential in addressing mistakes. Highly effective teams really need to embrace much more efficient ways of dealing with a wide variety of challenges—including human error.

Positive psychology focuses on positive emotions, positive individual traits, and positive institutions. This approach is a refreshing change from many schools of psychology, which focus more on analyzing the reasons for antisocial and other problematic personality types that often result in dysfunctional behavior. No doubt some folks do indeed have personality problems that predispose them to managing problems—such as handling their own mistakes—in ways that are not very constructive. But it is equally true that focusing on positive individual traits helps us to see and appreciate the strengths and virtues, such as personal integrity, self-knowledge, self-control, courage, and wisdom, that come from experience and being nourished in a positive environment.

The individual is very important in this context, but it is equally important to consider the organization as a holistic being. Understanding positive behaviors within the company itself entails the study of the strengths that empower team members to address challenges in an effective and creative way. Some examples of issues that should be discussed are social responsibility, civility, tolerance, diversity, work ethic, leadership, and honesty.

Obviously, the best leaders actually exhibit these behaviors themselves and lead by example, which brings us back to how specific individuals handle mistakes. When mistakes occur, does your organization foster a safe, open environment where people can feel that their best course of action is to admit what they did wrong? Do team members assume that their colleagues will drop what they are doing to help out in resolving any problems? Does the team avoid pointing fingers and the blame game to focus instead on problem resolution?

One manager mentioned that he did not focus so much on the unavoidable reality that mistakes will occur. Instead, he focused on encouraging his employees to acknowledge errors freely and then rated the entire team on its ability to work together and address problems productively, regardless of who may have been involved. Positive psychology gives us an effective framework for actually following through on Deming's directive to "drive out fear." The most successful organizations take mistakes and make them constructive learning experiences, leading to employees who feel a renewed sense of loyalty and commitment to achieving excellence.

Mistakes happen. Your challenge is to ensure that rather than demoralizing or paralyzing people, these missteps instead empower your team to be more effective and successful!

21.7.5 Positive Psychology in DevOps

DevOps focuses on improving communication and collaboration between software developers and the operations professionals who help maintain reliable and dependable systems. We often assess and evaluate existing practices and then make recommendations for improving the way IT teams function. Our focus is often on configuration, release management, and—these days especially— DevOps best practices. Bringing different technology groups together can result in some interesting challenges. We often feel like we are doing group therapy for a highly dysfunctional family, and many of the challenges encountered highlight the complex personalities and biases people often bring into the workplace.

We all come to work with the sum of our own experiences and personalities, which, by definition, means we are predisposed to having specific viewpoints— and maybe even more than a few biases. Many professionals come into meetings with their own agendas based upon their prior experiences. When conducting an assessment, we are typically asking participants to explain what they believe works well in their organization and what can be improved. In practice, getting people comfortable results in better and more useful information. When we bring developers into a room to talk about their work experiences, we often get a very different view than when we speak with their counterparts in operations or other departments, including QA and testing. The stories we hear initially sometimes sound like a bad marriage that cannot be saved. Fortunately, our experience is that there is also a great deal of potential synergy in bringing different viewpoints together. The key is to get the salient issues on the table and facilitate clear and effective communication.

Developers are often pressured to create new and exciting product features, using technology that itself is changing at a breathtaking rate. The QA and testing professionals are charged with ensuring that applications are defect free and often have to work under considerable pressure, including ever-shrinking timelines. The operations group must ensure that systems are reliable and available on a consistent basis. Each of these stakeholders has a very different set of goals and objectives. Developers want to roll out changes constantly, delivering new and exciting features, while operations and QA may find themselves challenged to keep up with the demand for new releases. What we hear is the somewhat biased perception from each side of the table.

Developers are highly skilled and often much more technically knowledgeable than their counterparts in QA and operations. This makes for some challenging dynamics in terms of mutual respect and collaboration. The operations and QA professionals often feel that developers are the immature children who lack discipline and constantly try to bypass established IT controls. This clashing of views and values is often a source of conflict within the organization, with decisions being made based on positional power by senior executives who may not be completely aware of all of the details of each challenge. The fact is that this conflict can be very constructive and lead to high performance if managed effectively.

By focusing on developing desirable behaviors, positive psychology moves from just identifying behavioral dysfunction to promoting effective and high-performance behaviors. The first area to focus on is honest and open communication. Seligman uses the term bravery to describe the ability to speak up or take the initiative, a key aspect of courage, which is often called for in the workplace. Integrity and honesty, along with perseverance and diligence, are also desirable traits that need to be modeled and encouraged in positive organizations. Successful organizations value and encourage these characteristics and their active expression.

We typically meet with each stakeholder separately and document their views, including frustrations and challenges. We then put together a report incorporating these observations that synthesizes all of our findings and suggests areas and methods for improvements. Although dysfunctional and distracting behavior must first be identified and understood, the next step of bringing all stakeholders to the table to look together for solutions and positive ideas for making improvements is the more essential intervention. Sometimes, this feels a little like horse trading. For example, one group may be convinced that only open-source tools are appropriate for use, whereas another team may be very interested in the features and support that come from commercial products. We often facilitate the evaluation and selection of the right tools and processes with appropriate transparency, collaboration, and communication. By staying focused on the positive proactive behaviors, we help stakeholders throughout the organization develop new communication patterns that foster more creative and productive collaborations.

Positive psychology focuses on proactively promoting the types of behaviors research has identified as being closely correlated with achievement, productivity, and positive interpersonal skills—three qualities essential for individuals on a high-performance team. Obviously, any improvement effort should begin with understanding the existing views and experiences of those involved. But bringing the stakeholders to the table and getting their management to support, reward, and model collaborative behavior are key steps along the path that leads to high-performance cross-functional teams and a more successful organization.

21.8 Conclusion

Individual personalities, as well as group dynamics, influence every aspect of organizational functioning, including attempts to implement agile ALM. Stellar IT managers learn to parley their finely honed people skills into an approach that balances individual team members' unique styles with the group's needs. By modeling positive qualities and encouraging a safe, open, team-first environment, savvy leaders guide IT professionals from every department to be productive contributors to the organization's agile ALM success!

References

[1] Sidaniusa, Jim, Felicia Prattob, and Michael Mitchella (1994). "In-Group Identification, Social Dominance Orientation, and Differential Intergroup Social Allocation," *The Journal of Social Psychology*, 134(2), 151–167.

[2] Byrne, Donn (1974). *An Introduction to Personality: Research, Theory, and Applications*. Englewood Cliffs, NJ: Prentice-Hall Psychology Series.

[3] Aiello, Bob and Leslie Sachs (2011). *Configuration Management Best Practices: Practical Methods that Work in the Real World*. Boston, MA: Addison-Wesley Professional.

[4] Juran, Joseph M. (1962). *Quality Control Handbook (2nd ed.)*. New York: McGraw-Hill.

[5] Friedman, Meyer (1996). *Type A Behavior: Its Diagnosis and Treatment* (Prevention in Practice Library). New York, NY: Plenum Press.

[6] Robbins, Harvey and Michael Finley (1995). *Why Teams Don't Work— What Went Wrong and How to Make It Right*. Princeton, NJ: Peterson's Pacesetter Books.

[7] Sullivan, Harry Stack (1972). *Personal Psychopathology: Early Formulations*. New York: W.W. Norton & Co.

[8] Seligman, Martin and Mihaly Csikszentmihalyi (2000). "Positive Psychology: An Introduction." *American Psychologist*, 55, 5–14.

[9] Seligman, Martin (2002). *Authentic Happiness: Using the New Positive Psychology to Realize Your Potential for Lasting Fulfillment*. Free Press, New York.

Further Reading

Abramson, Lyn Y., Martin E. P. Seligman, and John D. Teasdale (1978). "Learned Helplessness in Humans: Critique and Reformulation." *Journal of Abnormal Psychology,* 87(1), 49–74.

Appelo, Jurgen (2011). *Management 3.0: Leading Agile Developers, Developing Agile Leaders.* New York, NY: Addison-Wesley Signature Series.

Deming, W. Edwards (1986). *Out of the Crisis.* Cambridge, MA: MIT Press.

Friedman, Meyer (1984). *Treating Type A Behavior—And Your Heart.* New York, NY: Knopf.

Chapter 22

The Future of ALM

Technology professionals design and implement complex software processes every day. Some of software and systems lifecycles are very effective, and others are less than optimal. This book focuses on what you need to know to design better processes using agile principles. We are deliberately not describing a pure agile approach, as there are many other good resources out there that can help you do that. Our focus is more on the less-than-ideal situation, which we sincerely believe to be the norm in most companies. We have discussed the "elephant in the room," which is the reality that many organizations are not doing pure agile. This is not because agility does not deliver solid results—and nothing in this book should be viewed as criticizing agile or any of its principles. Rather, we think that it is time to have an open and honest conversation in the industry about software methodology, which, although it has evolved and improved greatly over the last 20-plus years, rarely fits neatly into rigid categories for those in the trenches who must design and implement today's complicated systems.

22.1 Real-World ALM

We appreciate and value sound frameworks such as Scott Ambler's Disciplined Agile Delivery and Dean Leffingwell's Scaled Agile Framework (SAFE) and, of course, Ken Rubin's seminal essential scrum. Many other knowledgeable agile thought leaders are doing fine work and promoting effective approaches to software development. But we caution folks to be mindful that agile as seen today includes an imperfect world of hybrid and customized practices, and we need to support them in a pragmatic and effective way. We value taking a broad view of software methodology in the real world and considering the many possible processes you could implement in order to create the best and most efficient processes for your organization.

DevOps, which continuously takes a cross-functional view of the processes that run your business along with the supporting IT services, is the key to driving your agile ALM. DevOps is very effective at improving communication and collaboration among all of the teams in the organization. We see situations that warrant more IT controls and governance than others. It is our goal to help you decide how to right-size and customize your processes to be the best fit possible for your business. More importantly, we believe that you need to be good at iteratively customizing and improving your processes over time. Please make sure that you remember to have a communication plan in place to ensure that all stakeholders know when you change the rules and exactly what the new and improved processes require. Not only do we incorporate continuous processes within our software lifecycle, in practice, we also *continuously* evolve our agile ALM.

This book is very different in that we believe that technology professionals, armed with the right training, can learn to creatively and iteratively design and implement customized and right-sized software processes using agile principles that will meet the unique needs of their business, thus delivering the highest level of productivity and quality. We expect and hope that this book will be the catalyst for many discussions on how to best handle the pragmatic and effective use of agile ALM, including some of the uncomfortable issues such as how to best implement agile in a non-agile environment. We especially do not expect everyone to agree with every aspect of our approach to ALM. Our previous book, *Configuration Management Best Practices: Practical Methods that Work in the Real World*, led many of our colleagues to write to us and connect with us on social media. We deeply value and appreciate input from our colleagues and hope that you will be in touch as well. Working together, we can each get a hand on that elephant and pool our knowledge for the benefit of all.

22.2 ALM in Focus

Application lifecycle management will likely be in the spotlight in coming years as the technology industry continues to evolve and seek new levels of efficiency. This focus is not only about developing code more quickly, but also addressing a wider need to adapt to the many challenges inherent in complex technologies.

Cybersecurity will continue to be a key concern, as malicious exploits threaten the technology infrastructure, while at the same time, we are constantly increasing our dependence upon technology and all it has to offer. Effective software methodology will be the most important determining factor as the industry learns to adapt to new challenges and grow in terms of scope and impact. The capability to develop software and systems more quickly and of the highest quality is a must-have, but the ability to understand and overcome ever-evolving challenges and obstacles is what can really separate your team from the crowd. We have no doubt that the industry is up for the challenge and will continue to achieve amazing results. Because we view human capital as being our greatest resource, improving the agile ALM can be the key to ensuring that all stakeholders ban together in a collaborative and productive manner.

22.3 Conclusion

In this book, we introduced our approach to creating a customized agile ALM methodology that is tailored to your organization. We applied agile principles and practices throughout our review and examination of software methodology going back over the last 20 years or more. We have discussed the "elephant in the room"—our reference to the fact that many IT professionals are using hybrid or customized approaches to agile. We advocate learning and using well-defined agile methodologies, such as SAFE, Disciplined Agile Delivery, and scrum, but at the same time acknowledge that there are valid and pragmatic reasons to customize your processes to align closely with your organizational culture and objectives. We believe that our technology colleagues in the real world are already engaging in continuous process improvement, resulting in agile processes that meet the needs of the teams and organizations in which they are engaged. We hope that the information presented in this book sparks your curiosity and motivates you to participate in this discussion. We hope that you will be in touch with us to share your views and experiences!

Index

REGISTER YOUR PRODUCT at informit.com/register
Access Additional Benefits and SAVE 35% on Your Next Purchase

- Download available product updates.
- Access bonus material when applicable.
- Receive exclusive offers on new editions and related products.
  (Just check the box to hear from us when setting up your account.)
- Get a coupon for 35% for your next purchase, valid for 30 days. Your code will be available in your InformIT cart. (You will also find it in the Manage Codes section of your account page.)

Registration benefits vary by product. Benefits will be listed on your account page under Registered Products.

InformIT.com—The Trusted Technology Learning Source

InformIT is the online home of information technology brands at Pearson, the world's foremost education company. At InformIT.com you can

- Shop our books, eBooks, software, and video training.
- Take advantage of our special offers and promotions (informit.com/promotions).
- Sign up for special offers and content newsletters (informit.com/newsletters).
- Read free articles and blogs by information technology experts.
- Access thousands of free chapters and video lessons.

Connect with InformIT—Visit informit.com/community

Learn about InformIT community events and programs.

informIT.com
the trusted technology learning source

Addison-Wesley • Cisco Press • IBM Press • Microsoft Press • Pearson IT Certification • Prentice Hall • Que • Sams • VMware Press